GERTRUDE JEKYLL'S LOST GARDEN

The Restoration of an Edwardian Masterpiece

GERTRUDE JEKYLL'S LOST GARDEN

The Restoration of an Edwardian Masterpiece

BY ROSAMUND WALLINGER

GARDEN • ART • PRESS

To my two men, John and Mark and to Geraldine Andrews
who believed the egg had wings

British Library Cataloguing-in-Publication Data
A catalogue record for this book is available from the British Library

Frontispiece: The Hot Border in June 1990

Printed in England
by the Antique Collectors' Club Ltd., Woodbridge, Suffolk IP12 1DS
on Consort Royal Satin paper
supplied by the Donside Paper Company, Aberdeen, Scotland

Contents

One of the herbaceous borders in July 1998.

Preface

This is a wonderful story. It is a story of detailed persistence which has restored and rejuvenated one of Gertrude Jekyll's most interesting gardens. The remarkable outcome, a living vibrating garden, shows that authentic restorations do not have to have a museum-like quality. Ros Wallinger has breathed new life and spirit into the gardens of Upton Grey. If she is to be taken at her word she knew nothing about garden design or plants when she and her husband John began this task. It is all the more to her credit that she has followed the plans, searched out the original plants and learned in the process. The book is partly a celebration of Upton Grey's return to prosperity but it is also an exciting story of Ros's own horticultural development. It is told modestly, but reveals her depth of understanding of Miss Jekyll's vision for this particular garden. As we have sometimes seen, meticulously following a blueprint may produce a stylised version of a garden; often it remains strangely inhuman lacking that extra 'spirit of the place' which gives a good garden its edge over the mediocre. It is to the Wallingers' great credit that the restoration of Upton Grey reflects the genius of Jekyll, as well as demonstrating her use of plants and colour. It is also a triumph for Ros Wallinger. Hard work and attention to detail must please the purist Jekyll scholar, but it is the emotional input which has produced a garden nourished and tended to evoke its Edwardian past.

Penelope Hobhouse

Bettiscombe
February 2000

Views of the restored garden

1998. Front of the house from the Wild Garden.

1994. View over the Formal Garden from the house.

1998. Towards the house from the Formal Garden.

Foreword

The garden of the Manor House at Upton Grey was designed in 1908 by Gertrude Jekyll for the influential Arts and Crafts figure Charles Holme. Today it is arguably the most authentic Jekyll garden in the world. All fifteen original plans for herbaceous borders, drystone walls, a wild garden and pond survive, and restoration to those has been meticulously carried out by the present owners, John and Rosamund Wallinger. However, when they decided to buy the house in 1983, they were completely ignorant of the garden's importance, as were the previous owners and the inhabitants of the village of Upton Grey. The Wallingers' initial research into the listed Manor House led them to a serendipity of remarkable facts, all of which are related here as the story unfolds. Photographs give a full visual record of the garden's decline, fall and rebirth over the century. Diary notes detail its restoration from dereliction to today's glory and to what Ros describes as a small monument to the Arts and Crafts movement.

The Manor House over the century

1906/7. The house and carriage sweep before Jekyll planned the garden.

Introduction

Discovering the Manor House, Upton Grey

'Right, that's it! We're moving to the country.'

Until 1983, John and I had lived all sixteen years of our married life in London, but in May of that year John came back from work in the City in a fearsome mood having had to park our scarred urban car five streets away from our house. The walk home through rain, puddles, and dog messes prompted his announcement. Having no intention of uprooting, I agreed – to help him over the bad patch.

I had grown rather fond of London. In the sixties my sister and I started The Square Orange Bookshop, in Pimlico, an ephemeral adventure but popular in its day. In the seventies I ran a small agency of cooks; an occupation which required no skill but gave me the opportunity to improve my culinary endeavours at other people's expense. In March 1977 I was chosen as one of London's five regional finalists in *The Sunday Times* 'Best Cook in Britain' competition. It was an astonishing and unmerited achievement, as most of my friends' stomachs acknowledged, but gardening was of no interest to me. Our terraced house overlooked a sixty by twenty foot garden which I adorned with a random selection of plants in pots, bought from whichever nursery I happened to pass. I had a graveyard of unsuitable and unnamed plants and that was the sum total of my gardening. We had brought up our son Mark in London and had a comfortable nucleus of friends around us. In other words we had spent the most important years of our lives there and we were in danger of becoming emotionally welded to the place. None the less John had made up his mind, so we put our house on the market and spent the following weekends looking for a house in the country. We saw several that we liked although none fitted all our criteria, but those Sunday night journeys back to London through streams of sluggish traffic always filled us with a sense of gloom and a longing to get back to the clean open spaces again.

One morning in July 1983, amongst the circulars that littered the doorstep, I found a black and white xeroxed sheet of paper. It announced 'An historic manor of considerable

1998. The house and forecourt as it is today.

architectural importance and dating predominantly from the Jacobean period'. The photograph was too blurred to make out what the house looked like but the price was attractive, £200,000, and about what we expected to get for our London house. So, on a cold, wet weekend in July 1983 we set out again to inspect houses to the west of London. The mysterious Manor House at Upton Grey was by far the closest. It was near Exit 5 of the M3 motorway, an area which would normally have been quite out of our reach financially.

We turned off the narrow winding road, down a weed-ridden drive indented with puddle-filled holes and over-hung with drooping, dripping chestnut trees. These trees have a melancholy effect in bad weather. At the end of their tunnel, the drive forked sharply to right and left. To the left lay a pleasant, one-storey cottage with a small granary above one end. Evidently this had once been stables for the manor house. To our right the drive curved around to a large rubble and mud oval area in front of an un-Jacobean and apparently Edwardian house, which looked every bit as disconsolate as the approach. It was shrouded in dripping climbers and weeds, *Polygonum baldschuanicum* and the unidentified vine-like creeper that, fifteen years on, I am still trying to kill. They climbed up the walls, over and out of the roof and wrapped themselves around the chimneys.

The photograph that appeared on the sales sheet in 1983 when the house and garden were becoming derelict.

March 1984. View over the Wild Garden from an attic window at the front of the house, showing weeds to the right growing over the roof.

The house seemed very large and dark. It stood, three storeys high, long and narrow with a deeply pitched roof, and either side of the heavy front door were leaded windows whose grimy panes revealed an interior every bit as damp as the exterior. Hung tiles covered bricks from above ground floor to roof eaves, and moss filled the joints where three large chimney stacks met roof tiles and the creepers. Curious round grey shapes were fixed just under the eaves and dozens of birds swooped in and out of small holes. They turned out to be a large colony of house martins. I have grown to love those hard-working courageous birds who leave a meticulously built nest in late autumn and return in spring find that sparrows have over-wintered in free lodgings and all but destroyed their labours. They are undeterred and start the building over again. Possibly sparrows rid those old nests of parasites. Whatever the reason, this sequence has come to reflect life in the garden – industry, creation, vitality, decadence – but a continual trust and determination to survive. The garden which surrounded the house was so dense with brambles, various mangy conifers and stinging nettles that we left it unexplored.

Cold, wet, curious and rather excited we returned to London knowing that we wanted the house and that it could be restored to a happy and comfortable state. We made an appointment to view the house more thoroughly the following weekend and I began to develop a peculiarly possessive feeling about Upton Grey from that day onwards.

Our appointment was at 11 a.m. the following Saturday. The sun was out and the approach still sombre but the overhanging branches seemed less melancholy as we drove up. An old white and rusting Ford was parked in the forecourt. It had been there the previous weekend and was to remain there as a sort of 'inhabited' statement for several weeks after we bought the house. Alongside the rusty frame was parked a silver Rolls Royce. On that incongruous car perched a pair of very high heeled white shoes and, leaning intently over detailed architectural plans that covered the bonnet, were the owners of the various bits, two men and a woman. To this day we wonder if all this was set up to encourage buyers. We were

March 1984. The front of the Manor House with weeds removed from the roof.

introduced to the owner of the Rolls Royce by the seller, a youngish, stocky fellow. The plans, we were told, showed how fourteen cottages could be built in the garden and that the house itself had already been divided into two.

It might seem odd that such lucrative ideas should be shared with potential buyers but the whole morning seemed so like a farcical fantasy that we accepted it as normal to Hampshire life. Eventually we were given a cursory conducted tour of the inside of the house. It was largely unfurnished, damp, and three rooms which were oak panelled were strangely dulled with a film of mildew. It felt like a house that needed extensive restoration, but not at any stage like a hopeless project. For the second time, we barely viewed the garden at all.

When we returned to London we set about arranging a survey. We talked about our mournful giant. The more we investigated and the more we talked, the more exciting the results and the feedback became. By September 1983 land searches and surveys were completed. 'It is', the surveyor said to me, 'a very drippy house'. Undeterred by that and by his report of dry rot, wet rot and wood-worm, we put in a bid for £175,000; £25,000 under the asking price. Then and only then, did we realise how much we wanted the house. Very gradually our bid and the asking price came together to meet at £185,000. Once our bid was accepted contracts were exchanged with remarkable speed.

In the spring of 1984 we moved into the cold manor house with builders and mice for company and the hourly peal of nearby church bells as timekeeper. The first photograph of 'new owners on site' shows a dilapidated table standing on very weed-ridden grass that had once been a bowling green. In the centre of the table stands a bottle of champagne. John leans out of an upstairs window, waiting for our first guests to arrive. With a group of friends, most of whom had strongly advised against buying, we drank to our daunting challenge. We never doubted that we would make it a glorious house and garden, and at no stage afterwards did either of us feel disheartened by the immense amount of work confronting us. Reward has always vastly outweighed labour and exhaustion.

April 1984. John at the window and champagne bottle on the table.

Chapter One

1983

Researching the House and Garden

Ernest Newton, *c.* 1900.

1910. Drawing by
F.L. Griggs for the
Architectural Press.

The winter of 1983-4 was very cold, reaching minus fourteen degrees centigrade in Hampshire. Icy draughts ventilated the house. Coming from warm, insulated London, I had never dreamt that England could be so cold. My fingers swelled to thick sausage shapes and my toes were covered with chilblains. During those cold winter months when the ground was too hard to dig, John and I started work on research into the house that was to lead us to the exciting discovery that we owned an entire, restorable Gertrude Jekyll garden. I now appreciate how lucky we were to buy the house at the onset of winter and when there was a great deal of work to be done on the building. It prevented us starting random work on the garden before we began vital research, because both weather and limited finances ensured that we moved slowly. I think there is a strong chance that, had we moved in with six summer months ahead and cash available, we might well have launched an ignorant and damaging assault on the dilapidated garden.

From the sales description of the house we knew it was listed Grade II. Houses in Britain that are of architectural interest are classified Grade I, Grade II★ or Grade II. So, in order to discover why the Manor House was listed, we began our research at the Royal Institute of British Architects (RIBA), in Portland Place, London. There we discovered that the architect for the Manor House was Ernest Newton, an important Arts and Crafts figure who was born in 1856 and died in 1922. We made notes, or took copies, of all the relevant material.

Ernest Newton was in his late forties when he designed the manor house for the wealthy textile merchant, Charles Holme. He built an Edwardian shell on the bones of an old Tudor farmhouse, and that wooden Tudor frame forms part of Newton's greatly changed building. It is described as 'Alterations and Additions to an Old House' in the Architectural Press's volume *The Work of Ernest Newton*. His house is dated 1907.

Early sixteenth century timbers have survived and are part of today's structure. The Edwardian frame also contains a fine early seventeenth century staircase and an oak-panelled room which may date from the mid-seventeenth century. During Newton's reconstruction in 1904-07 cannon shot from Cromwellian times was found embedded in walls, and a bag of seventeenth century coins was discovered in one of the massive chimneys. The coins had probably been hidden during the troubled years around 1644 when Oliver Cromwell's troops laid siege to nearby Basing House (one of the last strongholds of the Royalist resistance) and Roundhead troops had taken possession of outlying houses. The nearby fish and chip shop is appropriately named Oliver's Battery. Our panelled parlour room is known locally as 'Cromwell's Courtroom', so presumably suspected Royalists were put on trial here.

Newton, we learnt, was one of the inspiring turn-of-the-century architects whose use of English style and craftsmanship in buildings was to influence so many twentieth century designers. He was a founder member of the important and extant Art Workers' Guild. In his book *Dream Houses. The Edwardian Ideal,* the architect Roderick Gradidge claims that Newton was considered one of the finest architects during a period of magnificent house

1907. Newton's house immediately after his 'alterations and additions' to the original 16th century Manor House which is shown hatched on the plans below.

1910. The entrance. This is typically assymetrical.

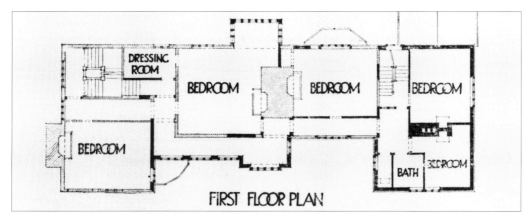

DRESSING ROOM

BEDROOM

BEDROOM

BEDROOM

BEDROOM

BATH

BEDROOM

FIRST FLOOR PLAN

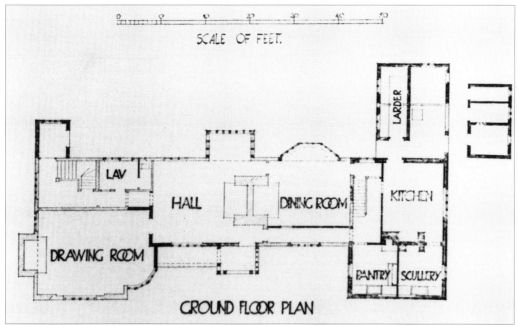

SCALE OF FEET.

LAV

HALL

DINING ROOM

KITCHEN

LARDER

DRAWING ROOM

PANTRY

SCULLERY

GROUND FLOOR PLAN

Ground and first floor plans of the house showing Newton's alterations. The 16th century Manor House is shown hatched.

1900. The original Tudor manor. Taken beyond the field that was to become the Wild Garden.

The same view of the altered house, *c.*1907, before Jekyll's plans.

The house from the end of the Wild Garden as it developed, deteriorated and was restored over the century

building. His meticulous architectural drawings show a gift for practical and sensitive houses, which were often built in the vernacular style, complemented by and complementing their surroundings. In the case of the Manor House, built over the timber-frame Tudor house, he chose to make additions in the manner of the original.

It was evident to us that the house was important and should be carefully restored. We grew increasingly fascinated as our knowledge deepened. Towards the end of our research at the RIBA we came across a footnote. It was the only hint that the garden might also be important. It read 'Garden possibly G. Jekyll'. I had heard of Gertrude Jekyll, knew that she was a nineteenth century Surrey gardener, and that her gardening boots had become almost as famous as their owner. I knew very little else about her. (It was several months before we learnt from knowledgeable gardening friends that the Jekyll family pronounced their name to rhyme with 'treacle' not with 'heckle').

We returned home and I continued researching Jekyll with books bought or borrowed from the library. It seemed strange that the house sales leaflet had not mentioned this important name and I wondered why. I came across a copy of Jekyll's obituary which impressed me profoundly; it had been printed in *The Times* in December 1932 under the headline 'Miss Gertrude Jekyll, Gardener and Artist'. It was a long obituary which summarised her life and gave praise to the great gardener. The first sentence read:

> *We regret to announce that Miss Gertrude Jekyll died at her home at Godalming on Thursday evening, at the age of 89. She had been failing for some weeks and had felt the recent death of her brother, Sir Herbert Jekyll, very much. She was a great gardener, second only, if indeed she was second, to her friend William Robinson, of Gravetye. To these two, more than to any others, are due, not only the complete transformation of English horticultural method and design, but also that wide diffusion of knowledge and taste which has made us almost a nation of gardeners. Miss Jekyll was also a true artist with an exquisite sense of colour.*

There followed eight paragraphs of biography, the last of which read:

> *Gertrude Jekyll, to whom we now bid a grateful 'Hail and Farewell,' sought ever for practical knowledge allied to beauty, and in that quest, whereby she may truly be said to have transfigured the gardens of England, she never grew old at heart or wearied in mind, was never discouraged by difficulty or defeated by failure, neither did she cease to share widely the fruits of her long and loving apprenticeship to Nature.*

How could not only the seller of the manor house but also the entire village fail to know that a garden designed by such a radically inspired woman stood at Upton Grey? I supposed that the financial hardship brought by the Second World War, coupled with a decline in the

1984. As we found it in a derelict state.

1992. A similar view with the Wild Garden restored to Jekyll's 1908 plans.

impractical luxury of gardening, and the fact that between about 1916 and 1983 the house had changed hands at least six times, accounted for the lack of interest. Perhaps because those intervening owners were not particularly wealthy, they built no swimming pool, hard tennis court or other destructive additions to the modest garden. As we were later to discover, the bones of Jekyll's 1908 garden were intact and restorable.

From late January 1984 onwards the hunt began to broaden. We made enquiries locally and in London and were told to contact Richard Bisgrove of Reading University. Richard confirmed that all surviving Jekyll plans were held in The University of California at Berkeley and that plans for nineteen numbered borders at The Manor House were included in that collection. John's firm had a branch in San Francisco and Jane Weller, the wife of his American partner, a keen gardener, found our documents and contacted John who ordered copies, for which he paid ninety dollars. We awaited the arrival of the important documents in optimistic excitement. As I knew so little about gardening I had no worries about re-creating a Jekyll garden to the letter, about living in a time warp, and I was happy at the prospect of copying a great master. I realised that I could not improve on her plans. We were also blissfully unaware of the costs in terms of time and money that this would entail.

As our search for information about Jekyll and Newton continued, we decided to learn more about the mysterious Charles Holme who had been mentioned at the RIBA as the owner of the rebuilt Manor House. We knew that Holme had founded an Arts and Crafts periodical called *The Studio* in 1893, but it was not until 1993 when the Victoria and Albert Museum put on an exhibition entitled 'The Studio' that I fully understood the importance of Holme, the man responsible for commissioning Newton and Jekyll to work at Upton Grey. In the catalogue for the exhibition *The Studio* was described as being, in its day, 'the most enduring and successful art periodical in the English Speaking Language'. Its contributors were an eclectic assortment of characters from a wide range of the applied arts. Gertrude Jekyll, Eric Gill, Phil May, C F A Voysey and even, to my surprise, the controversial Aubrey Beardsley, were among the many to fill its pages. *The Studio* was designed to appeal to the new rich, the post-industrial, middle-class art lovers, both men and women, the very class whose rapidly expanding numbers required housing that the Edwardian architects provided. It is said that between 1895 and 1906 more houses and offices were built in England than ever before in the country's history. The growing middle classes required manageable houses with modest gardens, close to the cities. Charles Holme, himself a keen gardener, was aware of the change in garden scale and design that this had brought about, and of a surging interest in the subject of horticulture. In 1907 and 1908 *The Studio* published *The Gardens of England* in four parts. By that date Holme's publishing company, named after his periodical, had opened offices in London, Paris and New York.

Between 1876 and 1902 Charles Holme lived in The Red House, Bexley Heath, Kent,

Charles Holme portrait by P.A. de Lazlo.

Edwin Lutyens at Great Maythem. He loved dressing up as a joke and is seen here wearing a mortar board and gown.

famous today because it is the house that Philip Webb built for William Morris in 1859. In 1902 Holme purchased several houses in Upton Grey and a great deal of the surrounding farmland. I believe he chose to settle in Upton Grey because it was, and still is, if property developers and road planners are kept at bay, one of the prettiest villages in Hampshire; and that he chose the site of the Old Manor House because it commands such glorious views over the surrounding countryside.

Hampshire's County Record Office in Winchester proved to be an invaluable source of archival information throughout our initial investigations in 1984. We are lucky that this county has such excellent resources. There, parish records, family archives and other useful material are held in files and on computer. Advice and help is available to the amateur researcher, so John and I spent happy hours reading, researching and copying documents. With what now seems like remarkable resolution, or optimism, I bought ten large albums and pasted in every item of relevance in chronological order.

It became important that I learnt the context of Gertrude Jekyll in the history of gardening in order to understand why a woman born over one hundred and fifty years ago should remain such an enduring influence on gardening, not only in Britain but almost throughout the world. Why had her obituary claimed that she 'completely transformed English horticultural method and design', an impressive feat for a woman born at a time when relatively few of her sex made much impact in the world of art, let alone horticulture. It is an interesting fact that gardening has acted as a barometer of social activity for centuries. Gardens reflect the climates, aspects and soil conditions of their environment, as well as the prosperity, relative stability and cultural status of their owners. With wealth and peace, the art of gardening flourishes. Variations in climatic conditions are evident in changing plant material, and I believe that the character of the designer is often reflected in how he adapts to nature.

A glance at gardens over the centuries shows how styles evolved, with Britain leading the way from the mid-eighteenth century, the era when landscape gardening was considered the greatest of our visual arts. As we had learnt through our research into Charles Holme, the Industrial Revolution in the nineteenth century brought about a marked change in life-styles and in most forms of art, in particular architecture and gardening. The aristocracy were no longer the sole arbiters of taste and the new, rich middle classes became a powerful influence

Gertrude Jekyll at Higham Bury, Polluxhill, Bedfordshire, wearing a pair of her famous (size 8!) gardening boots.

on arts generally. By 1850 the dilemma for gardeners was that there were quite simply too many unrelated styles of gardening vying for popularity. John Claudius Loudon (1783-1843) counted four: the picturesque, the gardenesque, the rustic and the geometric. The exponent of one form seemed unable to acknowledge merit in another, still less to use facets of all styles and make a composite art of all.

I learnt that it was Gertrude Jekyll who, towards the end of the nineteenth century, made one integrated art of so many disparate styles and who, by her books and articles, taught the world's gardeners how to develop them. To this new composite style Jekyll added an understanding of the use of colour. In *Colour in the Flower Garden,* first published under that name in 1908 and subsequently lengthened to *Colour Schemes for the Flower Garden,* she taught her readers how one colour can influence another and how the arrangement of colours fools the eye into interpreting foreshortened or longer perspectives. Her flowers were planted in drifts, like colours on a canvas. She evidently believed that her public and gardeners of every rank deserved the enlightenment of artists and philosophers. All this I was to learn as our Upton Grey garden unfolded its glory over the following years. Restoring it was to be like 'painting by numbers' and watching the full picture emerge. At no stage in the restoration of her masterpiece have I wanted to change any part. I have remained a contented disciple. To some extent this subservience is a result of ignorance but I have found that practical experience and learning confirm my trust.

Gertrude Jekyll was born in 1843, the fifth of seven children, one of whom died in infancy, into an affluent middle-class family, the very class that created the demand for new houses and gardens that she and the Edwardian architects were to meet. Even as a child she was a spirited, independent lover of nature and the countryside. Her father fondly called her his little oddity. At the age of eighteen she took the unusual step of moving to London to study at Henry Cole's Kensington School of Art (further education for girls was rare last century). Having completed her studies Jekyll continued to follow her artistic and independent interests, making friends in the stimulating world of art and craft, travelling throughout Europe and widening her horizons, socially, artistically and intellectually.

After the death of her father in 1876 the family moved to Munstead House near Godalming in Surrey where influential characters from the world of horticulture regularly visited her. In 1875 she met William Robinson (1838-1935), the determined exponent of natural gardening. She began to contribute to several of his publications, including *The Garden* and continued to write articles for a variety of publications until the year of her death in 1932. A keen and talented photographer, she provided illustrations for her own books and articles and, as her reputation spread, for other writers. Like most projects Jekyll undertook she practised this craft with a determined enthusiasm and like many nineteenth century photographers, she carried out the developing process at home. It is said that between 1885 and 1888 she took and developed over 900 photographs. Those taken for her book *Old West Surrey*, published in 1904, were accomplished works of art in a new, relatively untried field.

In 1883 Jekyll's mother gave her energetic daughter fifteen acres of land across the road from Munstead House, possibly to channel those energies and, before any house was planned, Gertrude started work on her own masterpiece, the garden at what came to be known as Munstead Wood. It was not until 1889 that she found the architect to whom she could entrust the building of her house. Jekyll was forty-six, Edwin Lutyens only twenty, when they met at tea with the rhododendron collector Harry Mangles. In the foreword to Francis Jekyll's biography of his aunt, published in 1934, Lutyens affectionately recalled that first meeting.

> *'We met at a tea-table, the silver kettle and the conversation reflecting rhododendrons. She was dressed in, what I learnt later to be, her Go-to-Meeting Frock − a bunch of cloaked propriety topped by a black felt hat, turned down in front and up behind, from which sprang alert black cock's-tail feathers, curving and ever prancing forwards.*
>
> *Quiet and demure, of few words and those deliberately chosen and deliberately uttered in a quiet, mellow voice − with keen, bright eyes that missed little in their persistent observation.*
>
> *She spoke no word to me, but on leaving, with one foot on the step of her pony-cart and reins in hand, she invited me to Munstead on the very next Saturday. I was there on the tick of four.'*

Thus started a partnership and friendship that were to last until the end of her life.

Munstead Wood is a fine example of Lutyens at his best in small vernacular buildings, and Jekyll describes it with pride and pleasure in her second book, *Home and Garden*. No doubt she influenced him in several aspects of the design, but her chapter on the house is written in unstinting praise of her young protégé. It is a poetic and loving homage to a house whose existence she had planned for over twelve years and whose adorning garden was already there, in maturity, to clothe and complete her house. Her energy was remarkable. The more I work with Jekyll at Upton Grey, the more I become aware of that energy. During her eighty-nine year life, she wrote over one thousand articles, some, as I mentioned, for *The Studio*, the publication closely associated with our garden; she designed parts of, or entirely, nearly four hundred gardens. She also supplied a large quantity of plants for those commissions from her own small nursery at Munstead Wood where she had an excellent head gardener and under gardeners, but employed fewer hands for her fifteen acres than most of her contemporaries. She mastered the craft of gardening as well as the art. In *Wall, Water and Woodland Garden*, published in 1901, she describes precisely how drystone walls are made, a craft she evidently practised herself. Of course she understood the propagation and division of plants, occasionally discovering a new strain which she introduced to the horticultural world, the most famous of which is probably the Munstead primrose. There were very few garden crafts that she had not mastered. All her paperwork was done in the days before photocopiers and electric typewriters! She was also her own accountant and secretary.

By 1900 Jekyll had become widely known and respected in the gardening world. Whilst she admired and supported William Robinson and his move from formal to natural planting, she also appreciated the qualities of the architectural, formal gardeners who, led by Reginald Blomfield the neo-classical architect, fought vitriolic verbal battles with Robinson. This was not the first time in garden history that admirers of the formal and informal styles of gardening had been at loggerheads.

Gertrude Jekyll wearing the feathered hat that she wore on her first meeting with Edwin Lutyens in 1889.

In his *English Flower Garden*, published in 1883, Robinson expressed his intense dislike of all formal gardening. He abhorred structured, disciplined gardens with neat flower-beds cut into manicured lawns which he scathingly described as looking like tarts on a pastry-cook's tray. His ideal was a wild garden where unmown and unweeded grasses would 'occasion no trouble'. As I was soon to discover at Upton Grey, our Wild Garden occasions a great deal of trouble. Natural effects, achieved with the discipline which is necessary in a small garden, require just as much work as formal gardening, especially areas around a pond or water garden where plants grow at a prodigious rate as, of course, do weeds. Growing a meadow of pretty wild flowers while controlling the very invasive dandelions, ground elder and nettles, borders on the impossible in my experience; a fact that Jekyll was well aware of because in *Wood and Garden* she wrote, 'wild gardening is a delightful, and in good hands a most desirable, pursuit, but no kind of gardening is so difficult to do well, or is so full of pitfalls and paths of peril.' The Victorian bedding-out system also suffered Robinson's scorn. The over-crowding of beds with blocks of coloured annuals, twice yearly replanted, was like 'the practice of cramming monstrous Chinese feet into impossible Chinese shoes' and the continual replanting of bedding flowers regularly left the ground 'like newly dug graves'. Robinson was inclined to extremes but they made for amusing and convincing arguments. Jekyll's talent was to combine the best of both formal and natural styles. She wrote: 'Both are right and both are wrong. The formal are architects to a man. They are undoubtedly right in upholding the simple dignity of old formal gardens but they parade its limitations as if they were the end of the art; they ignore the immense resources that are the precious possession of modern gardeners... Who is to play the very needful part of artist-gardener? ...the free gardener?' So Gertrude balances Blomfield with Robinson and produces complete, satisfying gardens that enhance nature while controlling it. 'Planting is to gardens as poetry is to words, the best use in the best context', she wrote.

I have taken courage from the fact that Jekyll was nearly fifty before she made a true impact in the world of horticulture. Shortly before she died she wrote that it had taken her half a lifetime to learn the art of gardening and the better part of the second half in learning how to use it. Gardening, as I was to learn, is a therapy, a pleasure and a hobby that can be practised at any age.

The Wild Garden as we found it in 1984, over-grown with brambles and incorrect trees. The photograph was taken from an attic window and the weeds in the fore-ground are growing out of the roof!

Chapter Two

1984

The Garden starts to unfold

Penelope Hobhouse.
Photograph by kind permission of Cynthia Woodyard.

In early 1984 word of our discovery began to spread to garden historians. Our first visitors were an intrepid group of horticulturists led by Gilly Drummond, whose fledgling Hampshire Gardens Trust was fast gaining support. She brought some of her key members to see the garden in February. Merrick Denton Thompson, Jean O'Neil, Victoria Wakefield and Penelope Hobhouse were among them. At that date the house was full of builders; John and I were busy painting walls and making curtains. We had done no work at all on the garden which was still in the over-grown, weed-ridden state that we had found it. I remember feeling ashamed that such important people should be expected to take an interest in what was, effectively, a very weedy, muddy and dilapidated site. But they were interested and encouraging, and from that day, for well over two years, Penelope Hobhouse was a patient giver of sound, practical advice. I think it was she who told me to start the clearing work near the house and work away. 'You may get discouraged if you start at the edge and work inwards'. Very wise.

The same month, Richard Bisgrove from Reading University came to see the garden. Over the years Richard has proved one of our greatest sources of encouragement; he can always revive flagging spirits with a few words of optimism. But my memory of that visit is very hazy. It was a cold, drizzly day when he struggled through dense undergrowth with me. I asked him how I should begin to tackle the jungle and he mentioned 'Roundup', assuming

that every literate person knew what that herbicide was, 'but it will only be effective if used in the growing season'. I wondered why; did not dare ask; knew nothing about plant physiology. There was so much to learn, so much to do. There still is. Gardening is an inexhaustible, fascinating subject.

During the bitterly cold winter months of January, February and March 1984 we spent the nights in a nearby flat lent us by a good friend. At the Manor House builders stripped out old pipes and electric wiring, installed a new plumbing and heating system and new wiring. The frail leaded windows were carefully repaired. Gradually the house dried out and started to become habitable and friendly. In the evenings I made curtains, and by day, dressed in a boiler suit that looked like a large kitchen cloth, I painted vast areas of repaired or re-plastered walls with a rather unwieldy roller-brush. For months hair and hands were flecked with paint. John joined in the work at weekends.

On warmer days, John and I wandered around taking photographs of every part from every angle. Although I knew very little indeed about plants and, at that time, nothing about how Jekyll's plans would look, I made notes on the state of the garden and its obvious defects. To the south-east of the house in what soon came to be known as the Formal Garden (because lines of walls and borders run straight and architecturally) drystone walls terrace the ground as it drops away from the house. These walls were collapsed and weed-ridden and the beds at their footings had disappeared. In the main herbaceous borders large trees had grown; a horse chestnut at least fifty feet high, a willow and a cherry tree among others. Two sixty-foot conifers stood on the Bowling Green. They were not on Jekyll's plan so we removed them, but to this day we have problems with subsidence where their roots once grew. Lawns were simply large areas of moss and weeds with very little grass, but were described as 'spongy-soft and comfortable to sleep on' by a friend's daughter. Nothing remained of a pergola which should have run from the house towards the centre of the Rose Lawn, and paving around the top terrace was broken and in need of repair. The area Jekyll named the Rose Lawn was only lawn (weeds and moss to be accurate) and there was no sign of flower-

1997. The same view over the Wild Garden after complete restoration to the Jekyll plans.

Gilly Drummond.

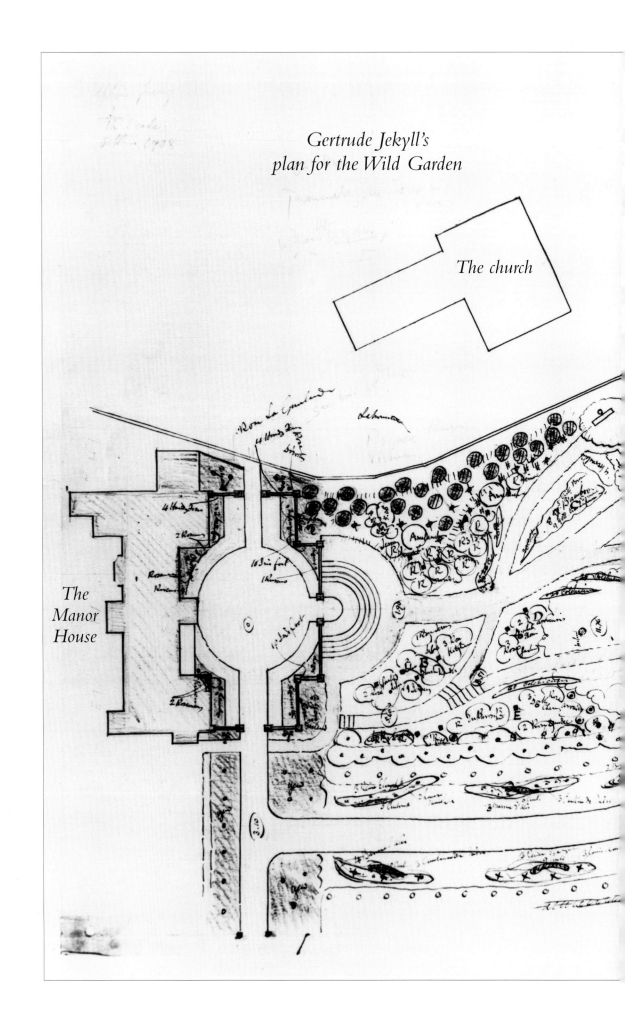

Gertrude Jekyll's
plan for the Wild Garden

The church

The
Manor
House

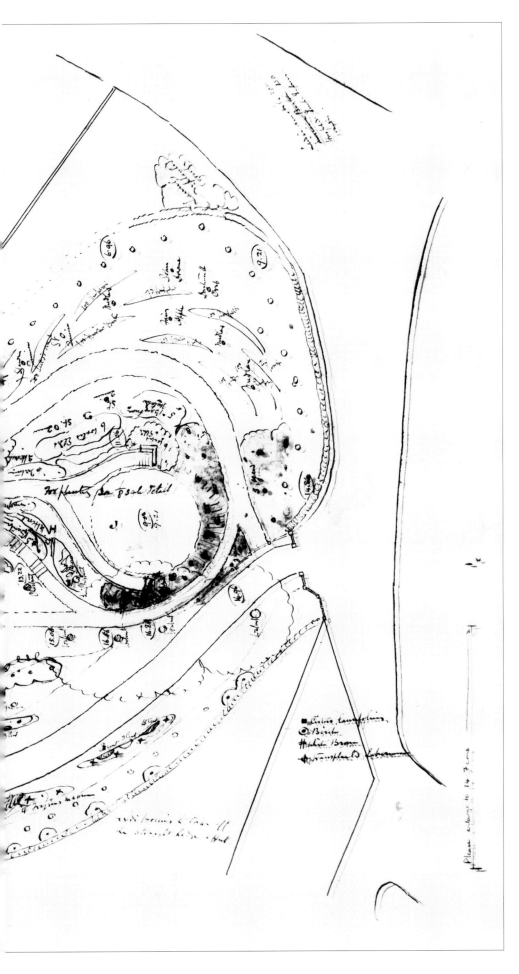

Our plans, and all those held
in the Reef Point Collection,
are the copies Jekyll made for
herself as references for
possible future changes in her
gardens so she uses
abbreviations and her writing
is often difficult to read. Very
few of the plans that she sent a
client survived.

1984. Towards the house from the Tennis Lawn.

1996. The same view with the garden restored to Jekyll's plans.

beds let alone roses. The few herbaceous borders that were at all evident were deep in weeds. Almost half of what should have been a yew hedge that surrounds the Formal Garden had died and was thick with brambles.

In the Wild Garden the situation was much the same but weeds here consisted of almost impenetrable brambles which were under-planted with a healthy crop of ground elder and nettles. The natural, spring-fed cattle pond had dried up and the small basin that remained was full of weeds. A great many incorrect trees had grown up over the century and it was some time before we were able to tell which were true to Jekyll's plan and which would have to be removed. Grass steps which form the entrance to the Wild Garden had reverted to a mossy bank.

On the first of May 1984, John's birthday, we moved in to a house which was still full of builders and largely uncarpeted but whose rooms were cheerfully light with paint. The weather was becoming warmer and it was time to start concentrating on clearing the garden. Until the Jekyll plans arrived later that month, there was a limit to what could be done safely. We did not want to lose a plant that might have survived from the 1908 garden.

1984. Removing the 50 foot chestnut tree from a flowerbed.

1984. Clearing the Wild Garden, looking towards the church.

Two months later, a similar view.

1992. The same view cleared and planted as planned.

Leucojum.

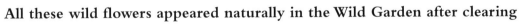

All these wild flowers appeared naturally in the Wild Garden after clearing

Pyramidal orchid (*Anacampsis pyramidalis*).

Fritillaria meleagris (purple).

Wood anemone *(Anemone nemorosa)*.

Oxlip *(Primula elatior)*.

Cowslip *(Primula veris)*.

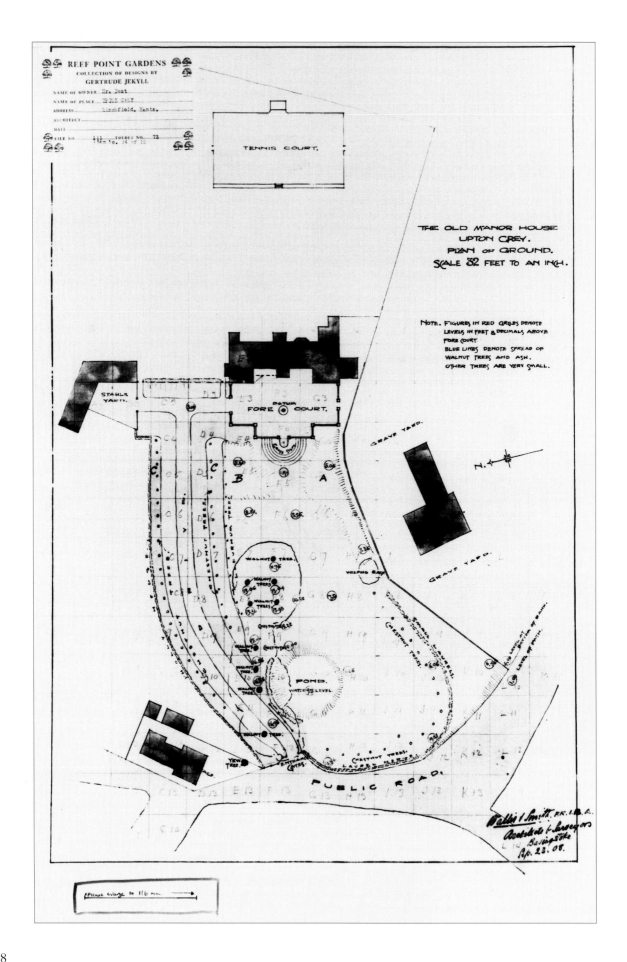

It may seem surprising now that most of Jekyll's plans are held in the USA. Some albums and plant lists are held in Godalming Museum in Surrey but the most important Jekylliana is in 'The Reef Point Collection' in the University of California at Berkeley.

Gertrude Jekyll died in 1932, leaving copies of many of her garden plans and several photograph albums at her house, Munstead Wood, in Surrey. Towards the end of the Second World War the Jekyll family sold most of Gertrude's estate to raise money for the Red Cross War Effort, and a substantial amount of her work made its way to London. In the late forties the American garden designer, Beatrix Farrand, an admirer of Jekyll who had visited her at Munstead Wood, acquired the collection of plans, some letters and photograph albums. Beatrix kept the collection at 'Reef Point', her house in Maine, and on her death, left the plans and albums to Berkeley's landscape architecture department. This became known as The Reef Point Collection. Farrand, herself a talented landscape architect, was responsible for some wonderful garden designs. One of her masterpieces was for Dumbarton Oaks, Washington, DC. With those plans, she left to posterity *The Plant Book for Dumbarton Oaks 1941*. As Mac Griswold and Eleanor Weller acknowledge in their erudite book, *The Golden Age of American Gardens, The Plant Book* is a remarkable document and describes in detail what should be re-planted, what might grow too large and what could be replaced without damaging the look of the garden. They claim that it is a book buoyed by the courageous assumption that a garden can live forever.

I owe Beatrix Farrand two debts. One is that inspiring sense of conviction; it makes me determined to soldier on despite being told that gardens are ephemeral and that ours, in its time warp state, is unnatural. The other is the fact that she saved Jekyll's plans for the world, making it possible, nearly one hundred years later, to recreate a horticultural work of art almost precisely to those plans, following colour, shape, texture, structure and proportion to the letter.

Gertrude Jekyll drew over two thousand plans for the three hundred and ninety-eight or so gardens she worked on and many of those that survive are held in The Reef Point Gardens Collection in The University of California at Berkeley. By no means all of those plans are for complete gardens; several are for special areas or for individual borders. Very few owners whose plans survive are able to restore today's gardens to the original designs. In many cases parts of the gardens have been sold for development, particularly in valuable real estate areas such as Surrey. Occasionally swimming pools and hard tennis courts have been built, and in a handful of cases the owners simply do not want to restore their adequate garden to labour-intensive Jekyll designs. Expense must also be an important factor in those decisions. It was the knowledge that very few other Jekyll gardens were complete or fully restorable that spurred our determination to make Upton Grey as accurate a living museum as possible.

Opposite: One of the two architect's plans that were sent to Jekyll prior to her planting plans. She usually worked with architects' plans, especially if gardens were too far from Munstead Wood for her to visit.

Jekyll's plan for Border 2, one of the main 'mirror' herbaceous borders. It took me well over a year, and much consulting with experienced gardeners, to decipher the whole plan.

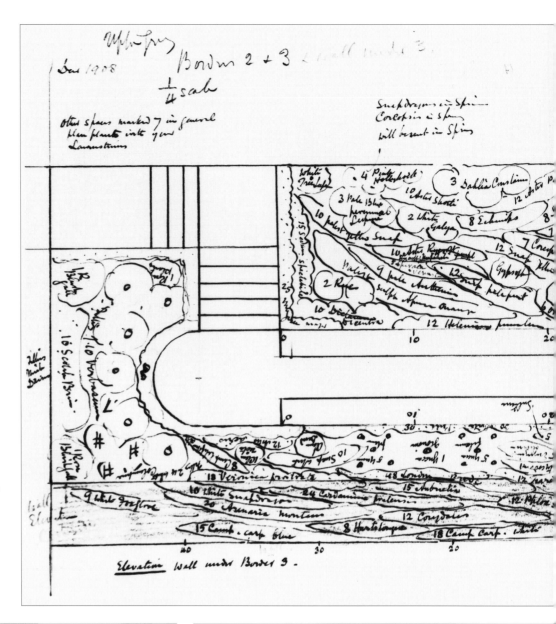

Below left: Border 2 in late summer 1998 from the centre looking towards the house.

Below right: Border 2 in late summer 1998 from the centre looking away from the house.

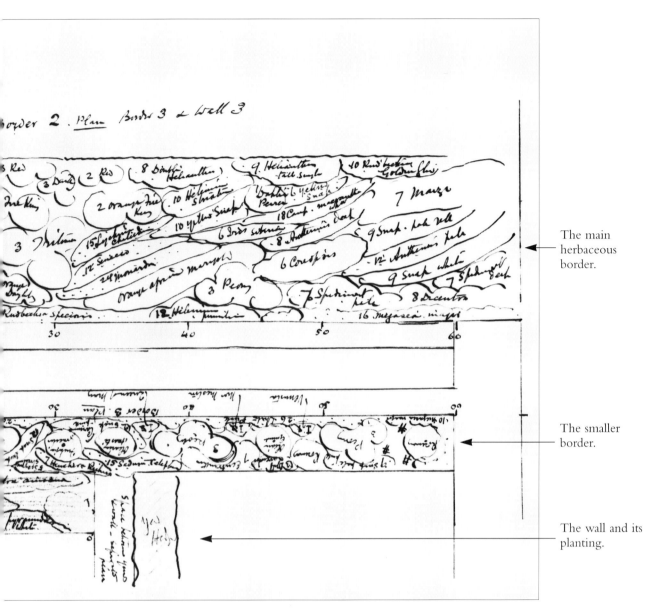

The main herbaceous border.

The smaller border.

The wall and its planting.

An overview of Border 2 from the house with the planted wall which is shown on the above plan.

Chapter Three
1984 and 1985
The physical work on the Garden starts

During the first two weeks of May 1984, while waiting for the plans to arrive, John and I manually cleared obvious weeds and brambles. My knowledge of weeds was as woeful as my knowledge of flowers and we had to be careful that we were not annihilating a survivor from Jekyll's garden. There were some plants that were evidently not weeds and, as spring drew on, I managed, with help, to identify them, and I moved them to a safe patch of well-dug earth in what had once been the kitchen garden. As I later discovered, a few of those plants were probably survivors from Jekyll's 1908 planting.

They included *Hemerocallis fulva*; various peonies; *Fuchsia magellanica* var. *gracilis*; *Acanthus spinosus*; hundreds of daffodils, some of which were the original Jekyll ones, and two roses; one a rare, delicate pink multiflora rambler called 'Euphrosyne', and the second a rose that has since proved to be my favourite (largely because it is a determinedly tough survivor with a tenacity for life that I wish my other roses had). It is called Blush Damask, but was known by Jekyll as Blush Gallica. I will write more about both those roses later. In the crumbling drystone walls we found hart's-tongue ferns and a very pale creamy-yellow *Corydalis ochroleuca*. Tall unpruned roses, most of which had reverted to rootstocks, a few chrysanthemums and a weedy aster failed to survive transplanting and they remained accusingly in the Kitchen Garden, like skeletons on a battle field. At every stage of transplanting I made notes of where I had found things in case they had stood in an original planting place on Jekyll's plan.

We sawed down, hacked down, dug up, and made enormous bonfires. We bought a large and very expensive canister of Roundup for killing weeds in the central areas of the garden, and SBK (Selective Brushwood Killer) for the nettles and brambles along our boundary with the church wall. I made a great many mistakes in those early-learning days, by far the worst of which was to leave a large spray-canister of Roundup beside some relatively innocuous insecticide. At the end of a twelve-hour working day I could become careless. I intended to kill greenfly but sprayed almost half the garden with lethal Roundup and only discovered the mistake when I returned the sprayer to the garage, to find the insecticide still unused. It was a lesson so bitterly learnt that I have never repeated it. But it is surprising how many gardeners do that. Today I check all canisters carefully before using them and with experience I recognise the different smells of the various chemicals; I also mark each sprayer clearly. Luckily for me that 1984 mistake was not as fatal as it might have been. Very few plants had been planted and therefore sprayed. Those old plants that I had saved and moved to the Kitchen Garden were obviously mature enough to recover from the dose, because most survived.

In our first six weeks of gardening we made serious investments in essential equipment which included a chain-saw, a Westwood tractor, spades, forks, heavy-duty secateurs, a trowel, buckets and a strong wheelbarrow. The Westwood served us faithfully for those first few years of clearing. It forged its way through the almost impenetrable jungle of weeds as well as through the odd boulder and tree root. We decided on a Stihl (024) chain-saw because, having hired one for two days, we knew the capacity we required, and the rest of the

Some of the plants that I found in the derelict garden and which I believe to be original to Jekyll's plans

Acanthus spinosus can be seen in the middle of the left hand border. This proved not only robust but very invasive.

Day lily *(Hemerocallis fulva).*

A peony that I found in the derelict garden and which I believe is *Paeonia officinalis*.

Rose 'Euphrosyne' (a rare rambler).

1984. Ros reading one of the plans with some difficulty.

equipment I bought from the local garden centre. I have kept an annual record of all garden expenses over the years.

John and I decided that, as he was working five days a week in London, we would need extra help in the garden if we were to see results in our lifetime so I asked Merrick Denton Thompson's advice and he had the answer.

To this muddled ruin of a garden came Terry Gould, the Californian who for just over two years was to work with me twice a week and help us restore the bedlam to discipline. Terry was about our age, strong and enthusiastic. He worked twenty hours a week and, when not gardening, studied herbal medicine. I am afraid that when you are working all daylight hours yourself, you tend to take other people's contribution for granted and not until he left, two years later, to help other aspiring gardeners, did I realise how lucky we had been to start with Terry. He was good company, full of useful knowledge and knew where to get practical things like hurdle fencing to protect the small yew hedge plants for their first few years. With his great strength Terry achieved astonishing results in those twenty hours a week.

A few days after Terry's arrival in May 1984, the copies of Jekyll's plans were delivered. I had imagined that plans would arrive, that I would order plants, seeds, shrubs and trees and that planting would go ahead smoothly the following year. When I unwrapped the plans the excitement quickly turned to dismay as I found roll after roll of sheets covered with quite indecipherable writing. I suppose I had expected neat, block letters but the manuscript was very sketchy. Several words were abbreviated (Ol. for *olearia* for example) and several names have changed over the century; tritoma has become kniphofia, megasea is now bergenia. To someone who had never heard of helianthus, let alone thalictrum, it seemed I was deciphering a coded language. The Reef Point plans are in fact Jekyll's own plans, not the fair copies that she sent clients. They were her record and reference points for when clients wanted advice on change in maturing gardens, and that accounts for her sketchy writing. Two overall architect's plans for the garden were included with the copies of Jekyll's hand-written plans. They indicated the gradients and dimensions of the terrain and were inscribed 'Wallis and

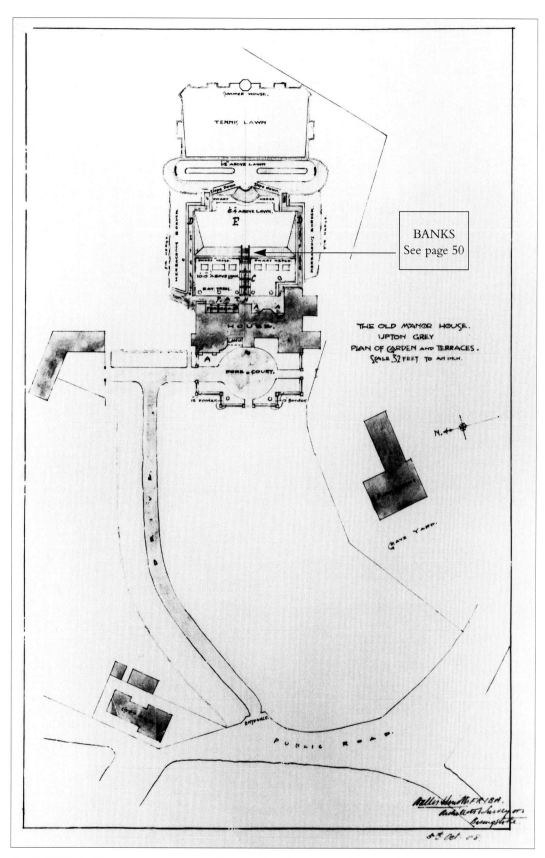

BANKS
See page 50

SUMMER HOUSE.

TENNIS LAWN

THE OLD MANOR HOUSE.
UPTON GREY
PLAN OF GARDEN AND TERRACES.
SCALE 32 FEET TO AN INCH.

N.

GRAVE YARD.

ENTRANCE

PUBLIC ROAD

April 1908. Architect's plan giving outline of the Formal Garden, showing Charles
Holme's grass banks. Gertrude Jekyll altered all this to give a simpler, less cluttered and
more sophisticated Formal Garden.

1992. Aerial view of the garden, showing the Wild Garden and pond to bottom left, and the Formal Garden, Orchard and Nuttery to top right. The church is to the right of the Wild Garden.

Smith FRIBA, Basingstoke'. Jekyll often requested that details of the garden's size and contours be sent her in advance of work, so saving time, particularly when the location was too great a distance from Munstead for her to travel. I have often wondered if she visited Charles Holme at Upton Grey. It seems probable as we are less than twenty miles from Munstead as the crow flies; she wrote for *The Studio* and would have known Charles Holme. The fact that no evidence of correspondence by letter survives with the Reef Point plans suggests that she communicated her ideas verbally at least some of the time.

In 1989 when I was unloading a bunch of reluctant dogs into the vet's surgery in Basingstoke I was astonished to see 'Wallis and Smith Architects', the very name that was on our 1908 architectural plans, written above the doorway on the adjoining building. I went in and asked if they kept records of work carried out at the beginning of this century. To my utter dismay I was told that seven months earlier they had burned all old files because they had run out of office space. That was one of the few threads of contact with the past that I have lost and I still regret that I did not at least look up their name in the local telephone directory as soon as our research started.

There was another snag, though not a major one. We had bought the Manor House and just over three acres. The stables, which now formed the adjacent cottage and garages, had been sold separately two years earlier, and I found that we only owned half the Kitchen Garden and Orchard. They and the Nuttery stand outside the Formal Garden and are not part of Jekyll's detailed plan so I allowed myself limited freedom to plant those areas with

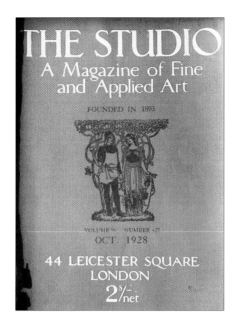

Two covers of
Charles Holme's *The Studio.*

appropriate fruit trees, vegetables and surplus stock from the planned garden. Terry and I found that we needed all available extra space for bonfires, compost heaps, greenhouse (to be built the following year), heeling-in and propagating areas. Happily the adjacent land was owned by a very cheerful local farmer and the more I encroached into his patch the happier he was to hand over the work.

The 16th May 1984 was my fortieth birthday. Again we celebrated in the garden with champagne, trestle tables and lots of friends. It was a beautiful, sunny day. Builders' debris was in piles all around the house and the lawn was still a soft luxurious layer of thick moss. House martins weaved in and out of the eaves, rebuilding their summer nests. All together we pored over Jekyll's plans, deciphering her writing, making lists of the plants, planning the future.

Throughout that summer, with help from serious gardening friends, I learnt to read Jekyll's writing and, once I was accustomed to it, the job of deciphering her abbreviations became easier. I also began to appreciate the art in Jekyll's gardens.

1984. Forecourt with builder's rubble and one of the enormous bonfire piles we made with debris from the Wild Garden.

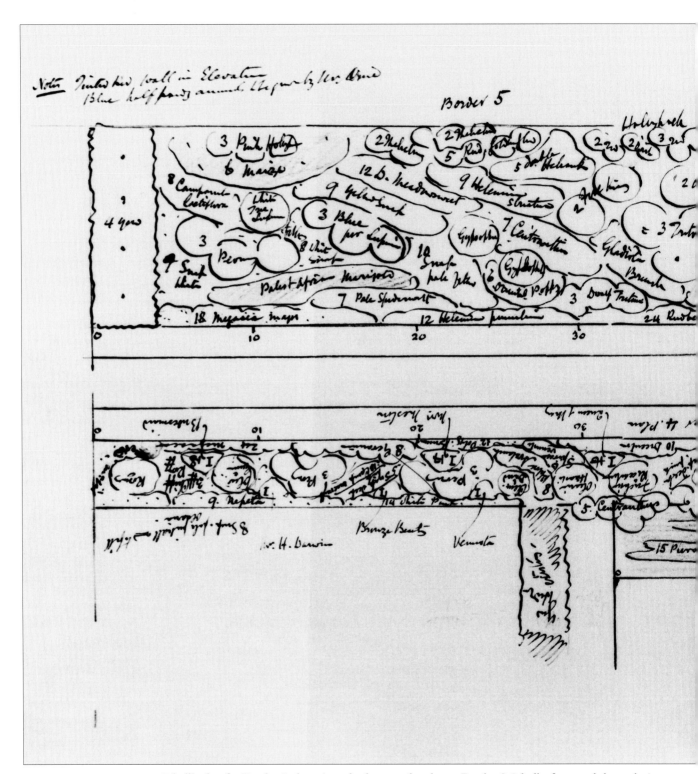

Jekyll's plan for Border 5, the mirror herbaceous border to Border 2. Jekyll often used the technique of planting borders opposite with similar colours but differing plants. In the main borders colours run from cool white, blue, pink at either end to hot orange and red in the centre then out to cool again. These borders are typical of the use of colours that Jekyll wrote about in *Colour in the Flower Garden*. Notice how the smaller bed and the wall beneath are also planted in drifts so that colours integrate gradually like Impressionist art.

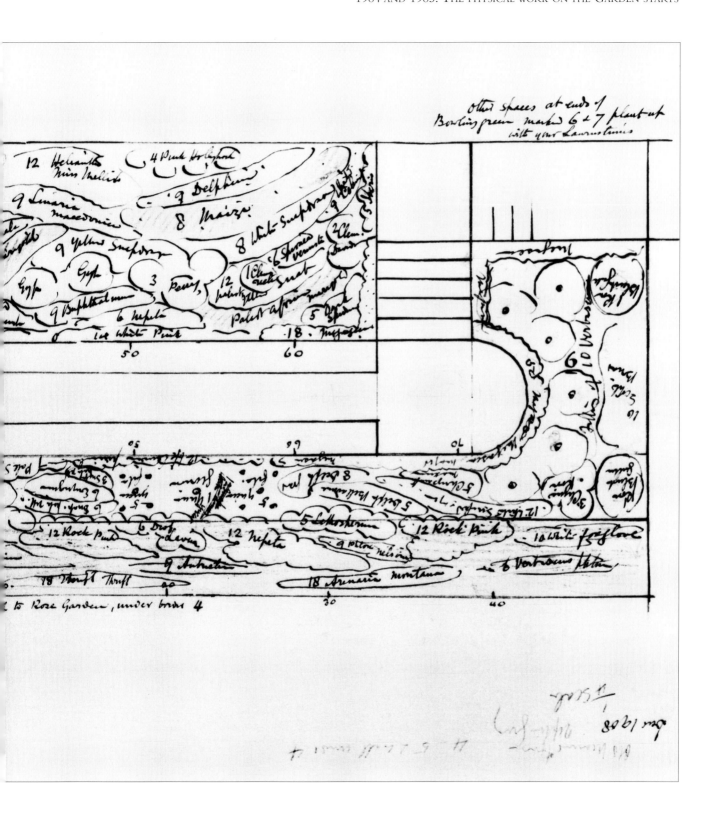

May 1984. Clearing weeds and trees before planting.

April 1984. Border 5 before restoration.

The restoration of one of the main herbaceous borders, Border 5 (page 38 and 39)

1985. Cleared (but for one tree) and the small yew hedge planted behind.

1986. Planted as on plans with hurdle fencing behind to protect young yew and plants.

1998. Border 5 planted and fully grown.   Photograph by kind permission of *Bo Bedre* magazine.

Biffo.

At Upton Grey we have both a formal and a less structured, more natural garden. Jekyll called the latter the Wild Garden. Both are balanced. Neither is an extreme example of its type. To the south-east of the house the formal garden has no curved lines; borders, paths, terrace and steps are straight. The Rose Lawn is a beautiful geometric shape, each half of which holds four trapezoidal beds surrounding a raised stone square bed. This is Gertrude working with an architect's eye. The planting is quite rigid but, where Blomfield and the architectural gardeners often planted those areas with nothing but roses, giving a harsh, unnatural effect, Jekyll edges the beds with *Stachys lanata* (first changed to *S. olympica* and recently to *S. byzantina*) and interplants the roses with lilies for wonderful mid-summer scent, and with old cottage-garden peonies to fill and soften the shape. Jekyll liked to mix peonies with roses, pointing out that some roses are too stark to stand on their own and that peonies make a perfect balance with their rich foliage and full rose-like flowers. The roses in our Rose Lawn are 'Mme Abel Chatenay', 'Mme Lombard', 'Mme Caroline Testout', 'Killarney' and 'Mme Laurette Messimy'. All are shrub roses from the nineteenth century, frail and disease-prone, and they need the comforting support of the glorious peonies, greedy feeders though the peonies are.

On the north-west side of the house lies the Wild Garden. The entrance drive runs alongside this. The Wild Garden has no straight edges. It is entered by wide, shallow grass steps which sweep in a semi-circle behind wrought iron gates. They take you to mown grass paths which wind through uncultivated and seldom cut grass. This is filled with daffodils, oxlips, cowslips and primroses in the spring and with fritillaria, wood anemone, forget-me-not, crocus, cyclamen and snowdrops through the year. Here the rambling roses grow in loosely supported columns and, as the paths move further from the house towards the pond, the planting becomes more natural: walnut trees (*Juglans regia*) and species roses are followed by bamboo (*Arundinaria medake* and *simonii*), meadow-sweet, aruncus and the popular then, fiendish now, *Polygonum cuspidatum* (Japanese knotweed) and magnificent but invasive *Heracleum mantegazzianum*. The trees are lilac, laburnum, birch, walnut and horse chestnuts which grow in groups. Medlar, quince, beech and crab apples grow singly.

In this garden which is small by Edwardian standards, I find the influence of several styles of gardening; rustic, romantic, geometric, natural and formal, those styles that had evolved, but never completely integrated over the centuries. Jekyll was too wise and open-minded to restrict herself to one style; she borrowed from many and let nature assist her. So, when Charles Holme commissioned Gertrude Jekyll to design the garden for his Arts and Crafts monument at Upton Grey, he chose the best in her field and the plans she gave him, dated 1908 and 1909, amply demonstrate that to me. This is not, however, the artist's own garden. Her commissions were designed to please her clients. There are letters with other plans that show she consulted clients on when they would be in residence, when the garden should be flourishing, and on our plans there is evidence that she agreed to accommodate either some of Holme's favourite plants or those he had brought with him in his move from Kent. For example, 'Use your own Laurustinus' (*Viburnum tinus*) is scribbled in a margin.

In July 1984 I bought four Jekyll books which had recently been reprinted; *Wood and*

Garden; Home and Garden; Wall, Water and Woodland Garden and *Colour Schemes for the Flower Garden.* At that stage in my ignorance all four were extremely difficult to digest. Fluently and beautifully as Jekyll wrote, if one has never heard of most of her subject, the reading can be very tedious. I put those books aside for a few years. The two books which proved invaluable in helping decipher Jekyll planting plans were Penelope Hobhouse's *Gertrude Jekyll on Gardening,* published in 1983, and John Weathers' *A Practical Guide to Garden Plants,* published in 1901. It was the indices that were enlightening. If an illegible word seemed to start with Asp, I went to those indices to choose likely plants and,

Ratty.

with common sense or advice, made selections. Penelope's book listed Jekyll's favourite plants. Weathers listed plants of 1901 and earlier, so if Jekyll only mentioned the species I could select a cultivar that was certainly available to Jekyll, and work from there.

Over the last fourteen years I have studied Jekyll consciously and subconsciously. Working with her plans during the day, while reading books by and about her at night, has made me feel curiously close to her spirit. Her books are peppered with philosophical observations which show her love of nature and her trust in God. 'The good gardener knows with absolute certainty that if he does his part, if he gives the labour… so surely will God give the increase.' Those beliefs may not be shared but they are nevertheless touching and reassuring. Armed with a dangerously small but growing knowledge of Jekyll, we renewed our attack on the garden.

Outgoings for 1984 were huge. Builders were being paid; furnishings, carpets and garden machinery bought. The heating bills for our large, draughty house were so high that for months I searched in vain for leaking oil pipes and refused to believe that so cold a house could burn up so much energy. Although we set thermostats low in order to economise (on very cold nights ice would form inside window panes), the hungry boilers devoured 5,571 litres of precious oil in nine weeks. Only after a couple of friends mentioned at breakfast one morning that, with all windows shut, they'd found a pile of snow on their window-sill did we double-glaze the whole house. Perversely, we also decided to buy two dogs. Dogs seemed a relatively cheap item as well as being, presumably, good company and burglar deterrents.

The Labrador is the standard choice of dog in Hampshire and the longer I live with them, the more I see why. We bought a black puppy with a large head, furrowed brow and intently serious green-brown eyes. Our dogs are named to suit their characters. First puppy was called Biffo because he looked like a thug and because he had won the litter initiative test. John lined up the nine puppies and rolled a ball for them. Biffo, in an energetic and clumsy scramble won the test, bowling siblings out of his way to reach the ball first. The second dog was to be Mark's birthday present and was intended to act as some compensation for moving out of London and away from his friends. He chose a fox terrier, a breed that looks like a Jack Russell with longer legs, alert faces and ears that hang at 'half mast', that is, half up and half down. The fox terrier is the dog which appeared on His Master's Voice record labels at the beginning of this century. The puppy looked minute compared to Biffo, yet she had a very beguiling face, bright brown eyes and a long nose; so we called the enchantress Salome. 'Bloody stupid name for a terrier', was the vet's greeting at each injection appointment. Today she is generally called Ratty because she is a quick, deft killer of rodents and small

Roses in the Rose Lawn

Rose 'Mme Caroline Testout' (HT 1890).

Rose 'Mme Lombard' (Tea 1878).

Rose 'Mme Laurette Messimy' (China 1887).

Rose 'Mme Abel Chatenay' (HT 1890).

Trees in the Wild Garden

Lilac (*Syringa* 'Mme Lemoine').

Medlar *(Mespilus germanica)*.

Walnut *(Juglans regia)*.

June 1997. The intention in the Wild Garden, Miss Jekyll believed, was to start with some formality and for the planting to become more indigenous and 'wild' as it moved away from the entrance until garden and landscape almost blend in the distance.   Photograph by kind permission of Heather Angel.

rabbits. The dogs proved good companions during the summer months but Salome began to show her true colours as hunter and wanderer as soon as she was big enough to jump over the church wall, so I devised a practical way to allow her limited freedom. She has a long rope, attached to an old bucket or empty oil canister, tied to her collar. She can run around but at limited speed and making a prodigious noise, so I generally hear her escape attempts. It is not an infallible device. If she escapes with ball and chain it causes havoc in neighbours' herbaceous borders. She is not universally popular in the village. We love her as one loves a tiresome old friend but I will not get another fox terrier when she dies. She is quite an age and is hanging on to life with stout determination – like the tiresome old friend.

Being novice gardeners we were lucky to have Jekyll's plans as our guide. With these and an agenda to follow, making a garden is far simpler than starting at random. We wrote lists of the following year's schedule and target dates, which was an excellent discipline because, although weather and plant suppliers can affect schedules, goals are a good incentive to flagging spirits. We spent the last three months of 1984 clearing, demolishing and burning in order to start 1985 with a partly penetrable garden and a comfortable house.

In November I ordered three hundred yew plants for delivery the following spring. These were needed to repair the many places where existing hedging had died. I bought them at minimum size and minimum price as we were in no hurry and they would have ample time to establish themselves. The last purchase for 1984 was eight panels of six-by-ten feet hurdle fencing. Terry erected this beside the formal garden to give shelter for 1985's new plants and the young yew hedge. Hurdle fencing is an old craft that uses hazelnut branches in a woven pattern to make an attractive rustic fence or screen. Most old gardens included a 'nuttery' where hazelnut (*corylus avellana*) trees were grown as a crop, not only for nuts, but for the wood which, being fast-growing and supple, has many uses ranging from providing material for fences, plant frames and beans, to rustic furniture. (I am told that William Robinson reluctantly tolerated rustic furniture because it rots quickly. It seems he was hard to please).

In December John and I drew up plans for the following year which ran as follows:

> Clear ground of weeds. Strip turf from formal lawns, i.e. bowling, tennis and rose lawns. Measure all beds to ensure that they are the correct size. Restore beds that are grassed over. Take trees out of beds (there were several, the biggest being a fifty-foot horse chestnut). Buy and store twelve loads of good manure. Make compost heaps. Re-build collapsed drystone walling, the stone steps and terraces. Double dig and manure all borders. Build the pergola. Make lists of every plant, shrub and tree on Jekyll's plans and investigate sources. Make lists of essential chemicals for pest control, weed control and disease. Make list of good organic treatments (blood, fish and bone etc.). Order roses; order seeds; order plants that could not be grown from seed. Investigate greenhouses with a view to buying a small cheap one the following spring.

At every stage I took photographs and most nights made garden diary notes. Both seemed so trivial at the time. Both were very useful in retrospect.

1985

During January and February Terry and I continued clearing the garden and removing small trees and stumps, both working very hard through all weather. I believe that, given a potential 7a.m. - 9p.m. working day spring and summer, I worked about sixty-five hours a week for the first two years. Terry worked a remarkably hard twenty hours (2 days) a week and John joined us at evenings and weekends to add a further fifteen hours. On that basis, two hard-working people can clear, plant and maintain a four-acre garden from virtual dereliction in two years. During winter months one person can cope alone. Modern machinery and the chemicals, which I am rather loath to use nowadays, speed results. One machine that saved us a great deal of time, and therefore money, was the JCB excavator. It can dig trenches or shallow basins and uproot small trees. In one day it can carry out work which would probably take one man two weeks of manual labour. We hired the JCB and driver in 1985 to make long trenches for yew hedging which was to surround the formal garden, and again in 1986 to dig out the pond basin. If possible heavy machinery should be used before the garden is established. This is an obvious point in retrospect but can be overlooked. In 1985 the lawns were not established so the JCB did no damage to grass with its heavy wheels. Another machine which saved us days of work was the turf stripper which we hired for two days in April 1985. It close-stripped the mossy grass layer off all green surfaces in the Formal Garden, rolling them up into huge bales which we used to make into a strong edge for compost heaps, which itself rotted down to fine compost material.

Both the Tennis Lawn and the Bowling Green needed hours of careful work in order to achieve a good firm surface. We were lucky that the foundation work for a Tennis Lawn had been done thoroughly at the beginning of the century. It is the precise business of levelling ground, of ensuring adequate drainage and adding the various layers of suitable soil that go to make the foundation of a grass court, which are costly and time-consuming. According to Reginald Beale who published *Lawns for Sports* in 1924, the following procedures are necessary. Once levelled the soil should be drained on the herring-bone principle (a four inch drain down the middle of the court with three inch spurs every twelve feet). Having done that and introduced the correct layers of subsoil (light, sandy, gritty etc) the main work is done. No wonder grass courts are rarely seen these days. Apparently we were left with the easy bit; the preparation of the top layer of soil and the sowing of grass seed, but John, Terry and I found that very demanding work. John was, and still is, in charge of grass (see page 48). In the spring of 1985, having stripped back to earth with the turf stripper, we lightly rotavated and then graded the area. We did this by attaching ropes to each end of an aluminium ladder and dragging it across the earth again and again until it was level. We followed this by treating the surface with weed killer (Roundup) in two separate doses. A month later we scarified it lightly with spring rakes, removing all stones at the same time. We then carefully trod the whole area with large flat-soled boots − and so did any available friends (who very rapidly found better things to do) − after which we top-dressed with sterilised topsoil which we buy annually from Surrey Loams. That was followed by 'heeling in' the surface; a similar process to 'treading in' but only the heels do the pressing. It is a comical sight to watch. It is slow, it is painstaking and indeed quite painful but it does give the correct compaction to the surface. Having consulted Sports Turf of Bingley, Yorkshire, we bought a fine grass seed mixture known then as F1 Highlight (chewing fescue, browntop and creeping red fescue but no rye). We broadcast the seed and finally top-dressed again. Grass is an expensive luxury; it costs about £500 annually and that figure includes no labour and no machinery depreciation. On those lawns the making of a good surface was such a labour of love that on-going maintenance is relatively simple. I do not play tennis so mine was a labour of loving others enough to do it well, as I kept reminding myself in a rather martyred way when I struggled out with glasses of cool drinks for the perspiring players.

After two years, when major work is completed, a garden of this size can be maintained by

Restoring the grass areas

1984. Grass areas as they were with very long grass, weeds and moss.

March 1984. Turf-stripping done.

May 1984. Terry rotavating the stripped and weed-free surface.

1998. One of the lawns restored and resown with a good quality rye grass seed. The Tennis and Bowling Lawns are sown with a rye-free 'fine turf mix' of grass seed.

Jekyll's use of drystone walls to replace grass banks

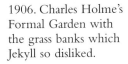

1906. Charles Holme's Formal Garden with the grass banks which Jekyll so disliked.

one person working a very long week, as I was to prove from 1988 until the beginning of 1991. I called that period my total immersion stretch and chose to work on my own in order to learn all aspects of gardening, not just horticulture but the running of machines and their maintenance. It also taught me one very good lesson, the value of a reliable gardener.

In the spring and summer of 1985 our priority was to get the structure of the Formal Garden completed. Having cleared out trees, brambles and roots, our next two jobs were to plant the yew (*Taxus baccata*) hedge which surrounds the formal garden and to tackle the drystone walls. Some of the original yew hedge had survived but where it had died, we filled the trench which the JCB had dug earlier with well-rotted manure and top-soil, and then planted the three hundred small yew that I had ordered the previous autumn. For the first few years of their life yew need plenty of water but once established they are tough survivors in most conditions.

The drystone walls, which terrace the garden to four levels, form an important feature structurally and visually. A little work had been started on the garden before Charles Holme consulted Miss Jekyll in 1908. To the south east of the house she altered his existing garden quite radically. Where Holme's house overlooked grass banks that sloped to a lower grass terrace (see architect's plan page 35), Jekyll designed drystone walls to drop to a Rose Lawn. In *Wall, Water and Woodland Gardens* she wrote of her dislike of grass banks with uncharacteristic feeling. 'Hardly anything can be so undesirable in a garden. Such banks are unbeautiful, troublesome to mow, and wasteful of spaces that might be full of interest'. Most gardeners agree with her; even with modern machinery like hover mowers they run to moss where scuffed and scorch in the sun. The drystone walls with which she replaces the grass banks are full of colour and interest in their season. As far as I can judge from photographs, Holme's Wild Garden was rather fussily planted. Gertrude Jekyll altered it to a calmer, more sophisticated garden with an entrance of shallow grass steps and rambling roses that lead to a small group of walnut trees.

Most of the drystone walls stand about four feet high and are made of local Bargate stone which is a warm buff-grey colour. They are planted in detail on her

1996. The same view with Jekyll's 1908 walls restored and planted proving that walls are both structurally pleasing and can be beautifully planted.

An interesting sequence! Jekyll's garden in its heyday, 1915 (right). As we found it in 1984 (below). Restored and replanted in 1998 (bottom)

Illustration from the *Studio Year Book* of 1915 showing Holme's Formal Garden from the Bowling Lawn.

1984. The same view before we started work on the garden.

1998. The same view today, with walls rebuilt and planted correctly.

51

Santolina chamaecyparissus and *Lavendula spica* 'Munstead Dwarf'.

Papaver rupifragrum.

The Rose Lawn showing the contrast between the rigid structure and the soft planting.

Photograph by kind permission of *Bo Bedre* magazine.

Rose Lawn and wall planting showing common flowers used to good effect

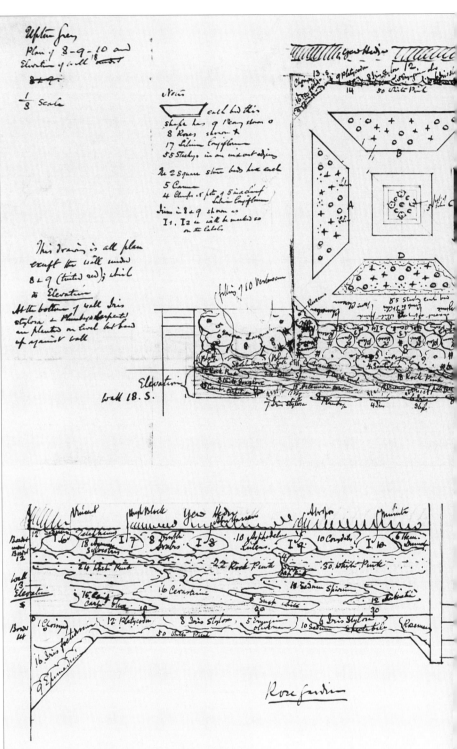

Gertrude Jekyll's 1908 plan for the Rose Lawn and surrounding walls. This plan shows Jekyll working with geometric formality. The area is very structured but the planting is quite cottage garden in effect.

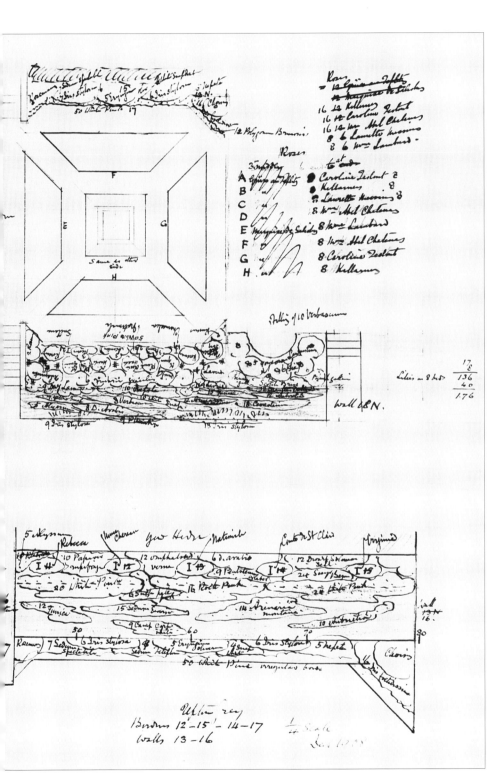

Steps to the Rose Lawn. Jekyll liked steps to be as shallow as space would allow.

Photograph by kind permission of *Bo Bedre* magazine.

Corydalis ochroleuca and hart's-tongue fern.

Walls in late summer with *Anemone sylvestris*, *Platycodon mariessii* and *Eryngium oliverianum* in foreground.

1984. Walls surrounding Rose Lawn before re-building showing their weed-ridden crumbling state. They collapsed when we tried to weed them so all had to be rebuilt.

1984. Walls rebuilt.

plans, as ever in drifts of appropriate plants, rock and alpine types mainly, but with some interesting varieties according to whether walls face north or south. Each wall has quite different micro-climatic conditions from its neighbour. The plants on the south-facing walls include *Arenaria montana, Armeria maratima, Pterocephalus perennis,* and on the north-facing walls shade-loving plants, including *Corydalis ochroleuca,* hart's-tongue ferns and *Cardamine pratensis.*

There are altogether twenty-three different plants in the walls alone. Nearly all the stone for the walls remained and was re-usable but the walls had collapsed and needed dismantling and rebuilding. We were given three quotations for restoring the walls, rebuilding the steps and repairing all the terracing. The lowest estimate came from Lindsay Clarke Brothers, landscapers from Farnham, so obviously they were the people we wanted to use but we had no means of telling how competent they were.

I telephoned Hampshire County Council. Merrick advised that I accept the lowest tender and promised to send an experienced waller to inspect the work as it went along. Lindsay Clarke sent a remarkably young man called Derek to do the job. He looked suspiciously like a cowboy builder but appeared to know what he was doing. He told me how to batten back the earth to a certain angle so that stones would lean into it, catching rain and protecting plants. He showed how the top capping stones should lie and explained that high walls like these should have a firm cement footing for extra strength (that worried me as it sounded rather modern). He then carefully dismantled the stones from the collapsing walls and laid them out in the order that they were taken down and were to go back. After a few days the experienced drystone wall builder came to inspect 'Derek-the-Walls' at work and declared him a fine builder. That is the sort of help that made life at the start of our restoration work so much simpler. Derek took about two months to complete the work and did a very good job.

On one plan dated 1909, across which she had written 'thrown out', Jekyll designed a third, very shallow drystone wall, to stand between the Tennis Lawn and the Bowling Green. Presumably Charles Holme decided against this low wall because it had evidently never been built. An odd decision we thought, and wondered if he had run out of stone or of money. In 1993 we decided to build the wall because we assumed that Jekyll had wanted it and because it was so beautifully proportioned and planted. By then Bargate stone was no longer available so we used Purbeck, a slightly paler local stone, as a substitute. That wall now completes the terracing very prettily.

While 'Derek-the-Walls' was finishing the stone-work Terry and I got on with the next

1985. 'Derek-the-Walls' at work.

priority business. Very evidently we needed a greenhouse if we were to grow as much stock as possible from seed. I had learnt the hard way that seeds cannot simply be sown in pots and ignored. In the early summer of 1985 I started the first trial sowings of seeds with no greenhouse for shelter. With pessimistic foresight I had bought many more seed packets than I needed. Most amateur gardeners do this because seeds are cheap compared to plants and you always want to reach that price level when post and packing is free. 'Add £1. 50 p. & p. if order is under £12. 00' is often irresistible and in 1985 £12. 00 provided a gardenful of seeds. Of the one hundred and eighty or so different plants that I needed there were over sixty that I could grow from seed, most of which germinated reasonably well. Those which did not and those that I knew I could not grow from seed, I later bought as plants, corms or bulbs to divide and propagate from over the years. My favourite suppliers – those that have the largest proportion of the seeds that I require – are Chiltern and Thompson and Morgan.

1998. The walls in the Formal Garden completed. The steps in the foreground are Jekyll's ideal 8cm rise with 45cm tread and the small wall is the one which Jekyll planned but Charles Holme rejected.

1984. The Rose Lawn before clearing. Behind and to the right are overgrown drystone walls, flowerbeds in the centre had disappeared.

March 1985. The Rose Lawn cleared but not weeded and beds not renewed.

Too many other seedsmen supply only mixed colours and Jekyll always specified colours, for example, *Campanula carpatica* 'white'. Those suppliers also have a wide range of species and cultivars. I buy most of my vegetable seeds from Suttons.

The first experimental seeds were carefully sown in trays of compost, tenderly watered and left in a sunny position. One night we had a violent rainstorm and the tiny seedlings were drowned. The next week I started again, this time leaving the trays in a sheltered position. We went away for a weekend during very hot weather and I came back to find seedlings shrivelled to death. As a result of this upsetting experience, I bought a very basic, perfectly hideous, metal and glass greenhouse which we erected in the summer of 1985. A do-it-yourself greenhouse is a lot harder to construct than I was led to believe. Ours was eight by twelve feet, with a four-by-four foot extension which can be kept frost free by a small economical heater. That size is quite adequate for basic garden needs. It took about a week, and some bad language, to construct, after which my subsequent sowings were safe as long as we never went away for summer weekends. I had a very good excuse for refusing invitations and staying in my beloved garden. By early May of the following year our greenhouse was full of healthy seedlings, enough to part-fill most of the herbaceous borders.

The other essential job, which all gardeners who are replanting from chaos must face, was to clear the earth of remaining weeds and then fertilise it. In June 1985 we sterilised all earth in the Formal Garden in a drastic way, which I know to have been correct and essential, but which I shall not repeat. We used a chemical powder called 'Basamid'. Because it is a powerful chemical it is only available in bulk quantities to farmers and people who have large areas to clear. (I have never seen it sold in garden centres). It must be forked lightly in to the earth, after which the treated area is sealed with black plastic sheets for about a month. This has to be done while the weather is reasonably warm in order for it to take effect. For six weeks that summer the Formal Garden looked like one of William Robinson's newly dug graves, and to some extent it was, because not only did all the weeds die (including convolvulus) but so, unhappily, did the worms. After six weeks the ground is clear, healthy and, although I have not needed to prove this for myself, I understand that it also clears ground of 'rose sickness', and it is then ready for double digging. Terry and I worked up good appetites digging ground to the depth of two spade-heads (known as double spit), filling it with manure and then replacing the earth; probably worked up quite a smell too – a subtle combination of sweat and dung.

1985. The greenhouse full of my first successful attempt at raising plants from seed.

In July, patient Penelope Hobhouse, who had been my constant source of advice for over a year, took me on a Jekyll lesson; a visit to Hestercombe in Somerset. Lutyens was responsible for the garden architecture and Jekyll for the planting but no doubt they worked

June 1985. The Rose Lawn with Basamid weed-killer and plastic sheeting on the newly positioned beds.

at both together. The 'great plat' is a glorious example of their partnership and the plans for Hestercombe are about the same date as ours, 1908. July is a difficult month for most gardeners as Jekyll herself acknowledged. 'There seems to be a time of comparative emptiness between the earlier flowers and those of autumn' (there certainly is a lull patch here at Upton Grey), but Hestercombe, with its magnificent stonework, geometry, mellow planting and beautiful structure appeared to me to be a garden that would be breathtaking in any season. (1998. Further restoration at Hestercombe includes a splendid landscape garden and lakes designed by Copplestone Warre Bampfylde in the eighteenth century and a small Victorian terrace by Henry Hall.)

I returned to shambolic Upton Grey more overwhelmed than encouraged but believing that we too could achieve great things, though on a rather smaller scale. My immediate problem was to find sources of all the plants on Jekyll's plans.

Plant Finder, that valuable book of information on plants and suppliers was first published in 1987, so until that date I had no means of finding a source for the plants I needed and had to rely on advice from friends. It was a slow process ordering first catalogues and then plants, with no firm idea of who could provide what. Luckily for us Jekyll did not design gardens for her clients with a plantswoman's priorities in the sense that they love and collect flowers for their rarity value or for individual beauty. She designed gardens as an artist. She loved the effect that sweeps of colour and texture create, and for those drifts she generally chose popular, reliable plants. She occasionally used structural plants like yucca, for architectural effect but, though they may have looked exotic, those she chose tended to be quite commonly available. For that reason, the great majority of the plants on our plans are still easily found, but there are one or two exceptions. Occasionally a virus has killed a cultivar, for instance to the best of my knowledge none of the *Iris germanica* or *pallida* cultivars on our plans survive and I have also had trouble tracing some of her dahlias and asters, so we have chosen close modern substitutes. Bressingham Gardens supplied most of the herbaceous material that I could not grow from seed, and Beth Chatto supplied the rare ones. In most cases I bought one 'marker plant' to put in the area which was to be filled with seedlings. That acted both as a place guide and to give me an idea of what the seedlings would eventually look like.

I was able to buy all but four of the sixteen roses for the Formal and Wild Gardens from Peter Beales, David Austin and Harkness. The search for the remaining four was to prove interesting and rewarding. Many of the herbaceous, perennial and annual plants were ordered as seeds and that was, of course, a great saving on buying plants (despite the cretinous mistakes

1996. The Rose Lawn with peonies in flower showing how well peonies look among roses. It was a combination that Jekyll loved.

Three peonies that we found in the garden in 1984 and which continue to flower.

I made at the first attempts with growing from seed). Plants that grow from bulbs, corms and rhizomes, in other words those that I could not easily grow from seed, I ordered from Kelways and Bressingham. At Upton Grey those groups include crocus, five different types of iris, corydalis, canna, dahlias and peonies. There are ninety peonies in the formal garden, a remarkable number considering the area they are to cover. They are planted in groups of three in almost every border. The fact that we found several (at that time unidentifiable) peonies in the derelict garden in 1984 proves that they thrive in alkaline soil. In 1985 I noted that I removed those plants to a safe area in the Kitchen Garden, but as I did not know their type or date of origin, I could not be sure they were not planted relatively recently. In order to be accurate I decided to buy peonies for the Formal Garden that I knew were available to Jekyll at the beginning of this century. Because our Jekyll plans state only 'peony', but no species, I chose two that were pale pink, double-flowered and pre-1908. They are 'Sarah Bernhardt', a *lactiflora* cultivar, and 'Lize van Veen', an *officinalis*. As I was to discover, peonies are the glory of this garden from May until late June. Having two species, I have an early and a late-flowering type; they smell wonderful and they positively love this fast-draining chalky ground and our cold winters when their tuberous roots are exposed to the elements. They are greedy feeders and I am a generous caterer, giving them compost, manure and organic fertiliser regularly, and phosphorus (P) and potassium (K) from time to time. I am told that fertilisers which contain a high quantity of nitrogen (N) will encourage lush growth at the expense of flower and root growth. Shrubs and trees were easy to track down and were supplied by Landford Trees.

Towards the end of 1985, as the days grew shorter and colder and as piles of debris grew, I concentrated on acquiring the skill of bonfire-making. Initially I simply dumped all burnable bits in a heap and armed myself with hundreds of matches, masses of newspaper and wood. But I only succeeded in getting the irksome pile to burn on a really hot dry day, often after wasting pints of paraffin. A wise local gardener and general handyman, John Smith, gave me this advice.

Close up of Peony 'Sarah Bernhardt'.

Peony 'Sarah Bernhardt' in the Rose Lawn.

Peonies 'Liz van Veen', an early, very pale pink, fading to white.

Formal Garden in winter showing the importance of good structure and simple outline. The design is geometric. There are no curved lines in the Formal Garden. See plan on page 66.

Cut your twigs, rose branches, debris, whatever, into small pieces about eighteen inches long. Take matches, newspaper and a large cardboard box to the site of your fire. That will obviously be an open patch, away from trees, hedges and all other flammable material. Divide the newspaper into separate sheets and crumple each into a ball. Pile these together and light them, then cover the burning mass with your upturned box. A funnel effect is now created, because no box is totally air-tight. Now lay your twigs in parallel lines over the flames. This is essential as there is very little heat in the flames at this stage and crossed branches will simply create a roof over dying flames. As your sticks sink into the burning box, add more, still in parallel bunches. Gradually build up the fire until the base heat is hot enough to take large pieces, logs and damp branches. Some evergreen leaves burn helpfully because they contain oil. Keep feeding the edges of the fire towards the centre with a long-handled fork. If earth and debris are very damp, sump oil will get the fire going. Soaked into a rag and ignited is the best method. Most garages will give away sump oil. Beware of petrol; it is quite effective but it burns fast without much heat and tends to ignite explosively. If weather is dry and windy, have a hose or several buckets of water handy. An uncontrollable bonfire is terrifying and it can run through dry grass. Very obviously, wear old and washable clothes. Every part of you smells after a successful bonfire. A good bonfire is immensely satisfying and the resulting ash is very good for the garden.

Christmas of 1985 was spent with my sister so I escaped all work. I gave most people gardening presents, and was given some excellent gardening things myself. I still have the heavy plastic-coated apron with deep pockets and a flap-up kneeling pad at its hem. I have only just used and only just appreciated the various winter tar washes and insect inhibitors for the fruit trees (I kept those in a box in the garage for ten years but they were still effective as far as I could tell). The Felco secateurs will see me out – which is a rule for buying that I apply more and more often these days – and the dozens of gloves that I was given were used and run through in the following years.

After Christmas, or as soon as the really cold weather starts, I hibernate for days on end. That means making up fires in all grates, reading instructive books and making notes of any relevant material. I had a great deal to learn in a relatively short time. Today, when people remark on how much I know for someone who only started gardening fourteen years ago, I have to admit that this knowledge is still extremely limited. It is a minute range in a huge field because I only know my plants, something about Jekyll, Holme, Newton and Arts and

Crafts, but almost nothing of subjects outside this area. Other people's plants are quite a mystery to me, to their delight.

By the end of December 1985 I was physically exhausted, fingers and toes were fat with chilblains, skin scarred and worn. But the garden was clean and cleared of all debris, its beautiful shape and structure evident. Like all good gardens it was a fine sight then, and is subsequently every winter, when only the 'bones' are showing. Good structure in a garden is as important as good planting. It can be strong or delicate, elaborate or simple, the key is to balance it with the architecture and environment. I was mentally sated with gardening, with plants, with old lore and new, but I was completely contented and happy. I learnt the importance of patience and timing (though I did not master them). Impatience is a kind of panic and a mistrust of nature. Trust in the future, a belief in something that felt like complete fulfilment, cocooned me and still does. A great many things go wrong, not only in my own small world of gardening, but on a shattering scale in life generally and yet there is healing and solace in nature. I had learnt some good lessons in those first two years.

The Wild Garden in winter. Although structure is important in this part of the garden there is very little geometric design and there are no straight lines.

Wrought iron gates to Wild Garden after cleaning and repainting. A description of the process is given opposite.

Chapter Four
1986

January and February continued bitterly cold. Coming from London where life was seldom extremely hot or cold, I had not been very aware of temperatures. Centigrade and Fahrenheit confused me. The day I really understood how horribly cold England could be was a January morning. I washed my hair and, with it still wet, walked out of the back door, along the terrace to the garage where I picked up some tools and returned to the house. The whole excursion took about five minutes. By the time I got back to the kitchen my hair was frozen into icicles. It does not say much for the circulation in my brain. It made me realise that I was not imagining the bitter cold and neither were the toes.

Almost everyone in Britain must have suffered a burst water-pipe at some time in their lives. It is an event which can be quite horrendous. I am tempted to wonder why caring, interfering governments have not seen fit to set up a body of people to offer counsel to burst-pipe victims who have suffered the shock of gallons of water flooding through their house. That January we had our first major pipe burst. It was about 10 p.m. We were going to bed when, to my surprise, I heard what sounded like a downpour of rain. I thought this odd as it had to be too cold for rain. I went to investigate and found a torrent of water tipping through three levels of ceilings from the top of the house to the cellar. This, I thought at the time, is the worst thing that has ever happened to us. Next day the plumber came with a smiling face, 'Never mind; this is what keeps me gainfully employed and my family fed'. So it does. We recovered. So did the house. Now every pipe is double lagged. Life is rarely completely bad. There is solace – remember how many destructive garden pests are being exterminated.

And there are the warmer days – days when winter sunshine colours everything with a gentle yellow light; when you think that this is the best country in the world, and so, apparently do the birds. All sorts of songbirds start to fill the air with warbling notes as do some very un-tuneful ones. Hibernation is coming to an end. Snowdrops are the brave pioneers. They send out their first flowers to spy on the retreating enemy, winter. In fact, *Iris unguicularis* have been doing this all winter but not with the military determination of battalions of snowdrops. I had assumed that their botanic name, *galanthus*, had something to do with that gallant nature. I discovered that the word derives from the Greek *gala,* meaning milk, and *anthos,* meaning flower.

These warmer winter days are times to spend doing maintenance jobs. During February and March I worked on restoring the three beautiful wrought-iron gates that stand near the house. They were in relatively frail condition, rusty, covered in a thin layer of green mould and in need of thorough cleaning and painting. The green mould must first be removed with a bleach wash, which inhibits the formation of more mould. Then rusty parts must be taken back to sound metal with a wire brush, and, in very intricate places, with a metal skewer. The gates are then left to dry thoroughly before painting starts. That should be done on a dry day when the temperature is above freezing. There are several types of paint which will do the job adequately. A coal tar bitumastic paint is excellent for metal surfaces but it dries to a very dull matt finish

1984. The same gates before renovating and before cherubs were replaced.

In 1985 I used a red oxide undercoat and then a good black gloss paint as overcoat. When I repainted the gates in 1996 they were in sound condition and I simply used 'Hammerite', a rust-inhibiting paint.

At the end of March 1986 England and I thawed back to spring life. The earth softened and dozens of bulbs burst through. The Wild Garden which, after clearing, looked rather like a bumpy field, began to turn yellow with daffodils. They grew, not only in controlled drifts in the correct areas on Jekyll's plan, but all over that part of the garden. Whilst the trees and brambles had remained, covering almost the whole area, there had been very little sign of daffodils. To our surprise, this year, for the first time probably for about seven years, those strong, resolute bulbs sent up a grateful flourish of golden-yellow. A few years later, Sally Kington, from the RHS's Lindley Library, came to help me identify which were the 1908 daffodils that Jekyll had planned. Almost certainly 'Emperor', 'Empress' and perhaps 'Horsfieldii', have survived and are in the correct places. There seems to be no sign of 'Barrii' or 'Leedsii'

The area in the Wild Garden where Jekyll's original drifts of daffodils survive.

Overall photograph of daffodils in the Wild Garden.

but two out of five drifts surviving years of neglect demonstrates how resolute some plants are. The other daffodils, those that cover most of the rest of the Wild Garden in contrary, muddled patches, have obviously been planted later this century. There were, to my knowledge, at least five other families living here at separate times and, during the Second World War, the house was divided in two and used by the Army or the RAF for recuperating personnel.

By late spring we had completed nearly all clearing work in the garden and most of the structural work. One important feature remained to be tackled. In April 1986 we restored the Jekyll pergola which runs from the house towards the Rose Lawn in the Formal Garden.

Close-up of those daffodils, including old varieties 'Emperor' and 'Empress' which were found growing in the garden.

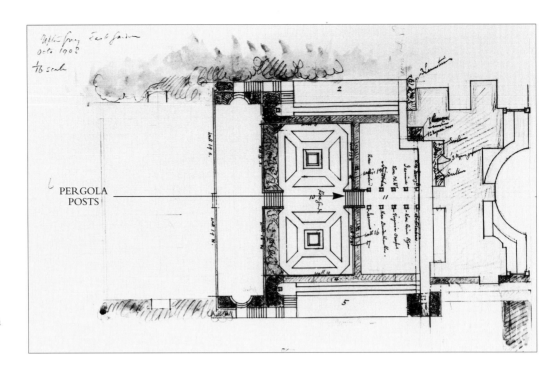

Gertrude Jekyll's plan for the top terrace and pergola.

The pergola is a feature in many Jekyll gardens and obviously its proportion is important. By reference to her book *Garden Ornament* we were able to choose what we believe is the correct height and shape of posts. On Jekyll's plan for the pergola she simply marked ten spots where posts and their named climbing plants were to be placed. I bought ten six-inch-square treated oak posts, each ten feet long, in order to stand two-and-a-half feet into the earth and seven-and-a-half feet proud. To carry the plants at the tops of the posts we bought seventy feet of very thick hawser (mooring rope) from a Southampton ships' chandler. This three-and-a-half inch diameter rope is old, oiled, and weathered. It is beautifully plaited, strong, heavy and relatively inexpensive. Any important sea port will have a chandler.

The pace at which both house and garden were eating up money was beginning to slow. I was trying hard to economise on plant material by growing from seed, dividing my plants or taking cuttings, but there were times when economy was not possible. For the pergola I needed two *Aristolochia macrophylla*. Each of those cost £10. They are now almost the more loved for being so expensive. Their elephant-grey stems enfold the thick pergola posts; their massive green leaves clothe them beautifully in summer. Its flowers are not spectacular,

Below left: *c*.1920. Postcard showing top terrace and pergola.

Below right: 1984. An exhausted Terry Gould by newly erected pergola posts.

1998. The pergola in winter. The rose arbour beyond the Tennis Lawn makes an important focal point in all seasons.

1998. The pergola in summer.

1992. From the house looking over the Tennis Lawn and the fields of Upon Grey in the distance. John and Mark playing tennis.

neither does it have the glorious autumn colouring of the neighbouring *Parthenocissus quinquefolia* (Virginia creeper) which changes colour through deep crimson to golden yellow in late October, but aristolochia is a wonderful structural plant.

We celebrated the second anniversary of arrival at Upton Grey by showing a small group of bewildered members of the Hampshire Gardens Trust around the fine bare earth, immaculately re-made walls and clean paving. There was hardly a flower in sight. To my shame, in retrospect, I was immensely proud of the fertile desert and did not realise how disappointed the group was until several years later, when someone told me that he had come on that first visit. I asked if he had enjoyed it. 'Well, frankly', he said, 'we were all a little surprised that you opened the garden at all. It's worth coming back today though!' Garden visitors are remarkably tactful to one's face; they are generally kindred spirits who put up with shortcomings and appreciate all the hard work even if results are a little disappointing. However, when I am out of sight but within earshot of them (behind a hedge for example) I hear wonderfully uninhibited comments. 'Nasty rose blight. Careless with her pest control. Pity about the dead tiarella'. I very rarely hear a direct criticism of Jekyll's planting.

Actually people went on reacting in that slightly disgruntled way for the first six years. It really took that time to re-create a pleasing Jekyll garden. Some parts, like the Rose Lawn, looked beautiful within five years because I had started with mature rhizomes of peonies and with roses as small plants. But the Wild Garden, which has no walls, terraces and fast-growing herbaceous plants of the Formal Garden, depends on trees and shrubs for structure. The Portuguese laurels, the walnuts and medlar trees will develop slowly and will not reach full maturity for some twenty-five years.

Different plants, and therefore different parts of the garden, reach their peak at different times over the years. Maintaining that peak in fast-maturing areas like herbaceous borders, whilst woodlands develop slowly, is important and, for a beginner, quite difficult. For the first few years I let rosemary, lavender, santolina and other small shrubs grow luxuriously. When, even to my inexperienced eye, it was obvious that they had become overgrown and out of proportion, it was often too late to cut them back to the correct shape, certainly not all in one year. It was not until 1987, as I will describe later, that I realised the error of my ways but we did not take serious steps to shape growth until the nineties. Most shrubs and structural plants should be carefully controlled as they develop. This was particularly

1997. Towards the
house from the Tennis
Lawn. This rich
expanse of green grass
gives perspective to
the picture of the
house and garden.

important at Upton Grey because, for economy, we had bought plants, trees and bushes at minimum size. Not all gardeners would do that, some with less time to wait and more money to spend like to start with mature, well-shaped plants, and today's garden designers often over-plant with the intention of thinning out as the gardens mature. That is rather an extravagant way of starting a garden. It depends on your priorities, and on your purse.

1986 was a happy summer. The weather was kind to young plants. We played our first games of tennis on the grass court. Well, to be accurate, others played and I watched or gardened. Grass is a wonderful surface for tennis. You can quite happily play in bare feet. The surrounding netting only encloses the ends and a quarter of the sides of the court because the ball does not bounce as violently as on a hard surface. For the first week after the netting went up I was distressed to find several, even more distressed than I, small balls of spikes rolled into the netting in hopeless tangles. They were hedgehogs who had wandered out of the adjoining Nuttery at night in search of worms. As untangling them was well nigh impossible I cut extravagant holes in the netting to release the little creatures (and I picked up a few flea bites at the same time because, although I never actually caught fleas from a hedgehog, they seem to make a few test bites for good measure). Nowadays we hitch up the netting overnight and the hedgehogs wander to and fro in safety.

From 1986 onwards, the Tennis and Bowling Lawn treatment has been roughly the same annually. In spring and autumn the grass is solid-tined, slit-tined or hollow-tined. It is then top-dressed with sterilised soil which is brushed in and the surface lightly re-seeded. For the following two weeks we act like living scarecrows while pigeons and crows do their best to outwit us and eat all seed before it germinates. Throughout the year the grass is lightly scarified and on damp autumn days the dew is switched off with a long, supple rod. We feed the grass in spring and early autumn and give moss or weed treatments when necessary. Sports Turf of Bingley were our guiding lights on grass.

As the Formal Garden matured I began to appreciate the importance of this laboriously tended expanse of green. It runs from the base of the Rose Lawn's drystone wall to a wooden seat in the rose arbour beyond the Tennis Lawn. In our garden Jekyll was careful to mark where seats should be situated, knowing that these are points from which to view beautiful parts of the garden. Seen from here the garden is well displayed as it rises above the rich green expanse and this, I am told by garden designers, shows the value of space in design: the grass

1986. The Atlantic cedar (*Cedrus atlantica*) to the left of the picture. It was not on Jekyll's plans so we removed it.

displays the beautiful structure of the whole area and gives perspective to a work of art. Where possible an allowance for views and vistas should be included in a garden.

While the Formal Garden had structure, shape and a considerable quantity of young plants enclosed in a ridiculously small (in height) yew hedge, the Wild Garden was in a state of limbo. We had cleared weeds, brambles and ugly cypress-type trees and we had faced the fact that eventually all the incorrect trees would have to come out if we were to return to pure Jekyll. That was the hardest decision for a beginner gardener. Some beautiful Japanese cherries, trees that I had learnt to love and rather covet in London squares, stood near the entrance to the Wild Garden. They were quite wrong and were the first to go. We cut those down ourselves. In June 1986 we bravely decided to have three large horse chestnuts (*Aesculus hippocastanum*) that stood alongside the church wall, taken down. They must have been over sixty years old and presumably planted at much the same time as Jekyll's plans were drawn up. I know, from contemporary photographs, that Charles Holme did not follow Jekyll's plans to the letter. I suppose that is the bane of all garden designers; clients pay for plans but are under no obligation to follow them strictly, although they may happily claim that theirs is a so-and-so's garden. As the horse chestnuts were so big we hired tree surgeons to fell all three. There is something desperately sad about felling a beautiful, fairly old and perfectly healthy tree. The trees had established a presence and a useful shelter in the garden.

I was in the kitchen making tea for the tree fellers, when I heard the eerie creaking, crack, crash, as the first massive trunk fell. There was a short silence, like the ominous silence between car tyres screeching and the crunch of broken glass, and then a second, very worrying, thud. I ran outside. The tree had bounced when it fell. First it fell where expected, and then, on the dry, hard chalk bank it had bounced eight feet to its left and demolished the wall along one side of the drive. Three rather shaken men stood over the giant, ruing the broken wall, and relieved it had not hit one of them. To me it seemed like a death protest from an innocent creature.

Once the conifers, cherries and horse chestnuts had been cleared, the Wild Garden looked

1996. The same view after removal of cedar. The Wild Garden is now well balanced with the house.

exposed, 'un-wild', and the remaining two incorrect trees, a yew and a large Atlantic cedar, looked peculiarly wrong. Neither was on Jekyll's plan but I knew, from an early photograph, that Charles Holme had planted the cedar in about 1907. Given that his tree was probably ten to twenty years old when planted, the cedar was about one hundred years old, massive, stately and ludicrously out of place in a small (by Edwardian standards) wild garden. Removing that tree was a very hard decision but one that, once taken, we knew to be correct. Convincing Basingstoke Council was difficult. In this part of Hampshire and perhaps throughout England, important trees have preservation orders on them. The Council could not understand that almost-Jekyll was not true Jekyll. Eventually I turned to Merrick again. He made the powers-that-be reconsider their decision but it was a slow process and permission was not granted until the second fierce storm, that of January 1990, split the great tree in half, leaving a menacing ravaged trunk and single branch that leaned accusingly towards the house, threatening revenge. It was sad to see destruction in such a small area, but it was, as the doctor says, usual to get worse before it gets better.

The Wild Garden will take twenty-five years to mature and to look as beautiful as Jekyll planned it. That is life. Some things develop, peak, and decay quickly, and some slowly. The art is to learn the pace and to control the fast performers so that near perfection is maintained. Having to clear almost everything before restoring the garden made our task far easier. Establishing a new herbaceous border in clear, fertile ground is so much simpler than planting amongst and under existing, established and greedy plants. The difference is like making a garment out of new cloth or trying to do the same with old, already used material. We were lucky; not many people are able to start with a clean sheet.

Over the years we have made very few compromises on Jekyll's plans for the garden, and only with Penelope Hobhouse's approval. There were three altogether. Apart from an eventual and reluctant compromise with the pond which I shall describe later, the other two were with planting. The drive which runs to the house beside the Wild Garden is edged with large horse chestnut trees and a holly hedge. Charles Holme evidently ignored Jekyll's plan,

The horse chestnuts (*Aesculus hippocastanum*) that line the driveway. They were not on Jekyll's plan but some had been there since before Charles Holme's days, so after consulting experts we left them (one of the very few planting compromises we allowed).

Grahame Stuart Thomas in the Rose Garden he created at Mottisfont Abbey in Hampshire.

as those trees are not on it. At the foot of the holly hedge two beds of tree peonies are marked. We have left the trees, as they are now in their prime, and we have omitted the peony beds. The other deviation from plans was in the Rose Lawn where Jekyll stipulated *Lilium longiflorum* 'in pots'. *Lilium longiflorum* is not fully hardy and has to be brought in to shelter in very cold winters. As there are about one-hundred-and-eighty lilies in the Rose Lawn, Penelope suggested we use *Lilium regale*; it is very similar, has a wonderful smell and is more robust. I tried both lilies. *'Longiflorum'* did not survive the first winter but *'regale'* is wonderful. No wonder Ernest Henry Wilson, who discovered the lily in remote west Sichuan early this century, considered it such an important find.

By the end of the summer of 1986 we had an exciting embryo garden of which we were unjustly proud. Oh, but I loved it all. I took to gardening like a convert takes up a new religion. Like all obsessions it was infuriating to everyone else because I could talk, read, think about little other than gardening, plants and Jekyll, and I never wanted to leave the garden. John was very patient, yet at the time I was obliviously ungrateful.

My knowledge was increasing. I re-read and now enjoyed Jekyll's books, and I started collecting second-hand books on gardening. My collection began with a search for the obvious; early editions of Jekyll, Robinson and important nineteenth century gardeners; later it extended to the general field of garden writers. The books are well read and well worn and I buy them simply because they have long been out of print but are a good reminder of conditions for Edwardian gardeners. Some are beautifully, wittily and wisely written – those by Jekyll, Margery Fish, and Vita Sackville-West for example. I find some authors, like Mrs Earle and the Reverend Dean Hole, write a little too floridly. Most of my books are written by women gardeners.

I believe that the greatest gardener of the second half of the twentieth century will prove to be Graham Stuart Thomas. His knowledge of plants in general is encyclopaedic; he writes well and informatively, and he is also a very talented artist.

When he made an appointment to visit this garden in the late spring of 1986, I had heard of him but knew little about him. He arrived on a sunny day when the garden was in a state of weedlessness, almost bare-earthed flower-beds, tiny, stick-like trees and pretty drystone walls. He was immaculately dressed in grey flannel trousers and a blazer; a good-looking elderly man with white hair and serious eyes. He brought with him Mac Griswold (whose book, *The Golden Age of American Gardens* I mentioned earlier). I showed them Jekyll's plans, my aspirations and inspiration, and left them to wander around. They had evidently come a long way to see precious little and their visit did not last long, but they were tactful and

encouraging. Graham came back with another important gardener, writer and rosarian, Hazel Le Rougetel, in 1994. They stayed for lunch, were full of gardening anecdotes and were fascinating company.

Lilium regale in the centre of the Rose Lawn.

Graham was probably the last living gardener to meet Gertrude Jekyll. She admitted few visitors in the last two years of her life, but with typical perception she allowed the very young gardener to visit her at Munstead Wood in 1931, the year before she died. He has written an account of that visit, which he kindly let the Hampshire Gardens Trust include in a display it mounted at Winchester College Memorial Cloister. It is enlightening and enchanting and Graham has given me permission to quote it here.

While studying the craft and science of horticulture in my early days in the late 1920s I had also been captivated by the art. A friend had lent me Gertrude Jekyll's Colour Schemes for the Flower Garden *which fired me with enthusiasm for graded colours in the herbaceous borders.*

On coming to work in Chobham, near Woking in Surrey, in June 1931, I lost little time before I managed to get permission to visit her renowned garden. And so, on a warm Saturday afternoon, September 6th, I cycled all the way through Guildford and Godalming to Munstead. There was only a hand gate to her modest and charming home amongst the trees on that sandy rising ground. She received me sitting placidly in a chair, welcomed me and told me to walk round the garden, pick a piece of anything I wished to talk about and come back to the house for tea. My notebook reminds me of graceful bushes of Leucothoe axillaris (L. fontanesiana) *and huge hummocks of* Gaultheria shallon *with neither of which I was familiar, and a carpet of* Cornus canadensis *just coming into berry. Having been brought up in limy Cambridge, I particularly remember these and huge banks of azaleas and rhododendrons, kept well apart.*

Hazel Le Rougetel.

73

But it was the colour borders which enthralled me. I had never seen anything like them before, although I was a little prepared in my imagination from her writings. Being rather late in the summer they were probably past their best, but a succession of colour was kept going by the expedient of putting in late flowering plants grown in pots to prolong the season. The main flower border was a grand size, some 200 feet long by 14 feet wide, though reduced somewhat for planting by the shrubs at the back against the stone wall. Some of the shrubs augmented the colour scheming; others provided interest earlier in the year, for this big border was developed mainly to give colour through July until late September. I saw the Michaelmas daisy border, which took over after the main border, and those leading to the Hut where she pursued her crafts. What was so remarkable about the colourings in the main border – from cool to strong and cool again at the far end – was the solidity of the whole, bolstered by the shrubs and great clumps of Yucca recurvifolia *and* Bergenia cordifolia *'Purpurea'. I have not forgotten the wafts of scent from* Lilium auratum *and also the delicate pink* Lilium krameri *(L. japonicum) and* Lilium longiflorum. *Golden privet, African marigolds, silvery senecio and santolina were all there, contributing their bit, likewise cannas and dahlias. At the back was a group of the dignified* Helianthus orgyalis *(H. salicifolius) not yet in flower; it looked like some burgeoning lily. This I took indoors to ask about.*

The much narrower pair of borders along the path leading to the Hut were about at their best. The gorgeous red, yellow and orange tones 'hit' one and caused the eye to fly along them coming to rest where the path was cleverly deflected to the left between hedge-buttresses, the more easily to take in the striking change to silvery grey foliage and cool colours, contrasted by the sober dark green fig, and bright blue Delphinium *'Blue Fairy'. Another plant I picked to discuss with Miss Jekyll was the comparatively rare* Ophiopogon jaburan, *which I learnt was pot-grown and plunged in position where an annual plant had spent itself.*

Then there were cool, damp positions graced by the new, lemon-yellow Primula florindae *and contrasting blue trumpets of* Gentian asclepiadea. *And of course, a combination of frailty with firmness, a froth of* Aster corymbosus *(Aster divaricatus) draping over bergenia leaves, a little feature I have often repeated. In those days hostas were practically unknown in gardens; at Munstead Wood one came across them grouped with ferns and also standing in pots by one of the water tanks.*

And so, in to tea. Miss Jekyll was still seated in the same chair looking very like the portrait by William Nicholson, painted eleven years previously, her hair neatly parted in the middle. We examined my few specimens and I think she was rather surprised at how few there were. But though her garden was well stocked it was at the time of summer flowers, well tried plants, not rarities. In fact I had brought with me a few photographs, in monochrome, including that of Lilium cernum *and* Lilium alexandrae *(L. noblissimum) which I had in my garden at Cambridge and I felt she did not take much interest in them! But in after years I have realised that not only was her sight poor – through those tiny spectacles – but her interest was in plants that made effect in gardens, not botanical rarities. She had after all been making her garden pictures for forty years and had assessed and assimilated all the salient points and uses of every plant she grew.*

Our tea was brought and we had it on occasional tables near by the sunny windows; thin white bread and butter and a preserve (I do not remember what) and some little cakes. Her mellow voice floated on through the words of wisdom she imparted about my samples and I came away deeply moved by all I had seen and heard. It was a pleasurable visit, long anticipated and a lucky one for me, because she died in 1932. William Robinson went to her funeral. We have all profited almost unbelievably from her examples and written words; most of what we do in our gardens today stems from her ideas.

Helianthus orgyalis syn. *salicifolius.*

It seems remarkable that one as young as Graham Stuart Thomas was in 1931, can have appreciated Jekyll so maturely and can have judged that visit with such perception. I have been lucky enough to meet many of today's great gardeners. I have often found them generous and patient friends or acquaintances, who give time and experience as generously as they share plants.

In the summer of 1986 a local newspaper wrote an article about us, illustrated with a photograph of me perusing Jekyll's plans. A few days later I was telephoned by a man who introduced himself as Colonel Kenneth Savill. He told me that his father had rented the Manor House from Charles Holme from 1916 until 1936, and that he had photographs from that period which he would show me. Colonel Savill arrived a few days later with two albums and a head full of memories. We walked around the garden together – the garden which had been his playground as a very young boy. He remembered trees, hillocks, beds, pond, and his photographs were excellent memory joggers. He had taken most of them himself with his evidently fairly rudimentary camera. Kenneth lent me his precious albums and I took them to Winchester where Eric Lane, a professional photographer, made copies for me. He now has his albums back quite unchanged and I have a valuable record of this garden from very soon after Jekyll's plans were executed. Over the years several people have lent me albums and photographs that make up a broad visual record of the garden from 1900 until today.

1918. Kenneth Savill as a boy in the Wild Garden with his parents who rented the house from Charles Holme. His albums of photographs provide me with evidence of the garden's development from 1916 until 1936.

By the autumn of 1986 we had a comfortable though still draughty house. We had two dogs and we had a garden that was becoming more exciting by the season. Looking at photographs taken in 1984 and 1986, the difference between them was startling. Whereas most of my 1984 photographs featured rampant brambles in an unidentifiable part of the garden, the 1986 photographs showed monochrome neatness. Beds, walls and tiny hedges completed a beautiful sepia pattern. Needless to say there was relatively little upkeep. Weeds had almost been eliminated, so very few germinated. Pruning was not necessary and pests and disease among strong, young plants is minimal.

Photographs taken from 1986 onwards show swathes of green lawn and increasing blocks of colour as dwarfs developed into giants and began insidious spreading into neighbouring areas. Because we keep so rigidly to our plans, I have to be very careful that plants do not seed themselves outside their areas. In those first few years I learnt which plants were likely to start a lawless invasion of another's territory, and I began to understand why some plants have almost disappeared from suppliers' lists. Apart from those that I had to accept I would never find (those that had fallen victim to disease or pest), one that I found hard to track down was the relentlessly invasive helianthus 'Miss Mellish'. It has turned from being one of my proud possessions to becoming an untrustworthy intruder. Its roots spread, quite literally, from one side of the border to another if I am not careful. 'United we stand; divided we multiply and over-run' applies to those and to many other invaders. A severed root develops into siblings and they turn into enemies too. Helianthus 'Miss Mellish' was sent to me from Germany by a garden visitor whose parents ran a nursery near Frankfurt. Despite its waywardness, knowing that this is one of the few gardens in Britain to have the flower, is very satisfying. I remember the anxiety I felt during Miss Mellish's first winter here and my delight when it reappeared (at an alarming rate) the following spring. Today the list of 'unfindables' is short and I no longer circulate it, but during the first six years at Upton Grey

The very rare but invasive helianthus 'Miss Mellish'.

Above left: *Linaria dalmatica* (substitute for *Linaria macedonia* which is lost).

Above right: *Yucca filamentosa*. A plant that Jekyll used often and which she admired for its structural beauty

I gave visitors lists of plants that I was having difficulty tracing. The plants that I have still not found are: *Gladiolus brenchlyensis*, dahlias 'Fire King' and 'Orange Fire King', asters 'Rycroft', 'Parker' and 'Shortii', *Linaria macedonica*, *Phlox subulata* 'Nelsonii', and most of the bearded iris cultivars. (In 1995 Phlox 'Nelsonii' was listed in *Plant Finder* as being available at Shepton Mallet in Somerset. By the time I made an order the nursery had closed and I believe the plant is now lost).

During the late autumn of 1986, Terry and I concentrated on the Wild Garden. We had cleared it of almost all incorrect planting and now began work on restoration. In order to be sure where various plants, trees and, most important, the pond, should go, we staked out the whole area into a grid of ten foot squares. There was evidence of a very small, dried up pond where we expected to find it but it had changed shape over the century. We hired the JCB again to dig out the forty foot diameter by three foot deep basin that Jekyll's plans stipulated. Having done that, the machine rammed imported clay blocks on to the exposed chalky surface. In our determination to be true to Jekyll where at all possible, we decided that our pond would be lined in the centuries-old way, with clay, and then puddled in. We all expected the pond to fill naturally with rain-water and were delighted to get a downpour a few days later. To my surprise, hours after a good drenching, the pond was quite dry. As the pond is at one of the highest points in the garden and in a part where the chalk level is very close to the surface, it is odd that a natural pond should ever have formed there, but it did. Chalk on clay can hold water and, over the centuries, ponds have formed at any point where a natural spring finds a basin. Puddling is traditionally cattle feet trampling mud and straw to form a water-tight basin. Because water tables in this part of Hampshire have fallen by twenty feet over the century, we no longer have a natural spring, so we had (with difficulty) to find the water pipe that runs from the main stop-cock in the road towards the house. After much digging we traced it and interrupted that pipe with a branch line and tap with which to feed water into the pond. That source of unnatural, treated water acted as a substitute for the spring. Ignorant of the properties of clay, we had ordered a lorry load of clay bricks from a local brick-making company as our lining material. I am now wiser and know that there are many different types of clay, some porous and some so fine that they are suspended in water in tiny cloudy particles. The 'brick' clay that we used will not hold water. Terry, John and I spent many hours treading in the blocks of clay, sealing the joints, filling the pond with tap water and returning the next day to find it empty, and we kept up this laborious system for several years, whilst a soggy bog developed on one side of the leaking pond. In 1992 we gave up, and had the pond lined with a plastic Butyl sheet liner. It does not show. It does not leak. It does not irritate. Now and then one has to bite the bullet and be practical. Anthony Archer-Wills, writer and expert on garden water-features, did this for us.

As 1986 drew to a close we began to see, for the first time, evidence of those tenets of good gardening that Jekyll believed so important; how structure and proportion make the fine bones of a garden outline and how colour and texture can prove so satisfying, even to the untrained eye. The garden was beginning to show signs of promise and maturity.

The herbaceous borders had put on a great deal of growth in one year. It was possible to see the colours drifting, as Jekyll planned, from cool to hot to cool again and to understand why

Fuchsia magellanica gracilis.

1998. The pond restored and edges planted.

1984. The Wild Garden. The grid stakes show where the pond should be positioned.

1985. Lining the pond area with clay bricks.

certain plants were positioned in certain places. Sometimes a path or steps are edged with scented plants. Jasmine, an unruly and vigorous plant, covers two posts of the pergola, and for one month of the year it is forgiven for its indiscipline as it intoxicates with sweet scent. Some plants have greater impact if viewed from below, for instance *Fuchsia magellanica gracilis*. *Gracilis* means slender, and its flowers are almost lost in herbaceous bedding, but seen from the foot of the drystone wall which it tops, the purple-pink flowers and delicate leaves are displayed beautifully against a blue sky. Even our customary leaden grey skies give it impact. A very different plant, *Yucca filamentosa*, takes on a stately magnificence when viewed from beneath.

Visitors, however, were still tactlessly surprised by how slowly we were progressing. Suffering as we were from Proud Parent Syndrome, we were happily undaunted by our two steps forward, one step back progress, and there were plenty of set-backs. At the end of a long day, the slightest hiccup can be demoralising. One of the many early failures was the depressing discovery that most tall herbaceous plants are flattened by a heavy rainstorm. Hollyhocks, *Zea mays,* helianthus and others, do not recover once they have hit ground level, and months of work can be lost in an instant. My diary notes; 'spent twilight hours propping up bits with makeshift sticks'. Two days later I ordered £80 worth of metal supports. Ten years on I find it hard to tell which is more irritating, collapsed plants or metal stakes that, on being rammed into the earth, hit a stone and bend. The Victorians went to enormous trouble to wind hazel twigs into plant supports and I have seen examples of those plaited frames in a garden in Dorset; they are almost a work of art in their own right. The owner told me that she takes five weeks in late winter making frames for herbaceous plants in borders of much the same dimensions as ours. I am not looking for cold outdoor work in mid–winter so I persevere with beastly metal stakes for some plants. But there are simpler devices which we have learnt to make with the hazel stakes. Short sticks encircling a plant

Giant cow parsley (*Heracleum mantegazzianum*). This and Japanese knotweed, two very invasive weeds, are plants Jekyll loved and used in several gardens. At that date their danger had not been established and they were considered fine 'wild' plants.

Phil Brailsford making small wicker hurdles for border support. These are made from hazel sticks from our Nuttery.

will hold tough string in a supporting grid. And, on the hurdle fencing principle, long thin branches can be woven into very attractive low supports for the edge of herbaceous borders to prevent plants from collapsing on to the path or grass edge. The nuts themselves are of secondary importance at Upton Grey because squirrels take all our nuts.

On a warm day I love to sit in the Nuttery, this miniature woodland glade under the light green leaves in their dappling shade, with a carpet of moss, primulas, bluebells or foxgloves at my feet, listening to birds and humming insects. In its season it is one of my favourite parts of the garden. The coppiced hazels have supplied wood for the small rose and clematis arbour that leads to the mulberry path beyond the Tennis Lawn and I sit on the remarkably comfortable home-made hazelnut bench thinking how good life is, if you simply allow it to be. No, on second thoughts this is waxing a little too lyrical. Realistically, this is a devilishly difficult area to keep weed-free. Cow parsley and dock are the nagging reminders that nature is not perfect and we are allowed to interfere.

Jekyll admired a number of plants which, over the years, were to prove problematical. Two of the worst are on our plans, but despite their relentless urge to spread I have planted both here because they are glorious plants in controlled conditions and they make very good focal points in the garden. The first is giant hogweed (*Heracleum mantegazzianum*), which is spectacularly grand and throughout the summer stands three feet high, like an exclamation mark at the far end of the Wild Garden where planting becomes more informal as it recedes from the house. It is acknowledged to be a dangerous weed and its cultivation is discouraged. I find it no problem as long as it is cut down before its flower head goes to seed; and if it does go to seed, those seeds seem to need months to germinate. The sad fact is that its seedhead is almost as beautiful as the flowering plant and we miss some of the glory. I imagine *heracleum* was, like the other invasive weed on our plans, very recently introduced to England in Jekyll's time, and that she admired the plant before it had established its unreliable reputation.

The second problem plant is Japanese knotweed (*Polygonum cuspidatum*). Jekyll often used it in her wild gardens, but it seemed lost to the world when I started my search. No nursery, garden centre or plantsman stocked it and no lists mentioned it. A local gardener recognised

The supports in place with *Rudbeckia speciosa* behind.

the name and promised me some of his stock. I was delighted to find this elusive thing still available, collected a clump from him and planted it. In 1988 a wise visitor told me that I had introduced Japanese knotweed to my immaculate garden and that its sale or distribution was forbidden because it proves so hard to eradicate. I have been watching with anxiety ever since. We still have it. It is very beautiful. It is very hard to destroy but mercifully it is not very happy on chalk, so has not yet spread dangerously. If it is waiting to take over, it is waiting a long time to pounce and forewarned is forearmed. I believe that Roundup, poured into the hollow stem, kills it eventually.

During the last months of 1986 I collected our first crop of home-grown seeds. This is best done on a dry day, well after morning dew has left the plants. I have learnt that most flowers will cross-pollinate with other colours of the same species and that, if I am to be accurate, I must isolate colours in various parts of the Kitchen Garden. (I am also told, but have disproved, that aquilegia 'Munstead White' will not cross-pollinate. Over the years it has set seeds that produce a very pale pink flower from cross-pollination with the deep purple wild aquilegia). I believe that small round seeds, like dianthus, tend to germinate more readily than, for instance, long or flat, hard seeds like eryngium. I know that some seeds need to go through a period of very cold temperatures to germinate and that some hard seeds need to be chitted (slightly nicked). I have very few total failures but, as I collect so many seeds, I expect my success rate is poor. It appears to make precious little difference whether seeds are kept in silver foil, jam jars or sealed plastic containers. Some are kept in the larder, some in the fridge, but the fridge seeds get in the way and are allotted less space every year.

Aquilegia 'Munstead White'.

Japanese knotweed (*Polygonum cuspidatum*).

Aquilegia vulgaris (wild colombine).

Bambusa syn.
Arundinaria simonii
with *Lupinus arboreus*
(tree lupin) growing in
the Wild Garden.

I continue to weed almost throughout the year and generally by hand into a bucket or barrow. I hoe in very dry conditions in summer and also in mid-winter when hands are suffering from the cold, but I am not happy with this method of weeding. I do not believe I kill weeds by simply uprooting them – I merely move them. They take a sensible amount of earth around their roots as they move and subtly re-establish themselves a few feet up the bed. Practically all the weeds are composted, although I do try to keep bindweed in a separate bucket and I certainly burn knotweed.

Since the winter of 1984 I have been using chemicals, though progressively fewer over the years. In 1986 I was using Roundup on stubborn weeds as well as fungicide on hollyhocks and roses and systemic insecticide on many plants and shrubs. Being on chalk, a soil which is relatively low in nutrients, it is necessary to feed plants and this we try to do as organically as possible. I give daffodils a liquid fertiliser after flowering, to strengthen their bulbs. I dead-head them in two or three stages, depending on the season, with a short-handled scythe. This is a quick and efficient way to carry out an essential job. I do not usually collect the dead heads as it seems unnecessarily hard work given that they quickly rot away in the long grass. They must of course not be mowed over until the leaves have fully died back. I give the roses a bi-annual feed of bone-meal, dried blood and potash, I use Vitax Q4 on all beds annually and I feed Growmore around the base of hedges and trees. All beds get compost and well-rotted manure annually. I am sure it is true that well-fed plants will fight the enemy (disease or bugs) with very little help from chemicals.

Over the winter, garden machinery is serviced. We had added a ten-bladed cylinder lawn mower, a small lawn scarifier and a rotavator to our collection. Winter servicing became quite a major expense until I learnt that a local man would do it on-site. This brought annual bills down from around £800 to £200. Ivor Wherrel has become a good friend and makes emergency visits whenever things go wrong. His van is quite bent-axled under the weight of all the machinery he carries around with him. The contents are treasures from machines older than he; black, rusty, bent bits of metal, all of which will come in useful if he hangs on to them long enough. He is a lesson in practical recycling, thrift and common sense.

We have always taken advice when buying garden machinery and are aware that gardens differ in their requirements. Formal lawns, particularly bowling, cricket and tennis lawns, must be cut with a ten or twelve-bladed cylinder mower. These give many more cuts per foot than the standard four or six-bladed model and consequently a finer cut with clearer stripes. Open meadow can be cut with a rotary bladed machine with the blades set as high as possible to allow wild flowers to set seed. Whether grass cuttings are collected or distributed depends on your standards, the length of the grass and the dryness of it. When re-creating or setting up a large garden, a strong tractor cum mower, cum puller-of-trailer is essential. Having slaughtered our trusty Westwood over those first three years of very hard work, we chose a Honda as replacement because it is a tough, reliable machine. Hondas are, however, expensive to buy, and so are their spare parts.

Towards the end of 1986 I dug up all dahlias and cannas and brought them into the frost-free garage where they were stored in large boxes between sheets of newspaper. It was a rather unconventional way to store them but it seemed to work, once I had learnt to sprinkle green sulphur powder on them to inhibit mildew. I continue to store dahlias that way but have better results with canna if I cover them partially with a little dry compost. The important thing is not to plant them out too early, a lesson it took me a good four years to learn.

In November I put fifty oxygenating plants into the pond. As water was continually leaking out and being tapped in, that purchase was probably not necessary. They sank to the muddy bottom of the pond and may or may not have survived. A death in this garden is usually a very minor set-back because there is so much other life, destruction and regeneration going on.

Almost the last garden event for 1986 was the arrival of two bamboo, *simonii* and *metake* for planting in the Wild Garden. These came from Andrew Sutcliffe of Kent who, in our telephone conversations, sounded like one of the many expert enthusiasts that the gardening world nurtures. These bamboo are the only plants in the garden that I have not come to terms with and if I am honest I think I would do away with if I were not recreating the master. I am aware that they were very popular with Victorians and relatively new to English gardens last century so perhaps Charles Holme asked Jekyll to include them. For the first few years in the Wild Garden they were inoffensive enough because they were small and slow to grow. At their best they stood insignificantly beside tree lupins which grew beautiful yellow panicles of flower below laburnum trees that leant over them, reflecting the yellow beneath with their own yellow racemes. It was an arrangement of rather unnatural planting but it was attractive. Fourteen years on the rapacious bamboo have to be cut back regularly or they stifle the tree lupins and spring up worryingly in the surrounding grass paths.

Anemone sylvestris. This was the plant that Jekyll chose for the Formal Garden. I misread her writing and planted *Aruncus sylvester.* Very soon I realised my mistake and replaced aruncus with the correct plant moving *Aruncus sylvester* to the pond where it is planned.

Aruncus sylvester syn. *dioicus* by the pond.

Climbing rose 'Mme Caroline Testout' bent and pegged down. In 1987 I had not been able to find the shrub form so I used the climber.

Chapter Five
1987 and 1988

1987

From January 1984 until the end of 1986 I had kept garden notes in the form of a once-a-week summary in large notepads. From 1987 onwards I made an almost daily agenda of short notes, written in a series of Five Year Diaries. It is full of absurd observations – 'Beastly cold. Ice on water butts. Dark by 3. 45' – all are events that occur naturally every year, but that I still notice with surprise and which I have remarked on inanely every year. When not making profound observations, I was making lists of the plants that I still needed and of those that I suspected were incorrect in the garden. One glaring example of the latter was *Aruncus sylvester*. Reading Jekyll's plan I had made out what looked like 'Aron. . . sylvester'. It grew in a narrow bed at the top of a wall above the Rose Lawn, immediately beside the box hedge. Having discovered that a plant did exist under the name *Aruncus sylvester*, I assumed that that was what Jekyll meant, bought one and put it in. Very soon I realised that it was far too big for the narrow space, so returned to my indices for help. There I found *Anemone sylvestris*, a favourite Jekyll plant – another exciting bit of decoding. I took aruncus out and put in the very pretty small white anemone. Actually there was a six-month gap between removal and the correct one going in and I made the mistake of putting in Japanese anemones (another Jekyll favourite) as temporary fillers. They are hideously difficult to get rid of – I still have them, and *Anemone sylvestris* has an annual struggle against the Japanese, or my spade, as I try to remove the intruders. Amateur gardeners tend to be impatient with nature. It is not wise.

The stately aruncus was not wasted. Beside the pond in the Wild Garden Jekyll planted *Spirea aruncus*. When I searched for it in an old encyclopaedia I discovered the name had changed to *Aruncus sylvester* and subsequently to *Aruncus dioicus*. I put the large plant in its correct position at the water's edge where it looks splendid. In fact midwinter it is by far the most beautiful plant in the Wild Garden. It holds its head erect through almost any weather. Its common name is 'goat's beard' and it is classed as a herb. When spiked with hoar-frost they are magnificent and when covered with soft balls of white snow they are gently pretty.

February started with irritating news. Two of the roses that I needed for the Rose Lawn, 'Mme Abel Chatenay', an early Hybrid Tea and 'Mme Lombard', a Tea, were not available for a third season. The beds looked sadly lop-sided with only two of the five planned roses in position. In 1985 I had planted 'Mme Laurette Messimy', a China rose, and 'Mme Caroline Testout', an early Hybrid Tea but, as I was to discover, only one was truly correct. Over the following years I watched in amazement as 'Mme Caroline Testout' put out branches nine feet long. It did not dawn on me for some time that I had the climbing variety. In those days it was not available in shrub form in Britain. The fifth rose on Jekyll's plans for the Rose Lawn is 'Killarney', an early Hybrid Tea. I found this description of it in T. Geoffrey Henslow's *The Rose Encyclopaedia*, published in 1914. 'Killarney. HT. Flower flesh shaded white, suffused pale pink, large semi-double, long bud opening well. Growth vigorous, free flowering'. Evidently it was a popular rose in its day, but no current British rose catalogue

'Killarney' (HT 1890). A rose which is so rare that when I was given it there were only three sources in the world.

Rose Lawn showing Gertrude Jekyll's eye for geometrical design

Looking down on the Rose Lawn in June.

Detail of the Rose Lawn with roses 'Mme Caroline Testout' and 'Mme Abel Chatenay' and peony 'Lize van Veen'.

Photograph by kind permission of Heather Angel.

The 'mirror' half with roses 'Mme Laurette Messimy' and 'Mme Lombard' and peony 'Sarah Bernhardt'.

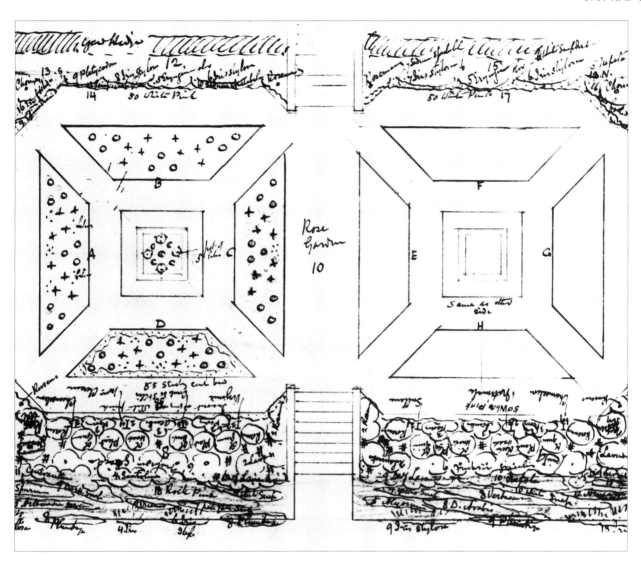

Gertrude Jekyll's plan for the Rose Lawn.

The Rose Lawn in winter showing Jekyll's eye for structure and geometry in design.

The Wild Garden in February looking towards the house.   The same view in March with daffodils.

The winter pruned climbing rose 'Desprez à Fleurs Jaunes'.

The rose the following June.

mentions it, so I gave up the search for 'Killarney' for a few years. The rambling roses for the Wild Garden had been planted the previous winter. I lacked only two roses there, they were 'Kitchener' and 'Euphrosyne', neither of which could I find in any rose growers' lists. I supposed I would never find them.

Terry Gould had left us at the end of 1986, as arranged at the outset, and I gardened alone for a few months. January and February are not busy months in the garden. Most winter jobs are maintenance and it is easy to find an excuse for delaying them until the weather warms. In early February I insulated myself in thick gloves as protection against both ice and thorns, and made an attempt to prune some of the large climbing roses that had been growing up against the house for years. Until I visited the late Peter Wake at Hambledon a few years later and learnt exactly how to winter-prune climbing roses I was in blissful ignorance and my roses grew more tangled and stalky every year. I now know better and often regret the knowledge because the work involved in doing the job well is hard and painful. Midwinter when all leaves have dropped and sap is no longer rising (but thorns are as plentiful as ever) carefully untie the rose from the wall, lay it out and cut out all unnecessary growth. Having done so pin it back to the wall in a fan shape to allow maximum air and light. In cold weather when hands are numb and gloves inhibiting this is the slowest and perhaps the worst of jobs. If I were a rich, idle gardener I would simply buy a new plant every six years and have done with it.

Towards the end of the month I bought myself a video camera and started walking around the garden, struggling with camera and muddled memory. The results are not good, but they are a 'better than nothing' record.

March is probably my favourite month. The days grow longer, and when the sun does shine, it gives a clear bright light that comes as an unexpected and happy surprise after months of gloomy darkness. Snowdrops, daffodils and crocuses flower in the Wild Garden. The first flowers of the Formal Garden start to open; the south-facing drystone walls are filled with pale colours of early spring but there are large expanses of good bare earth. A few lively green shoots are appearing through the surface and weeds are still controllable. There is promise, birth and optimism everywhere, not least amongst the birds who start to build nests in hideously vulnerable places. Bantams and ducks, which from 1989 onwards became an important feature in the garden, start laying eggs in March, undeterred by frosty nights and the hungry foxes whose new-born cubs need feeding.

The diary for March 1987 is peppered with good intentions, most of which I seem to have got round to doing, eventually. Early in the month I wrote, 'terrible lull in gardening notes, though not in gardening. Fully determined to write diary to date but there's a ghastly bat flapping around the house (J. is away) and I'll have to put out lights and stick head under sheets until tomorrow − braver by day − I hear the foul thing flapping'. We live close to the Basingstoke Canal Tunnel, where thousands of bats live, and from time to time a few set up

The Wild Garden in April looking from the house.

house in our attic. In those days I was frightened of bats as I was of birds in the house. Today I am wiser and braver. I catch birds, if I can, and release them or at least usher them out of the window. Bats move out of their own accord.

I also remarked on how wonderful the Kitchen Garden looked after I had struggled around it with the new rotavator. I always find the sight of freshly turned earth satisfying. I noted how many hundreds of lily seeds I had collected and wondered where I was going to sow such a number. Ten years on I know that a bare minimum of seed heads should be permitted to ripen; the plants are weakened by such fertile reproduction and I need nothing like that number as replacements. Things that seem so obvious to a moderately experienced gardener today were certainly not obvious to me then.

APRIL 1987

I seem to have spent most of April exhausting myself trying to clear weeds from around the pond. Generally the garden notes are happy but several entries simply read, 'too tired to write diary, "zzzzz"'. A few of the regular hiccups are noted; 'most hollyhocks seem dead so I'll have to collect seeds this year and grow new plants for '88. Dahlia bits (i.e. tubers) look sickly. I bought more in case mine haven't survived storage'. Two weeks later, 'most didn't – very mildewy'. (Remember the green sulphur powder).

The month ended with the customary list of what was in flower, what was sickly, plus general observations. 'Over back-breaking weekend I dug back the drive then trimmed it with the sharpened half-moon to give a beautiful edge. Still have to do other side. I am dead-heading daffodils – hope that proves worth the effort. I do that with a scythe which is gentle rhythmic work, quick and rewarding. Grass is heavy with their decapitations (when John is watching I pick them up and compost them, otherwise they decompose *in situ*). Must cut sprouts off chestnut trees. All lawns have been lightly scarified then raked over to remove thatch, after which they were top-dressed with sterilised earth. The earth was brushed in, then I seeded lightly at about 2 oz per square yard. Exhausting business'. The top-dressing is done biannually with special, sterilised and very expensive earth. I maintain that we spend more on the Formal Garden's grass than on any other part of the garden – much more. 'They need twice weekly mowing and look in very good condition. April seems the busiest month. I dare say May will seem even more hectic and thus onwards. My hands look ghastly and all gardening gloves leak. A hot month'.

MAY 1987

My diary notes: 'Weather colder. Fertilised and dug all beds lightly to avoid damaging late-flowering plants like rudbeckia which have only just started to throw up their green shoots. Went to laborious lengths to dead-head bergenia and to remove old leaves; may prove waste of time'. It is, in fact, a job well worth doing because the plants are an important feature in this garden. Their fresh green shiny leaves are handsome and visitors regularly remark how a plant that they had considered rather dull can look so striking. Given even half the care lavished on, for instance, roses, these old favourites are every bit as striking as their greedy neighbours. It seems unjust of gardeners to dismiss a simple robust plant as being dull because it is undemanding and consequently rather neglected. Sometimes plants take on almost human characteristics. I find this is particularly so with the really reliable and well-behaved plants that Jekyll admired and used in most of her gardens. Antirrhinums, bergenia, nepeta and centranthus are examples of the large range of worthy plants that are a little like the dull, sometimes irritating, old friend who is always there when needed but never dramatically exciting. They are quite unlike the exotic, fickle lover who expects constant attention but gives little reward. I have grown to love the simple old faithfuls and I try to remind new gardeners not to ignore the basic needs of these poor wretches. Treat them well, use them to their best advantage, because they can outshine many plants and compete with the best.

'Have one day a week help from local gardener. He spends all eight hours on grass. Peonies 'Lize van Veen' and 'Sarah Bernhardt' healthy. *Prunus lucitanicus* miserable'. (Those bushes took eight years to become established enough to put on growth; presumably because they are planted on a high chalk bank). 'Weeping ash is always the last tree to put out leaves and is still in tight bud'.

'I cleared a patch around the pond, very slowly, and found a beautiful green and white

Bergenia cordifolia. A reliable and underrated plant.

flower with grassy leaves. Hope it survives'. It turned out to be *Ornithogalum*, (Star of Bethlehem) and it did survive.

Olearia phlogopappa. A favourite spring shrub with most visitors.

'Pond level dropping' *(plus ça change)*. 'Planted out artichokes, marigold and asparagus seedlings. *Olearia gunnii* syn. *phlogopappa* dead'. It died every year for the first four years because it grows in a frost pocket. I don't know how GJ managed to keep it alive at Munstead Wood, if ever she grew it. It is such a beautiful, surprising plant. It has pretty, long, grey leaves and a profusion of small daisy-like flowers in the spring and early summer, at a time when the borders really need flowers, so I keep several cuttings going in a sheltered place beside the greenhouse and replant whenever necessary. I never manage to grow it from seed. By 1991 herbaceous plants had grown around to protect it from all but bitterest winters and the pretty bush has become the unrivalled favourite of our spring garden visitors.

The garden looks wonderful now. Everything is under control – JUST. Can I/we/they keep it up. The yellow phase is over, only *Alyssum saxatile* continues its triumphant Cornish butter yellow. Blues and mauvey-blues take over, led by the bluebells in the Nuttery, the *Nepeta mussinii* in walls and the bluish-mauve aubretia; this is not as sombre as it sounds because young leaves have a lively, often yellowy, colour about them. There are two dramatic white blocks that catch and startle the eye, one is double arabis, the other *Cerastium tomentosum*. The wild, self-seeded columbines (aquilegia) are beautiful with their leaves of green-tinged-purple that sit in unfolding swirls beneath blackcurrant-coloured flowers, so delicate and so graceful. The white columbines, 'Munstead White', are reluctant to cross-pollinate and are correct for our GJ plans'. (After a few years they set seeds that produce very pale pink flowers. Those seedlings seem to have a little of the wild columbine colour in them so I simply dig them out). "Munstead White' flower later, well on into summer'.

Ornithogalum (Star of Bethlehem).

The Nuttery with blue-bells and primroses.

'The very pale *Corydalis ochroleuca* and the hart's-tongue ferns that grow in the drystone walls have made such a determined effort to survive these last eighty years and the wall rebuilding that I am loath to move them from their secure footing. They are only a few feet out of place and will soon spread to their correct positions so I will leave them in peace for now'.

Later the cool mauve, blue and yellow phase will change to bright colours with the heat of summer. The drifts of colours in Jekyll's borders do reflect this gradual change with the seasons but they maintain a disciplined move from cool to hot to cool again with greater or less emphasis, according to the month. At Upton Grey the colours in the main borders become stronger and hotter as summer progresses and this surprises our late summer visitors. They come expecting to see a cottage garden, planted with soft pinks, greys and blues. At least once a week someone asks me if Gertrude Jekyll designed the borders as they see them. 'Did she really use canna?' It is odd that she should be remembered as a pastel-shades-only gardener when one of her most important contributions to modern gardens was her brave use of strong colours. Perhaps it is because people think of English flowers as being gentle soft colours, and they are largely correct in that belief; the late-flowering hot-coloured herbaceous flowers were almost all introduced to England from the seventeenth century onwards. Most of our indigenous flowers are pale shades and they bloom in spring and early summer.

Right: *Corydalis ochroleuca.*

Far right: Hart's-tongue fern (*Phyllitis scolopendrium*).

Top left: The Hot Border in May.

Top right: The Hot Border in June.

Above: The Hot Border in July.

Right: The Hot Border in August.

All show gradual change of colours as summer progresses.

The Roman bank leading into the Nuttery.

Towards the end of the month I wrote, 'wandered around the garden this evening and, feeling tired, resolved only to look at the good bits. Can't avoid the depressing sights though. The bank behind the Nuttery is a mess, perhaps I will grass it over'. (It was never possible to do so, being far too steep and rocky. Eventually we made a very small drystone wall at the foot of the bank to retain crumbling soil and then planted the bank with simple flowers like foxglove, omphalodes and pretty *Plantago rosularis*).

'Greenhouse seed-trays are perplexing. No *Penstemon glaber,* sadly, and I was so excited to have found that parent plant. Trade delphinium seedlings haven't made any appearance though mine have sprung up well'. I found this often happens with delphinium seeds. My comparisons between commercial and self-grown seeds is reported in October 1988. 'Phlox are nearly all hopeless so far; odd because last year's seeds germinated very well and very fast. So much for looking at the good bits. Tomorrow I'll spray. That's an undemanding job. That'll cheer me up'.

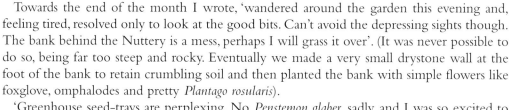

JUNE 1987

Early June. 'Pond still leaks. Nearly all irises are flowering this year. Their colours show how carefully planned GJ's schemes were. They carry the coloured drifts of blues through to yellows and on to purples, echoing the wall planting beneath and the beds around. *Asphodeline lutea* flowered this year, for the first time. It is a strange, tall, yellow flower. Not sure that I like it much yet. Masses of house martins nesting under eaves. Sky is positively peppered with them at dawn and dusk'. Looking back over the diary notes I am interested to see that I wrote 'not sure that I like it much **yet**'. It seems that I had already accepted that I would learn to appreciate a Jekyll flower, given time and enlightenment.

Mid-June. 'Cold. Some odd proportions in the beds. Anthemis, lychnis and monarda are huge and dwarfing the flowers that are planted behind. Still no phlox seeds germinated so have planted substitute snapdragons to fill gap this year. GJ wrote on our plans 'filling snap'

Asphodeline lutea, a curious flower.

Penstemon glaber. This species is robust, neat, pretty and is my favourite penstemon. It is one of the plants that visitors most admire, perhaps because like the other plants growing here at the foot of the box hedge, it gets very little nutrition and no pampering.

so I use them in emergencies (which I have each year, in differing places).' The value of annuals in a garden is often overlooked. They can fill gaps in borders on a temporary basis; they can be planted out at any time of the growing season in larger or smaller quantities according to spaces they are to fill; they can add valuable colour to dying areas around them; they are easily grown from seed and they are very cheap.

'Pond still leaking'.

'Poured with rain again. It seems that my trousers have been hanging out to dry for well over a month. Some plants happy, some hate it. Remarkably wet month altogether; weeds a serious problem. Fruit ripens later than usual but I have to pick strawberries early to beat the birds'.

Towards end of the month. 'The garden is wearying me. Both it and I are suffering from too much rain and cold. I feel like a ninety-year-old in sole charge of a ward of sick patients. So many plants have mildew/black-spot/slugs/green-white-black fly, or are simply stunted. Roses die in bud, so do other flowers. One eight-hour-a-week gardener is not enough. I must delegate more. Haven't even started work on, or groans about, the Wild Garden yet. I'll do that (grumble) next month'.

June 30. 'VERY hot day. Got back from Wimbledon tennis to find greenhouse contents very wilted. Tomatoes completely collapsed'.

It may seem rather desperate now but I never felt defeated. One of the garden visitors asked me which I loved best, my garden or my husband. I answered that although I make much more effort for the garden than for the husband it is because he is less demanding and I have three months a year off from the garden. I love the husband throughout the year. The winter break is quite a healer and a reviver.

Almost defeated Ros.

Rose 'Blush Rambler'
on the pergola with
*Parthenocissus
quinquefolia* in the
foreground.

JULY 1987

This is 'Beau Geste Month'. The dead and dying troops are propped up in semblance of life
and in an attempt to convince visitors that the borders are strong and healthy.

July 4. 'Opened for our first paying public visit, St John Ambulance Charity. NOT a great
success. Altogether about thirty people came, which at 70p per head, and OAPs and children
free, meant precious little for the charity. My God other people's children are a trial; still, I
don't suppose a day looking at gardens is their idea of fun'. John argues that we should charge
twice as much for children, not discount them. He says they make a racket and break things
and parents should be discouraged from bringing them. 'We knew almost every visitor. In
other words most were loyal friends and locals. We open again tomorrow for the Red Cross.
General reactions to garden polite, tactful, though not much enthusiasm – some admiration

for grass though. That should please John, who deserves it'.

July 10. 'Greenfly virulent and ubiquitous. Lilies look and smell wonderful. Roses look small and miserable. To be fair, 'Blush Rambler' and 'The Garland' on the pergola are temporarily glorious. The rest leave lots to be desired'. In 1985 Harkness was the only rose nursery that supplied 'Blush Rambler'. I had spent weeks looking for it before I was told about the excellent publication *Find that Rose* which lists roses available in the UK and their sources. The Harkness catalogue introduced it as being 'rescued from a cottage garden in Old Warden, Beds'. I suppose it was Harkness who had found 'Blush Rambler' and rescued it from oblivion. This and most rambler roses do well on our thin, chalky soil, but very few other roses on Jekyll's plan are healthy here, despite generous feeding.

'Heather Angel' (the well-known photographer) 'came to take some pictures for a book to

Aristolochia macrophylla and rose 'The Garland' on the pergola. Rambler roses grow well on this chalky soil but few other rose species are healthy here.

Rose piece about 22 cm (9in.) long

Cut at a slant just above a bud joint

Plant about two thirds of stick into earth in a sheltered part of the garden

Remove all thorns above and below planting level

Remove all leaves

Cut at a slant at a bud joint

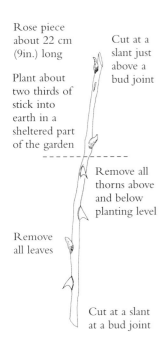

Rooting a rose cutting.

The cutting 18 months later.

be called *View from a Window*. She may not use ours, as plants aren't mature. She is a very impressive photographer, so I hope she does include us. Michael Tooley' (writer and tutor at Kingston University and a Jekyll expert) 'brought a couple from Cheshire to see the garden'. I like Michael. He amuses and encourages and knows an enormous amount about GJ. Best of all he identified the mysterious 'S' word on Jekyll's plans. He tells me it is *Sisyrinchium striatum* – a whole new name to me'. For the following two years I bet people that they would not be able to decipher that perplexing squiggle and I only lost the bet when a cunning visitor told me she had been tipped off by a friend. Ours are copies of the plans Jekyll kept at Munstead Wood as reference points for her own use, not the ones she sent the client, so she had not troubled to write clearly and she often used abbreviations. Once word gets about that a Jekyll garden is being restored a collection of experts appears out of the woodwork to look, comment, encourage and enjoy her work. They are almost always positive and helpful, and, in 1987, they all knew more than I did.

Amateur gardeners, I suppose, like amateurs generally, take their subject seriously, trustingly and unquestioningly. For the first few years I read all gardening books and articles and followed advice religiously. Where I could not find advice I followed instinct and it proved right or wrong in normal proportions. There is no doubt that the best but the most painful way to learn is through one's own mistakes, and occasionally those mistakes lead to revelations that can prove quite enlightening. Following advice from weekly newspaper articles I wrote the following in July: 'Did a monumental job and cleaned out and sterilised all seed trays (about sixty). Tomorrow I'll sow my own seeds – *Iris germanica, Hemerocallis dumortieri*'. Today I find it odd that I collected and planted seeds immediately. It is simpler to collect and keep all for sowing at once in the cold greenhouse in February. Some do germinate better if sown immediately but I tend to forget where I sowed them. Ten years on I do not sterilise the seed trays in bleach, but I do use fresh compost for seedlings. I certainly do not bother to sow seeds of easily divided plants like hemerocallis and iris and I now wonder why I ever did. I have far too many bearded iris and, because they are such beautiful plants, I am loath to compost surplus stock. In those days I collected their fat seed-heads and sowed them out; quite why I cannot remember. I never did find an exciting new colour; they all flowered an insipid version of pale blue. I have often tried to, although never succeeded in, breeding a good new colour or shape of plant. It is fascinating work playing God with nature but I seem to produce weaker or simpler plants, a reversion to old, pre-hybridised types which makes me believe that the older genes are stronger. Reading the Michael Tooley and Primrose Arnander book entitled *Gertrude Jekyll; Essays on the Life of a Working Amateur*, I realise that Jekyll herself did breed, discover and introduce new strains of plants to the world of horticulture, but that process took an inordinate amount of time and garden space. Sometimes Jekyll gave her precious discoveries to nurserymen to market and benefit from financially. Getting a new strain of plant accepted required, and still requires, years of persistent presentation at RHS shows.

Towards the end of July 1987 I began to experiment with rose cuttings. I call gardening my fertility substitute and, looking back, see a continuing thread of urges to propagate, graft, reproduce and so on. Rose cuttings can be taken from soft wood in July and from hard wood in September. I read up the 'plastic bag' method for soft-wood cuttings and followed instructions meticulously. I took pencil thick pieces, eight or more inches long, removed most leaves, dipped the cut ends of twigs into hormone rooting powder, sank the twigs into a large, plastic flowerpot filled with compost and then enshrouded all in a plastic bag. Within

days the wretched twigs suffocated, mildewed and died. A few weeks later I started again with hardwood cuttings. This seemed to me to be a more natural way of treating life and it proved more successful. Robust pieces about nine inches long are cut at a clean angle, defoliated and pushed carefully into a slit trench. There are always a few odd straggly pieces of wood that I wedge in for good measure, simply to get rid of them. To my surprise those spindly bits over-winter just as well as their fellow sticks. They grow roots, not only from the slant-cut base but also from odd nodules along the stem and when all are dug up for inspection a year or so later, the successful flimsy cuttings often outnumber the thicker ones. It seems that Gilbert White in his *Natural History and Antiquities of Selborne* also noticed this because in November 1760 he wrote, 'Larger shoots will not root so readily'. On the whole ramblers seem to strike best, followed by most climbers; China and Tea roses do all right and Hybrid Teas do badly. Species roses are generally very easy. So far I have had no success at all from 'air-layering' cuttings. That means almost severing a climbing or rambling rose's stem, wrapping the wound in damp moss and enclosing it in a small plastic bag. The one success I had took root about three months after incision but, by mistake, I hacked off the successful piece whilst pruning and discovered the shrivelled, root-growing twig days later, on the compost heap. I remember thinking 'Thank goodness I cut that off myself and that it had not been done by husband or gardener'. I would have found it hard to take lightly.

Sisyrinchium growing behind *Eryngium oliverianum*.

Hemerocallis dumortieri.

The box hedge, having been reduced in height by half. This and shrubs like rosemary and oleaira are cut with the hedge trimmer.

Gardening, studying nature and working with nature encourage contemplation. Gertrude Jekyll peppered her writing with philosophical observations. They are as relevant today as a century ago. One I enjoy is, 'The garden is a grand teacher. It teaches patience and careful watchfulness. It teaches industry and thrift and above all it teaches entire trust'. I'm not sure that either my patience or my careful watchfulness were much in evidence when I destroyed my one successful 'air-layered' cutting, but I appreciate a good excuse for being thrifty.

July 19. Diary notes are as usual: 'Pond Sinking. Bugs and mildew bad. Is spray effective/ correct? The *Stachys lanata* which surrounds beds in the Rose Lawn makes a beautiful edging. It has furry grey-green leaves which last throughout the winter. But it needs constant manicuring to keep it in shape'. Today new, more compact cultivars of stachys are available, I would not use them here but I accept that many of them are improvements on older varieties and are easier to control.

In 1987 I was beginning to learn the art of 'on-going' gardening, that is the necessity of cutting back plants as they grow, in order to maintain good shape and health. It took us twelve years to experiment with trimming bushes like rosemary and olearia into shape with a hedge-trimmer because it seemed a little like taking a sledge-hammer to crack a nut, but the petrol-driven hedge-trimmer makes a better and a quicker job of controlling a great many shrubs here. In 1998 we literally sliced in half the box hedge which stands along the top terrace above the Rose Lawn. If Gertrude Jekyll had told Charles Holme how high the hedge was to grow she certainly did not bother to mark it on her plans; probably she assumed he had common sense enough to control it at optimum height. I did not. Several people said it was a pity that the view over the Rose Lawn was blocked by the thick box hedge. I listened but did not react, thinking GJ perhaps wanted to create a room effect. Odd because I dislike 'rooms' in gardens, they are artificial and claustrophobic. In 1998 my mother posed the question so determinedly

Stachys lanata syn. *S. byzantina* as edging to Rose Lawn beds.

that I asked Richard Bisgrove what height the hedge should be and in his tactful, gentle way he suggested cutting it back by half to just under two feet. We did so with the trusty hedge-trimmer and, having halved it, cut a dip in the centre along the top so that it would grow strong new shoots from within and not put on too much extra height as it greened over.

July 22. 'Picked spinach and a few French beans. Beans all coming up at once, as usual, despite four-week gap in planting. Must have pruned raspberries too late as we haven't had any. Birds had a few. All strawberries eaten by birds. Fruit cage simply protects them (on the inside) from dogs (on the outside). Next year I shall concentrate on garden and pick fruit at Janaway fruit farm. Far more efficient'. I assume every gardener makes this kind of resolution and most probably fails to keep it. I certainly never did, so struggle on with home-grown produce riddled as it is (when I get it) with slugs, bugs and disease.

July 28. 'Hot borders looking good where they've stood up against rain. Look better from upstairs window'. I noted regularly that gardens look better if viewed with perspective, and seen from a window above is often the best view. 'Wet. Cold. Not good gardening weather. Not good gardening – Period'. (Grammar and spelling in my diary is atrocious, and comments are always rather staccato). Even GJ, whose garden at Munstead Wood always displayed successful shape or colour in some part, acknowledged that July is a difficult month in the south of England. Unless I keep a careful watch over the herbaceous borders, some plants become quite engulfed by their vigorous neighbours and may never appear at all. *Senecio maritima* tries to disappear completely every year. It is a tiresome plant and needs coddling. Constant monitoring is essential.

AUGUST 1987

'Colours are smudged and gaudy. The effect is of a pantomime dame who has rushed the heavy make-up job. I have just finished pruning the rambler roses because I read that this should be done immediately after flowering. It's far earlier than for other roses but it seems logical because this is a pruning that goes right back to the base of the plant so they will need plenty of time to re-grow. I have cut back about one stem in four'.

'Cut back *Campanula latifolia alba* var. *macrantha* and divided most'. This campanula was probably introduced by GJ and was eventually marketed in 1933. 'I have begun to realise that Jekyll's planting for 1908 would have needed thinning by 1911. Borders looking very crowded. Next year I'll plant fewer annuals, for instance snapdragons, and I'll thin out the anthemis'. Yet again I noticed that constant monitoring is essential.

SEPTEMBER 1987

'As always, gold, rich sunset reds and surprisingly beautiful'. As both Jekyll and Capability Brown drew comparisons between music and gardening, I call this the final crescendo time of year. The glorious colours of autumn are loud and strong before they die away with oncoming winter. The composite flowers like rudbeckia, helenium, dahlias and helianthus fill my autumn borders with burnished copper, gold and deep ochre reds. The asters play a gentler theme with their faded, blue-tinged colours. 'Things beginning to die. I've started cutting back plants like peonies – always a bit impetuously. Rather looking forward to winter. Feeling weary. Garden going over, full bloom and collapsing and so am I'.

OCTOBER 1987

'Last Friday, the 16th, at 3 a.m. all southern England was shattered by hurricane storms. Five hundred trees in London's parks have been uprooted'. (Later reports say many more). 'Kew has

The colourful centre of the Hot Border.

lost hundreds of old and rare trees. We lost two large horse chestnuts, most of the medlar, the last walnut, an apple tree and a hazel. Branches have been ripped off nearly all chestnuts along the drive and all but three panels of hurdle fencing blew down. Winds were 94 mph in London, and stronger in places near the south coast. We were woken at 3. 05 a.m. by the sharp crack, crack, like rifle shots, as whole trees and branches snapped in the gale. We got out of bed and watched the storm from our bedroom window. It was dramatically exciting; awesomely ferocious. Actually rather more dramatic now that we know it was the worst storm for over two hundred years. Extremes are compensating. Temperatures at storm time were remarkably high. Winds were followed by floods in several places, though not too bad here. Today we're back to winter temperatures. Cold, frost and thin ice on pond. Electricity came back on Sunday. Some places still cut off'. Despite the massive damage all over south-east England, the thing that really lives in our memories is the almost bestial low-noted roar of the wind interspersed with the sharp cracks as branches split. What ferocious power nature commands.

Autumn colours in the main border – *Rudbekia speciosa,* kniphofia. In 1987 *Senecio maritima* disappeared altogether. We have to replace it every year.

The main compost heaps which rot down with no help and into which we put all vegetable matter except bindweed and knotweed.

Rose 'Jersey Beauty'.

Rose 'Mme Abel Chatenay'.

NOVEMBER 1987

(Roses) 'Mme Abel Chatenay', 'Mme Lombard' and 'Jersey Beauty' finally arrive three years late.

Pond still leaking'. Then follows hibernation time. December, January and February are cold, slow months and the garden is very undemanding. In 1995, when I was giving talks in New Zealand, someone asked me how, for a three year period, I managed virtually single-handed. My answer was that every winter I have a couple of months a year off from gardening. 'Good Heavens', she said, 'We don't have any months off at all. It's year-round gardening here'. I'm pretty sure I couldn't cope with that; those New Zealanders are mighty hard workers.

The winter of 1987 rolled on into 1988. Days were short, dark and cold. When we lived in London I had dreaded the onset of winter. Now I began to look forward to those months of hibernation, long evenings in front of fires, time to read ordinary books, not only on gardening, and I always enjoy the prospect of several weeks of absolutely no outdoor work.

1988

In January I bought two loads of what must have been the country's most expensive manure. It came to £70 and to my utter amazement I was charged Value Added Tax. The stuff was reddish raw and full of lumps of Hampshire flint and chalk. I had ordered it without first asking the price – always a foolish thing to do. It came from a farmer neighbour who had put up somewhat grumpily with our yapping fox terrier for years, so I considered this fair do's and did not complain. Needless to say I did not repeat the order and have bought really good manure from a local girl ever since (for £10 per two loads).

I stack the manure beside the main compost heaps in the Orchard. When a heap has matured, I mix the manure in with it and this makes a good, rich dressing for our rather poor chalky soil. I use it when planting and fork it lightly into beds each autumn. About every six years the borders are thickly covered with rich compost, double dug and plants are lifted, divided and replanted. Having the space to compost garden debris is a great luxury. There are eight compost heaps strategically set in various parts of the garden. The objective is to make journeys to compost heaps with heavy barrow as short as possible. Nothing is done to speed decomposition except occasionally to cover one heap with a large piece of old carpet. In the Wild Garden the

Frost over the
Rose Lawn.

January. View
across the
Bowling Lawn
from the
Nuttery.

three heaps consist mainly of mown grass and horse chestnut leaves, and they do take a relatively long time to decompose – about a year. Although they make a good mulch for top-dressing these leafy composts provide very little nutrition. In the Orchard we have a bonfire patch which is occasionally dug over to recover the very good ash and earth subsoil. Beside that is a compost heap which consists of herbaceous debris and grass cuttings. At the other side of the Orchard are the four main heaps. One of these is the manure heap and the others are, again, mostly herbaceous debris and grass cuttings with a few leaves added each autumn. These heaps are rich in worms and more nutritious and they decompose relatively quickly, within about seven months according to the season. Very stalky herbaceous plants are sometimes burned, but they are a good means of aerating the compost heap although they decompose slowly, so we use them in moderate quantities. Not many weeds survive those heaps but I do try to avoid composting bindweed and Japanese knotweed. Turning compost heaps is good winter work. That and heavy digging are about the only outside jobs I can bring myself to do when temperatures are below freezing (and those only if the fork will get through the frozen earth).

In March 1988 I suffered another calamity – the death of some very precious 'twigs'. The saga had started in September of the previous year when John and I had taken a rare holiday and driven to France for a few days. We came home via Paris. My long-suffering, but fed-up-with-gardening, husband took me to Roseraie de l'Haye on the outskirts of the city. It is an important rose garden based on the Empress Josephine's collection at Malmaison; all beautifully displayed and cared for. I wandered around in an increasing fog trying to learn about or identify roses and suddenly came across a rose that I thought was lost to the world, 'Mme Caroline Testout'; not the fairly common climber but the shrub form. In great excitement I headed back to the gardeners' lodge by the entrance and passed an even more incredible find, 'Reine Olga de Wurtemberg'. Neither had appeared in any British rose catalogue for years and I believed them to be extinct. At the lodge I explained to the head gardener about our garden, how I had given up hope of ever finding those

Shrub rose 'Mme Caroline Testout'.

roses and that I would very much like to buy a plant. To my great joy he led me straight back to the roses and then and there cut off pieces, which he took to the lodge, wrapped in damp newspaper and gave me. There is so much good, generosity and trust in the world of gardeners.

I had little idea how I was to transform those twigs into viable roses but could not let myself down by admitting it, nor would my indifferent grasp of the French language have enabled me to. John and I drove home that day and I asked my wise friend Hazel Le Rougetel how to cope with the precious bits. Patiently Hazel explained and, following her advice, I selected a sheltered spot near the kitchen door where I could watch and water the plants as necessary. I made the slit trench, put a little sand in it, dipped the freshly cut stumps into hormone rooting powder and jammed the treasure trove in. For weeks I watched over them. Some turned brown and apparently died but a good few kept up a healthy look of life even as winter sped on.

The Easter school holidays of 1988 started in late March. They were cold and wet. Mark and friends brought drenched bicycles to dry out under shelter by the kitchen door where the valuable rose cuttings were entrenched. The next day they set off on a ride – right across the rose cuttings. I had given up the daily inspection of my treasures and it was not until the following day that I discovered the pathetic twigs that lay strewn around the muddy patch. About eight stumps with thin white roots lay smashed and twisted in the mud. I put them all back into a trench but they were too immature to recover. I remember the anguish well, but also a slight feeling of pride that I had managed to get them to root at all. I wrote to the head gardener of Roseraie de L'Haye explaining my sadness. In truly magnanimous spirit he promised to send me more pieces the following autumn, and did. I took more care the second time and now have splendid plants to remember the French gardeners by. All gardeners must have similar moments of tragedy. Close your eyes, take a deep breath and start again. Nature will heal you and your plants, so never give up.

Climbing rose 'Reine Olga de Wurtemberg' (1881).

105

1989. The Wild Garden in spring showing drifts of daffodils that reappeared after clearing.

In the spring of 1988 the Wild Garden put on a wonderful display of colour with aconites, daffodils, omphalodes, wood anemones and all sorts of wild flowers whose names I had yet to learn. None was planted by us; they simply and defiantly came up through thick tussocks of grass after decades of neglect under brambles and ground elder.

The plants that often give greatest pleasure are those that flower at unusual times; I am always happily astonished by the beauty of *Iris unguicularis.* They are in full flower in February and early March when so little else is out and they continue to flower if picked regularly. They stand in thick clumps of pale mauve flowers above thin, light-green leaves, a delicate complement to the early spring flowers, aubretia, alyssum and corydalis, that fill the drystone walls. Vita Sackville-West gives an affectionate and amusing description of this iris in *Some Flowers*, originally published in 1937 but recently republished by The National Trust.

Regularly at this time of year I marvel at how many slugs appear to have survived what should have been a devastating winter. In spring they make up for that period of fasting with a vengeance and particularly enjoy making unsightly holes in the lush, green bergenia leaves. I can ill afford to lose these good structural plants at this time of the year so I kill them by squashing them between two flat stones. Their death is quick and painless but the process of finding and dispatching them is not.

The bicycling rose tramplers went back to school in April and I got down to serious gardening again. I was still getting one day a week's help from the very hard-working local gardener, John Smith, and seemed to be able to manage quite well with that arrangement though, with hindsight, standards were not very high. The weed-killers, Gramoxone and Roundup, make regular appearances in my gardening notes. There was a reckless use of chemicals in those days. I suppose I reckoned that money saved on gardening help could usefully be spent on unnatural killers. I certainly reckoned that some could be spent on Spanish Cava, a very good champagne substitute for a tired body and jaded palate. Having drunk relatively little throughout my youth I found this bubbly source of merriment went quickly to my head and I decided it was time I got used to a little alcohol as garden and gardener matured. One of the good things about taking up gardening in middle age is that most great gardeners are rather old – it has taken them all those years to learn their enormous subject. This is a world in which I feel comparatively young, if rather well worn.

I had hoped that once planted according to Jekyll's plan the garden would develop tidily along her carefully measured lines but I soon discovered the folly of that optimism. As I often noted, plants need continual control and care. Jekyll wrote, 'All gardening is the reward of well directed and strongly sustained effort'. With hindsight I believe that the only person who

Fritillaria meleagris (white).

can monitor this sort of museum garden accurately is the on-site-all-the-year gardener but
even I, who live with the plants, have to refer continually to plans to be sure that things are
still accurate. I use annuals as fillings where a gap appears in a border. These I bring from the
extra stock in the Kitchen Garden. I remove them the following season or when the gap has
been correctly filled. Another useful trick I have learnt from Jekyll is to fill border gaps, as
they appear, with plants in large terracotta pots. 'Contrivances' she called these. She tended
to use plants like ophiopogon which fill a space with structural green leaves rather than with
colour. This contriving is quite hard work because plants must be potted up and brought on
during the early summer months, and when they are positioned in the herbaceous border
they must be watered regularly as they tend to dry out quickly. In our garden 'contriving' is
temporary adjustment, not permanent change. I am confident that Jekyll never imagined her
gardens would be held in the unnatural time capsule that ours is. Upton Grey simply serves
as an accurate example of a complete Jekyll garden and, not being an artist gardener myself,
I am happy to obey her rules and keep it thus. The borders which are off plan, like those
around the stable cottage, are planted by me, albeit only with plants which Jekyll used in her
gardens. They have a fleeting glory but none of Jekyll's long season of beauty, her structure
or her careful composition. Try as I may I cannot improve on the master gardener.

At the end of each year I make notes of what seeds or plants to order for the following
year. By 1993 we were self-sufficient in all plants. Nowadays I keep either seeds or cuttings
from year to year and have a back-up supply of most plants of varying size and age in the
Kitchen Garden.

In May 1988 I noticed that some of the *Iris germanica* were rotting. I referred to my
growing library of gardening books and learnt, a little late as usual, how to manage them.
First and most important, they must not be planted too deep. Like peonies, they must lie near

Lychnis chalcedonica
growing behind peonies.

the surface of the earth; their rhizomes should be slightly prominent above ground level. The flower stem should be cut right down after flowering and the leaves removed as they die, or cut back to half their height in late summer. Every four years or so in July they should be dug up, the young side rhizomes removed and replanted and the old central part thrown out.

Towards the middle of summer I finally accept what has died the previous winter and reluctantly throw it out. It takes some time for me to give up all hope of saving a plant, but it is hard to persist optimistically coddling a late May twig which is leafless and black.

In August 1988 we deposited the dogs in local kennels – a sad and rather expensive business – and took off to France again for what was to become our annual five-day holiday. We returned at the end of August to find the herbaceous borders a riot of colour. They must have been fairly colourful for weeks but working so constantly in the garden I had failed to stand back and look at the garden as an entire picture. For the first time the impact of returning from a short holiday made me realise that the garden was not a series of colourful borders but a complete picture. I remember not liking the strong reds, oranges and yellows that filled the centre of the Hot Border and I felt uneasy at the splendour of the pillar-box red *Lychnis chalcedonica* which stands between yellow daisy-flowered *Bupthalmum salicifolium* and kniphofia, the 'Red Hot Pokers'. Today, a more mature and braver gardener, I appreciate the value of vibrant colours that end the season so majestically and I have also learnt to look at a garden from a distance whenever possible. Standing too close to a border gives much the same effect as standing too close to a painting; you may appreciate the fine brushwork as you may the choice of plants, but the composition of each is better judged with perspective. I enjoy watching garden visitors sit on a Jekyll-positioned seat and take in the whole view of the garden as a complete picture.

SEPTEMBER 1988

I was still making the mistakes typical of amateur gardeners but probably more frequently. I did learn from them and recorded them all faithfully. 'Threw out nearly all lettuce – bolted. Sown all at once and too tightly'.

Rather bemused diary notes point out that plants are collapsing. It took a long time to learn

Detail of *Lychnis chalcedonica*.

that very few of my herbaceous plants stand up unaided and even longer to learn when and how to stake or prop the various plants. We evidently needed many more metal frames. As they are expensive I experimented with straight hazel stakes set in squares with strong string running between them to form a grid. It was better than nothing but not ideal. Two years later I tried using sheep wire for supports (the five inch square open fencing wire) and placed it above plants early in the year, raising it as they grew through. That is effective and strong but it is important to remember to raise the wire regularly, otherwise it remains ten inches or so above the ground hugging lower stems and is both virtually useless and immovable. (Metal frames also need to be raised as plants grow). The earlier that plant props are installed the better. Admittedly metal frames look unsightly until plants grow to cover them, but I have learnt the hard way that trying to erect supports midsummer is very vexing.

The Hot Border in 1989 showing *Kniphofia* x *praecox* and *Bupthalmum salicifolium* along path.
Photograph by kind permission of Andrew Lawson.

Above: *Viburnum opulus* (known as Water Elder by GJ).

Right: Autumn dew hangs on a cobweb suspended from *Fuchsia magellanica 'Riccartonii'*.

My old-fashioned single African marigold.

The beautiful variegated sweetcorn, *Zea mays* that Jekyll often used for late summer structure in herbaceous borders.

OCTOBER 1988

'Dug up and stored potatoes; half earthed-up in boxes. Most have worm holes'. What a waste of time that was. I have subsequently learnt only to store sound produce.

1988 seemed to have been a very wet year and I marvelled that water tables in this part of Hampshire are said to have dropped some twenty feet over the century, as most of this garden was a constant bog. I was trying to take seed-heads of selected annuals like snapdragons and marigolds but found it difficult to get them dry enough for storing. In order to breed only what I believed were old colours, mellow yellows and soft whites, I planted seedlings out in blocks of one colour well away from each other in the Kitchen Garden in an attempt to prevent cross-pollination. It is not infallible; bees cover a lot of territory. Amongst the marigolds I noticed that some of my own seedlings had become simpler, almost single-flowered with open centres. I kept seeds from those flowers only, and over the years have almost eliminated the large double, rather harsh-looking modern hybrid flowers. I love these old-fashioned African marigolds with their excellent rich green foliage and valuable late flowers. They are planted in drifts which lead the cooler yellow herbaceous plants through warm oranges towards the centre of the Hot Border. Used thus they give strength to the colour flow and they bloom on until the frost hits them. I find that the yellow marigolds are more fertile than the orange and I have to be careful to isolate plants that I wish to breed from, or the crop becomes monochrome. As I wrote earlier I discovered that if I use my own seeds year after year the resulting plants become gradually simpler or weak, so from time to time I buy commercial seeds as an outcross.

Mid-October. I tried to take hard-wood cuttings of the shrubs choisya, *Virburnum opulus,* and philadelphus. They were simply nine-inch sticks cut at a leaf-joint, with foliage removed from all but the top, then stuck in the earth with no preparation and no care. I had about sixty per cent success with choisya, thirty per cent with *Viburnum opulus* and none with philadelphus. A little later that autumn I learnt, from one of the increasing number of garden visitors, that a jar filled with water in which willow leaves have been infused for a few hours makes a good substitute for hormone rooting powder. Simply hold stem ends in that liquid for a couple of seconds before planting. One of the pleasures of having visitors to the garden is that knowledge is shared, and some remarkably good tips learnt.

Hiccup of the month was top-dressing for the Tennis Lawn. 'The topsoil for autumn dressing was riddled with stones and lumps of clay. Unfortunately I dumped it all from the trailer on the middle of the Tennis Lawn before I realised the problem and for the last two days have been picking lumps (buckets and buckets of them) off the grass. John was very patient as I had ordered what I thought was a good, cheap deal and the grass is his pride and

joy'. Sometimes the initial cost of quality proves to be better value than the cheap offer.

Late October. 'I am hoping to get seeds from the beautiful variegated *Zea mays* that grow in the main border but so far the best are infertile – typical of nature'. Some visitors are surprised to see the plant they know as sweet corn growing in the herbaceous border, and initially I was amused that Jekyll used it here. I asked an old gardening friend if this was unusual and he told me that in the 1920s maize was often planted in herbaceous borders and that it was also sold in Covent Garden flower market where it was valued for its striking variegated foliage.

John Smith, our once-a-week garden helper stopped work here after 1st November as there was little for him to do midwinter and he had plenty of indoor work in other places.

That winter I pruned the apple trees. We have good old trees of Cox, Worcester, Russet, Bramley and other fine-tasting apples. The following summer each tree put out dozens of elegant long shoots but by the autumn they proved to be useless, fruitless shoots. Now we summer-prune lightly and annually, and winter-prune heavily only every three or four years, in order to control the trees and keep their shape.

The Orchard showing the apple trees, Cox, Worcester, Russet and Bramley with spring bulbs that have been planted over the century in the grass.

Climbing rose 'Lady Waterlow' (1903). This is one of my favourites. It flowers throughout the summer and into winter and is very healthy.

Chapter Six
1989 and 1990

1989

I limp through January with the usual reiterated notes on the state of my chilblains. February was altogether brightened up by the arrival of a third dog. Because our Labrador, Biffo, had only one dropped ball, we were advised not to breed from him, so the poor fellow was neutered. John decided to buy a close relation of Biffo's – his nephew. Nephew immediately became Neff and, like his uncle was soft, black, square-headed and remarkably clumsy, although utterly gentle. Since the day he arrived he has rarely stopped wagging his tail. He got on well with the other dogs as he was sensibly servile to the older two and keen to please anybody. Neff bumped his way around the house as favourite novelty until April, when our fourth dog arrived. In retrospect this seemed like masochism from house-proud me but I think the logic must have been that Mark had the terrier, John had two Labradors and I had nothing cuddly (except of course for John). A friend who breeds collies gave me a puppy. He arrived very loved by her and became very loved by me. He had bright black eyes, a sharp pointed nose and, even as a small puppy, masses of mottled grey, white, and brown fur that stood up like quills but which was remarkably soft. The collie had come from deepest Suffolk so, as Neff was a shortened version of Nephew, we abbreviated Country Cousin, and called the puppy Cuz.

APRIL 1989

'Planted canna out; some under plastic tunnels, some in beds'. That was very stupid and, predictably, not one plant survived the several frosts that followed. Instructions on over-wintering the corms were not precise enough for a beginner and between 1986 and 1991 I managed to kill most of my valuable stock annually – and to lament it in diary notes. Over the century cannas had become unpopular bedding plants. In 1989 few nurseries stocked them and the few that were sold were expensive. Jekyll, however, knew the structural value of those stately plants and used them in several of her clients' gardens. I have the purple-green leafed variety which grow to about four foot and put out red or orange gladiolus-shaped flowers in late summer and autumn. In the right context cannas are beautiful. At Upton Grey they make a strong feature amongst the regal lilies at the centre of the Rose Lawn, continuing the season of that area's interest well into October. In April 1991 I wrote, ' I have found the answer to keeping canna alive over winter. Lift them in very late autumn, generally in November after the first light frost. Take them to a dry shed and cut off all leaves, shake most of the earth from roots, then dust with sulphur powder. Put the corms in a long, flat cardboard box and leave them in a frost-free place for a few days to dry off. Then lightly cover them with DRY compost. A piece of newspaper over each box will keep the light off. I don't ever cover corms completely with compost – never have enough'. I now treat dahlias similarly but leave them in a box with no compost cover. Probably the most important thing is not to plant the cannas out too early. Mid-May might be safe. Late spring frosts are far more damaging than the early autumn ones.

Mid-April. I noted how wonderful the climbing rose 'Lady Waterlow' is. This is a rose that we found growing against the house in 1984. It seems to have taken me five years to notice it, and certainly to appreciate it. At that date neither I nor any visitor knew which rose it was

Canna indica and *Lilium regale* in the centre of the Rose Lawn.

Canna indica - detail of foliage.

1989. John, Mark and friends top-dressing the Tennis Lawn.

and we lived in ignorance until Graham Stuart Thomas identified it for me a few years later. 'Lady Waterlow' flowers in spring and continues to carry plenty of buds through until Christmas or until the weather turns really icy. It is virtually disease free and a good shape. The flowers are salmon pink, deeper or paler according to the season. I really cannot fault it. 'Lady Waterlow' is a climbing Hybrid Tea introduced in 1903. Here it grows in a wretched footing which it shares with an unstoppable honeysuckle, against a south-facing wall of the house. It is not on Jekyll's plans but as it grows against the house it does not interfere with her layout and is allowed to remain.

At the end of April the grass is again tined and top-dressed. I am now used to that performance and value the good it does to lawns, but in 1989 I felt differently. 'The Tiner tined adequate green turf into pretty black patterns of mud. Then one hundred and eighty bags of expensive 'Perfect Top Soil' were brushed into the holes and with any luck, in a few days time, we'll be back where we started. Meantime the Tennis Lawn looks like a field and the birds think so too. They are pecking it to pieces'.

April 30. 'After weekend of really productive grass-gardening for John (possibly to make up for disaster with top-soil the year before), it didn't seem so bad doing absolutely no outside work today. It poured with rain and was hideously cold. My, it makes me feel gloomy. It was all rather dark and aimless. I could have painted some walls but went shopping instead and bought an incredibly tight, and therefore uncomfortable, denim skirt. That should inhibit the Mars Bar intake. Tonight a sharp frost is expected. One compensation for days like this is that going to bed with an electric blanket is a real treat'.

JUNE 1989

Mid-month I wrote, 'Very, very tired, so much has happened in the last two weeks'. That was my reaction to two exhausting events; one, quite a success, the other a catastrophic failure.

The first, not the catastrophic event, was our first garden opening for the National Gardens Scheme. Quite why we decided to open on two consecutive days after the woeful attendance at 1988's opening I do not remember. We had not made much effort to publicise the event; I had pinned up no yellow signs, except at the entrance to our drive, and had sent out no warning postcards. May 1989 was one of the hottest on record. There was a sort of

Cartoon 'Don't **EVER** give up'. This cartoon was drawn for me by the patient husband of a Californian friend who had come to a talk I gave in San Francisco.

spontaneous combustion in the garden. Everything flowered early and consequently a great many plants flowered at once. That weekend was sunny and glorious. Peonies, roses, irises, a few very early lilies and some herbaceous plants were in flower. (This happened again in 1996 but that year, because the winter had been bitterly long, spontaneous combustion was in mid June). From 1. 30 p.m. until 5 p.m., that last weekend in May, John and I took turns to sit by the gate collecting money; pounds and pounds for the excellent charity. I think we had over a thousand visitors in two afternoons – far too many for a small garden. I hope they were not very disappointed and that they did manage to see the garden through the crowd. The Formal Garden looked as beautiful as it ever had but the Wild was very immature: four-foot high walnut trees can make a rather disappointing woodland glade.

And the dreadful failure? – I had been asked to give a talk for a nearby garden club in early June 1989, and because I was fairly preoccupied with the physical side of gardening had given the proposal neither enough thought nor enough dread. The subject was to be 'The Work of Hampshire Gardens Trust'. Since 1986 I had been on the committee of the rapidly expanding first gardens trust in England. Gilly Drummond was chairman, inspiration and driving force. She had helped us at Upton Grey and I especially wanted to show my appreciation for all she had done. Gilly provided me with a carousel of about thirty-five carefully arranged slides with notes. It all seemed worryingly simple. Of course I practised the words but could not run slides at home as I had neither a projector nor a screen.

The date of 'Disastrous Talk' was June 8th and happened to be the official Fourth of June picnic day at Eton in Mark's penultimate year at school. The talk was due to start twenty miles from Upton Grey, at 8 p.m. in the village hall in Overton. As usual, on important occasions, I arrived absurdly early, dressed to the nines in Fourth of June kit, spattered, by then, with various items of picnic and grass stains, and with my feet crammed Robinson-style into horribly tight shoes. I waited in the car park until the first person arrived, climbed out of the car carrying carousel, notes and bag, tripped and spilled the slides everywhere. A kindly person helped me gather up bits and, once in the hall, we started to re-carousel the slides. Of course, being unnumbered, I had no idea which order they should go in and far worse, I did not know they should go in upside down. With trembling hand I spent the intervening hour trying to remember which slides went with which notes. As several photographs showed houses which were completely new to me, I decided only to reinsert those I recognised – sixteen out of the thirty-five. My talk was due to last forty-five minutes. At 8 p.m. the audience was seated; eager faces watched the screen, lights went out and the ordeal started. The words came out stilted and nervously soprano. When the first slide appeared upside down I wanted to run away but ploughed on and slide after slide – all sixteen – had to be inverted. Perspiring profusely I wound up the talk. Lights went on. I glanced at the clock and saw to my horror that I had only talked for fifteen minutes. There was complete silence. No clapping and no questions. The grim-faced treasurer strode up to me and asked what he owed me. 'Nothing. I'm sorry. It was dreadful'. He agreed and walked off. But one very kind woman came up to me with a remark that helped me resolve to learn from the bitter experience. 'It will be better next time. I have three ducks which I'd like to give you'. Life is never completely black. Those ducks proved to be the start of great things at Upton Grey. I kept Aylesbury ducks for many years – just to remind me, never give up.

Having recovered from these ordeals, I got back to serious gardening – a good therapy for most things, even if the garden itself is causing problems. Come to think of it, garden problems make a good distraction from the major bumps in life.

Ducks on the pond.

JULY 1989

'Tree Lupins are COVERED with greenfly. Bamboo look rather sickly. I feel a bit sickly too. Could it be all that praline ice-cream we had for lunch or is the ghastly, miserable rain rotting me as well as the plants'. The bamboos looked small and disappointing for the first eight years here. In 1994 they suddenly burst into worrying activity. They grew not only up but in all directions – one of the many wicked plants that I describe as waiting to pounce. They lull gardeners into a false sense of security then burst out all over the place. Japanese knotweed also does this very effectively – so, in a less alarming way, do helianthus 'Miss Mellish' and *Acanthus spinosus*. Watch out for ambush plants.

After a brief period of rain, June ended with a hot spell. Most plants loved it but the hollyhocks were covered with rust and have been riddled with it most years since. I find that the single types are a little more resistant than the double. Spraying makes precious little difference, so I do not bother.

Most of July I spent twelve hours a day in the garden. The ducks arrived and settled in happily, unmolested by dogs as they were too big for the fox terrier to get her jaws around and the Labradors know better. Foxes, I was to learn, only invade our garden during their cub-breeding months of late February through to mid-May, so nowadays ducks are penned in at night for those sixteen dangerous weeks, but they are free to roam for the rest of the year.

At the end of July I discovered a mole burrowing across the Orchard towards the Tennis Lawn. Moles under tennis lawns are about as dreadful as dry rot in the house. I killed it with smoke pellets, poor thing, or perhaps I just scared it away. Anyway, the hummocks stopped short of the sacred grass and never came back.

Far right: *Platycodon grandiflorus* var. *mariesii*.

Right: *Clematis heracleifolia* var. *davidiana*.

AUGUST 1989

'The planting at the edge of the pond has turned from a pretty, controlled profusion of greens, yellows and blues to a tangled mass around a very unattractive, khaki-coloured patch of stagnant water. The ducks are making no inroads at all into the thick scum. Don't entirely blame them'. Ducks do keep ponds clear of duckweed but they also stir up mud at the bottom of the pond disturbing the oxygenating plants and valuable water lilies, and they make rather a mess of the banks. Nothing in nature is perfect.

The first half of August was very dry. 'Nothing grows so I do very little gardening and am practising pottering. I won't water borders because it takes hours and because I'm told plants will not develop good roots if the surface is watered too often. Greenfly and rust on hollyhocks seem to be reduced, luckily. The astonishing weather-forecasters still enthusiastically promise sun and high temperatures when most of the country must be crying out for rain'. Extreme dryness in midsummer often brings a winter-like lull in gardening.

Autumn in the Wild Garden.

SEPTEMBER 1989

The autumn flowers always please, probably because by now the fading flowers of summer are beginning to wilt, and therefore the vitality of late-comers and second-bloomers is especially valued. One of my favourites is *Platycodon grandiflorus* var. *mariesii*. It has blue or white bell-like flowers, a little like *campanula persicifolia* and is of the same family. *Clematis heracleifolia 'davidiana'* makes an annual impact on autumn with its soft blue flowers and beautiful foliage. The daisy-shaped flowers (compositae) which dominate our autumn borders produce an optimistic, opulent display of gold and clear yellow. They seem to complete the cycle of colouring which has run throughout the year from yellow, blue, pink, orange to red and then back again through orange, pink, blue and yellow – like Jaques' seven ages of man, I often think, but less macabre. And autumn in the Wild Garden somehow puts one on trusting terms with death. The trees and shrubs are so beautiful. As winter approaches they drop their rich foliage making the ground beneath look like a reflection of that dying glory. Then the frosts come. Dormancy starts. I do hope death will come and go like that. It needs no sting.

Throughout the year people greet me with 'How's the garden?' I like that. It rings a change

1990. The pond in the Wild Garden with chestnuts beyond after tree surgery.

from 'How are you? Are you well?', which require, and indeed want, no response. In winter I reply 'Asleep, luckily' – and like a good child, it sleeps with very little waking. As it sleeps I continue to work, but greatly reduced hours. This is gardening on borrowed time. I spike the grass, where the machine has not reached, with a huge unwieldy fork. When the weather is dry and not ice-cold we mow lawns with the blades raised about half an inch above the summer cut. I dung and mulch all the beds, slowly, laboriously. I cut things, prune things, shape things, edge, strim and tidy generally. All these are jobs that, strictly speaking, could wait until spring but are wisely done now in the short daylight hours. Plants that have been brought in from the terrace to over-winter need a little care too, though neglect often does indoor plants less harm than too much attention. Minimum watering, a little feed and lots of light seems the best treatment. Our house is never very warm, despite its voracious appetite for fuel, so over-heating plants is not a problem.

JANUARY 1990

'Still gardening on my own and enjoying it. The four dogs play around. Salome makes dark green circles on the grass when she pees and these develop a brown centre'. Fortunately only female dogs cause damage to lawns.

January 25. 'Another violent storm which, in many south-eastern areas, has completed the uprooting job started in October 1987. The storm started at 8.30 a.m. and continued until 7 p.m. Electricity and telephones are cut off. This is a more localised storm but just as violent in mid-Hampshire as its ubiquitous predecessor. However, as there was no leaf on deciduous trees, there was less wind resistance and the overall damage was not nearly so devastating as in 1987. Because this garden is virtually re-built, and we have only a few full-grown trees, we suffered relatively little ill-effect. The copper beech and the *Acer cappadocicum* in the Wild Garden survived, as did the horse chestnuts along the drive, but our huge Atlantic cedar which had been a whim of Charles Holme's and never was on Jekyll's plans, split in half, so

The chestnut trees two years later.

sealing its fate'. Now I made another serious mistake. Because their quote for cutting and clearing was much lower than those from reputable tree surgeons, I hired a gang of 'off-the-road' cowboys. They felled the tree but left a terrible mess and I had to employ someone else to help me stack away the enormous logs, proving, not for the first time, that the cost of good workmanship would have been better value than the cheap offer.

January 29. 'Mammoth amount of work all week clearing branches and burning bits. Electricity back at 6 p.m. for first time since storm. Most of Hampshire seems still to be cut off'.

By pure chance we had already arranged that the following month we would have the horse chestnut trees that line the drive cut back by about one third. That was a specialist tree-surgeon job and expensive, which took about five days to complete. Tilhill of Farnham did the work for us. A neighbour had told us that one or two of our trees were looking diseased and he was worried that large branches might fall into his garden. The cut-back looked drastic immediately afterwards but has proved well worth doing as the trees are much healthier in consequence and much better shaped – this time an example of spending more money but getting better value.

FEBRUARY 1990

Sunday February 4. 'Only gardened for four hours. Terrible thunder and lightning immediately overhead. Nearly had heart attack. Poured. Floods all over west coast. Sowed snapdragons, marigolds, belladonna delphiniums and *Pterocephalus parnassii* in warm end of greenhouse and others in cold bit'. Until 1993 I heated the four-by-four foot, closed off section of our greenhouse with a small cylinder heater. It managed to keep frosts off plant trays within close range but not those by the glass sides. In 1994 we bought a simple and effective Calor gas heater for the main greenhouse and electric cabling for the small area; after which we were able to give dozens of trays of seedlings a good start and have them ready for planting out in late spring. The flooding I mention had started in early January. Without the greenhouse and its heating, seven weeks of rain would have set our garden schedule back too far. The annuals have to be ready for planting out in early May if the borders are to have the required balance, and we would not have made that deadline.

Pterocephalus parnassii syn. *perennis*. This was one of the plants that I was unable to find until the *Plant Finder* was published in 1987.

The pond in winter.

MARCH 1990

Francesca Greenoak had made an appointment for a garden interview. I was expecting the person who wrote such sensible and enjoyable articles for *The Times* to be an old woman. To my surprise she turned out to be young, beautiful, intelligent and full of sparkle. She wrote a very generous article about us under the heading 'Reliving Past Glories' which was published on Saturday March 3rd 1990.

In the spasmodic way that gardeners do, we have kept in touch since. I enjoy the gardening world and the friends I have made, very wise, generous-minded, and in some cases, entertainingly prickly, but I have not been fully accepted into their intellectual circle and remain a bit of a specialist oddity. If you have a career in the media or in finance you know in advance who the important people are. If you make gardening your career you find it is a closed world of seriously successful people who do not bother to venture outside their happy world and do not need the suspect bonus of fame to fulfil themselves. When Andrew Lawson telephoned to ask if he could photograph the garden throughout the seasons of 1990 and 1991 I agreed happily but, never having heard of him, hardly mentioned him in diary notes. I do remember carrying out a cup of tea to him at some stage and, in the brief minutes that I talked to him, being very impressed by his love and deep understanding of nature in every aspect from birds to insects and the smallest weeds. Andrew Lawson is one of our best horticultural photographers.

In the spring of 1990 remarkable Rosemary Nicholson added a small Gertrude Jekyll section to the exhibition at her Museum of Garden History in Lambeth and our garden was included. Items were beautifully displayed and it was very flattering to us. Sally Festing, whose biography of Jekyll was about to be published, wrote an article about Upton Grey which appeared in the Royal Horticultural Society's magazine *The Garden* later that summer. I considered that article, and being mentioned in her book, were a great compliment to GJ herself and to us as her labourers.

There probably are sermons in stones and good in everything but there are sad times too in the garden. There was grieving in that violent spring of 1990. Two of my ducks had mysteriously disappeared and by April I was left with one duck. It now had no mate and no companions so she followed me around the garden and would wait for me patiently by the door. She became known by me in rather a maudlin way as Beloved Duck and by John as Roast.

Roast, the duck.

A drystone wall in late spring.

APRIL 1990

It was a strange spring and the frosts were vicious. The dicentra, which had looked beautiful at the beginning of the month, were badly hit. After a severe late frost there is no solution but to cut it back to ground level and hope that it re-grows. So far it always has and I have to cut it back to some extent almost every year. The cannas, which again I had planted out too early, all died. We had very cold nights and warm, sunny days, which made the shock to plants all the more lethal. I divided *Iris unguicularis* and wrote in my diary 'Wrong?' It was wrong. It should be done in late summer, but they did not seem to suffer. If you want to be safe, follow the rules but sometimes you get away with breaking them.

My diary notes: 'hacked small branches off base of chestnuts. They protest at having been coppiced at the top by branching out yet more vigorously at the base'. Nobody had warned me of that.

I made my own potting compost on April 2nd. It was leaf compost mixed with earth and reused old peat. On April 23rd I reported on germination. 'Useless; full of lumps (probably the leaf compost bit) and riddled with weeds. The top is damp where watered and' the bottom bone dry. Nothing germinates. False economy'. Experienced gardeners probably know this but I was surprised to find that, although it looks so rich when thoroughly decomposed, pure leaf compost seems almost sterile, virtually nothing grows in it. Yet again I learned the folly of false economy and today I buy a good quality commercial potting compost.

April 11. *'Good Gardens Guide* has just been published (for the first time I think)'. Now, there's a good way to make malcontents of gardeners. In 1990 we were flattered to be included at all, albeit with no star. As the years go by I seek higher and higher ratings and fundamentally, if I am really honest, want to score better than friends whose gardens are also included, even though I do not deserve to. When being assessed there is always the temptation to make the sickening excuses all gardeners are prone to; if only you had come last/next week before the drought/frost/winds. That is assuming you recognise the guide's inspector. I now understand what a French restaurateur goes through with visits from Messrs Michelin and Gault et Millau.

Looking at my garden diary I see that I made my usual muddle about the dates that we had agreed to open for the National Gardens Scheme. This is the type of blunder I make all too frequently, thinking of one thing whilst doing (and muddling) another. John was fifty in 1990 and for months we had planned his party. It was to be a lunch for about one hundred and fifty people on Sunday June 3rd; our first ever big party. There was to be a marquee over the Tennis Lawn; water and electric cables were to run from the house to the kitchen tent in the Orchard and the house was going to be open for our guests to use and pass through.

April 12. 'To my horror I find we are listed as opening the garden on June 3rd. How can I be so incompetent? This weekend I'm going to paint large signs saying Garden NOT Open. Actually, the further I get from the awful dawning point the merrier I feel about it. It can't be the end of the world if the odd visitor from afar wanders around while we're lunching. But we'll certainly have to have a heavy on the gate – Stewart?' Stewart is old, frail, small, kind and light.

April 29. 'Finished clearing all mess around ex-cedar tree and burnt piles of branches. Over last few days I've mowed all lawns, strimmed long grass, re-made compost heaps, coppiced Nuttery (too late, sap is rising), sowed more seeds and transplanted some seedlings to Kitchen Garden. Roast laid two eggs all on her own (i.e., no mate), but sensibly doesn't sit on them. Trusting and rather tragic. I took them home and made very good chocolate cake with them'. April is one of the busiest months in the garden. I often wrote up notes days late, repetitive and muddled, but I had to get the garden ready for the Big Party.

MAY 1990

The first of May 1990 was the date of John's fiftieth birthday but as I said we had decided to celebrate later in the summer when weather would be warmer and the garden looking its best. As it happened we chose to celebrate on one of the very few days that summer when it poured with rain.

May 8. 'Cleared all rushes out of pond'. I thought I had but I had not. They come back regularly and if I manage to control them, *Iris pseudacorus* takes over the invasion. Four years earlier Penelope Hobhouse had warned me that controlling plant growth around the pond would be one of my greatest difficulties. How right she was. At the damp, clay-filled pond edges weeds grow at an alarming rate and even the intentional plants spread relentlessly out of their alloted area.

Mid-May. 'Jane Brown took me to Goddards – a wonderful Lutyens house. Garden higgledy piggledy'. Goddards was amongst Lutyens' earliest commissions, designed, when he was thirty, for Sir Frederick Mirrielees at Abinger Common, in Surrey. It was the first time that I had seen a Lutyens house both inside and out and it showed me the importance of attention to detail in good architecture. Everything from window and door handles to drainpipes and guttering were designed with care and made with pride. The mellow brick and stonework were echoed in the garden where the planting, too, was mellow and comfortable. I suppose Lutyens was largely responsible for the architecture of garden walls, dipping-well, flagstone work and brickwork.

Like Hestercombe's 'great plat' which also has plenty of structure, the garden would look beautiful with little or no planting because, as I noticed, there had been little upkeep and the garden was running to seed in a delightful way. Two things struck me that day. First that the on-site gardener and owner, like me, has so much more control and more vested interest in maintaining a garden to high standards than the part-time employee – Goddards was run by one part-time gardener and occasional help. The second point was how very different our properties are. Goddards almost grows out of its garden. 'Marriage', in the sense of a complete compatibility of house and garden, describes the work of Lutyens and Jekyll there. A different impression is created at Upton Grey. Newton had no part in this garden's design. Jekyll was both garden architect and plantswoman here. The pergola which links the house to the Rose Lawn is strong and beautiful in both proportion and planting and it balances well with the heavy Edwardian architecture. The difference here is that this garden 'displays' Newton's house, quite dramatically, whereas Goddards' garden almost clothes Lutyens' house. Like all great garden designers and landscapers, Jekyll had an architect's eye for proportion, structure and texture.

Next day. 'White furry stuff all over box hedges. Clouds of it fly out when they are shaken. Sprayed all with systemic insecticide as it seems like woolly aphid judging by description in RHS book'. Odd, I had never noticed it before. Neither had I noticed much disease on any old fruit trees, shrubs or plants until we started clearing the garden. Obviously I was upsetting the balance of nature somewhere so I started to be more cautious and to use fewer chemical 'cures' as the years went by.

May 23. 'Weather hot and quite dry. Funny to have bluebells out at the same time as delphiniums'. In 1998 the bluebells were beginning to flower by April 12th, which shows how much flowering dates are affected year to year by the weather.

'John cuts grass edges using a plank as guide. Takes hours. Waste of time'. In retrospect I wonder if it is. My edging leaves very wobbly lines which, over the years, rather run out of control. While using a plank does take longer, it maintains the correct lines, and makes the edges and corners look crisp and smart.

For most of the summer of 1990 I gardened an average of seven hours a day. It is quite possible to work in the garden a full twelve hours on an English summer's day, so a day taken off completely is easily compensated for. At weekends I worked fewer hours but John helped, so we kept up the rate; all of which proves that one person with modern equipment can manage a five-acre garden if working full time.

May 24. 'Only three hours gardening as TV South came to film here from 9.30-12 with Stefan Buczacki and others. Nice day. Nice bloke. Programme goes out 6.30 p.m. Friday'.

On the subject of growing media interest in the garden, at some stage the previous year Jane Brown had brought a journalist to see the garden. His name was Adrian Higgins. As the garden was so immature I forgot about it and never asked which publication he was writing for, neither did I mention it in my garden notes. It was to prove the most important article ever written about our work here, which suggests that allowing journalists and broadcasters to absorb the garden at their own pace tends to result in more personal and enthusiastic reports.

JUNE 1990

John's momentous fiftieth lunch party gets very little space in garden notes. 'Extraordinary day. The big Wal lunch. One hundred and forty people and so delicious. Sunny morning (it

Ros and animals.
Photograph by kind permission
of Christopher Sykes.

had been seriously dry for weeks), then 12.30-2.00 downpour. Most people arrived with umbrellas which got snagged on the rose pergola as they walked through. Then sun came out magically and the rest of the day went flawlessly. Roast, feeling lonely by the pond, waddled down with the last guests and joined us in the marquee for crumbs. Dogs ate any meaty bits'. Stewart at the gate turned away a few garden visitors but let in anyone who had driven from afar. There were few and they came and left unnoticed by us.

By the end of the week the tent had been taken down and all the mess cleared away leaving very little damage to the garden except a few tent pole holes in the Tennis Lawn; this came as a relief to me as *American House and Garden* magazine had telephoned to ask if they could send a photographer the following week to illustrate the story submitted by Adrian Higgins. I was delighted by that, having, as I said, forgotten all about the previous year's interview. The prospect of being read about in America was very exciting, and of course, to me, all being relative, the garden was looking beautiful in its sixth year. The article's editor told me that the photographer was to be Christopher Sykes, a very well known name in that world, but not to ignorant me. For the following few days I beavered away in the garden 'tidying and propping and taking dead bits off things'. I prayed for good weather and got it. I did not

Campanula lactiflora and peony 'Sarah Bernhardt'.

write anything about that important day in notes other than to remark, 'Borders looking good. Reds and yellows nearly all out but meadowsweet is weak. Hates this drought'. In retrospect, I doubt that all of the yellow herbaceous plants were flowering as early as that but obviously things looked all right.

I remember the day quite well. As there was a lot of gardening to do, I did not get dressed or 'made up' for the event. I wore rough jeans and had my hair tied back in a bundle. Christopher Sykes arrived, to my surprise, with, I think, two assistants. I showed them around and, because Roast and dogs kept getting in the way, moved off to another part of the garden to work. The photographing team were still snapping away at about one o'clock so I asked them if they wanted any lunch and, having got myself into a bit of a cleft stick when they said yes please, went to the village shop to buy some of its excellent cheese and bread. For about an hour we sat in the kitchen

A group of visitors in the Formal Garden.

eating bits and discussing gardens and the gardening world. Christopher was apparently photographing English gardens and their owners for an issue of the American magazine which was to be subtitled *England Today*. He told me that, after lunch, they wanted to take some photographs of me at work and asked what I would like to be doing. The lawns needed mowing so I got out the large cylinder mower and started work on the Tennis Lawn expecting to be stopped for a pose at some stage. It was about 3 p.m., which is feed time for the dogs, a time when they are particularly attentive and as always Roast followed me around religiously. I was striding up and down with the mower, surrounded by the four dogs and the duck, who walked with a strange sort of goose step as she tried to keep up. When I had finished mowing it was evident that Christopher and his team had taken any photographs they wanted. They thanked me and drove off into the evening leaving a rather disappointed group of animals and me. I assumed they had decided not to photograph us after all.

For the following few weeks I proudly told friends that the garden had been photographed for *American House and Garden*. The wiser ones told me that it was common enough to be photographed but very rare actually to feature in the magazine, so as the busy summer went on I rather forgot about it. We had a few more Garden Open days and as a result of the television programme hundreds of people came. Proud as I was that so many wanted to see the garden, I found open days absolutely exhausting – far more tiring than a hard day's gardening. Either my patient father or a friend from the village would come and help me take money at the entrance – lots of it. At the end of each day I wrote a cheque to the charity for the takings and hid the tins of cash away until I had time to go to the bank. My 'burglar-proof' hiding places are ingenious. I often searched for those tins for months – I still come across little stashes of coins from time to time.

Managing the visitors' cars was the greatest problem. A local farmer let us use his nearby field for parking. But a nearby field is not nearby enough for the decrepit old people who make up a large percentage of visitors. They want, and sometimes need, to drive up to the house, where there is just enough space for ten cars if parked carefully – not enough space for dozens driven rather erratically by a frail body whose head only just appears above the dashboard. A game of fair-ground bumper cars would describe the ensuing performance more accurately than parking. Inevitably there is some poor old soul who needs a lavatory and in those days we were not set up for that. The afternoons were enlivened with questions and frank comments from the visitors. Mostly I enjoyed those and I learnt a lot, but everything loses its appeal in overdose. I wish I had taken photographs of the parking bedlam but I did not. I suppose I had not enough sense of humour or enough time to immortalise the chaos.

Garden Open Days are notorious for allowing the passing burglar to do a speedy recce of the house and its vulnerable points. All doors had to be locked and curtains drawn. I often spent as much time turning the house into a small fortress and setting up signs directing cars to parking, as I did running the rest of the day. By the end of 1990, and in only a few days opening, we had had over one thousand seven hundred visitors. National Gardens Scheme did well by us and they were great supporters in return. It is an excellent charity.

JULY 1990

We lunched with Prue and Martin Lane Fox at Hazelby House near Newbury this month. That sort of garden leaves me with a profound feeling of inadequacy as well as a vague hope that I might achieve similar standards here. High levels of tidiness are really all I aspire to, as I have no intention of changing Jekyll's scheme of things. I simply want perfection in what Jekyll prescribed – a rather lofty aspiration. Martin had one part-time and two full-time gardeners to help him achieve near perfection. He also had a considerably larger garden than we have. I explained that I was spending two years working entirely on my own to learn the art of gardening, but experienced gardeners do not understand that. I left Hazelby thinking it one of the most beautiful gardens I had ever seen, but John felt it was a little too contrived, though I daresay he was trying gently to be tactful to me.

As usual, garden notes report that the very hot July was 'making the herbaceous borders fall over'. By that I meant that plants were collapsing. They continued to fall over despite stakes and metal supports, often taking their props with them. These are times when nature is at best a perverse child and at worst the enemy, even the visitors were beginning to comment on the garden's and my rather dilapidated appearance. At times like that one of their favourite questions is 'which gardening chore do you like least?' Or at the end of a long day at work 'what is the straw that really breaks the camel's back?' Answers vary according to the season and nature's temperamental wiles. In my case the last straw is often the dogs rampaging through the flower-beds, but winds that knock down a year's growth in one gust, gloves that develop holes in fingertips, ants that climb up a trouser leg and literally bite all over before escaping, despite thumps and pinches from the enraged bitten, are just as bad. Quite often my short fuse mood shows when garden groups arrive late towards the end of a busy day. One delightful visitor, seeing my prickly mood said gently, 'there is life after gardening you know'. I bear that in mind when I've gone just a bit too far. Stop for a minute, sit down, breath deeply and enjoy life. She followed it up with her name for gardeners which I suppose is old hat but I liked it and it drew a weary chuckle. 'Gardeners are flowers, they are buttock-ups'.

On the last Open Day of 1990 an old man and his daughter arrived with the crowds. They turned out to be very important visitors – ones I would never have met had we not opened to the public. I had noticed their arrival. They came early and slowly, and disappeared into the crowd. They left at an even slower pace, towards the end of the day when numbers had thinned to a trickle. As they shuffled past I asked if they had enjoyed themselves. 'Oh yes', replied the daughter, 'my father used to garden here in 1917 for a Mr Savill'. That Mr Savill was the father of Kenneth Savill, the person who had lent me his photographs of the garden, and who had lived here from 1916 to 1936. (The family who had rented the house from Charles Holme). We sat together and talked about the garden in those early years. The old man said it was very much as he remembered it and proceeded to describe in remarkable detail where the old ferneries had stood, the water tanks or wells and his memory of plants. He asked if I had cut down the vine whose grapes he remembered had tasted so fine. They were fine, and I had. The poor plant had survived the century but the house was very damp where its roots grew up against the wall and, as it was not on Jekyll's plan, it was mercilessly hacked out. Dreadful. Today I would at least attempt to take cuttings before destroying an old plant.

It was chance meetings like that which led me to people who had known, or were relations of, Charles Holme. One person I always enjoy seeing is Charles Holme's grand-daughter, Joan Flower. Joan has been a source of a great deal of valuable information about Holme and the early history of the garden and she has allowed me to make copies of some of her relevant photographs. Now I have a comprehensive record of the house and garden from before Jekyll and Holme came here to the present day. Joan's photographs, plans and articles which are now on display to visitors, make the garden tour more interesting and, to some extent, unusual.

Charles Holme's grand-daughter Joan Flower. She has been a great help with photographs and information about her family.

The garden notes for August 1990 read like October in a normal year. I complained about a bad fruit harvest and was cutting back raspberry canes, gooseberries, acanthus, helenium and stachys. Almost annually I made notes about impossible stachys because by about this time of the year I have become really fed up with cutting it back. As I noted before *Stachys lanata* needs regular cutting because it is an old variety that becomes straggly as it ages, and it flowers on long disproportionate shoots – modern cultivars are better shapes for use as edging plants. Possibly because I only took up gardening in middle life, I had formed no particular attachment to old-fashioned cultivars, some of which have become rare over this century. I have no nostalgia for the old plants and when I do find them, excited as I am by the discovery of a near-extinct specimen, I very rarely find it an improvement on its modern replacement. Like *Stachys lanata*, both helianthus 'Miss Mellish', which I have mentioned as being a really rewarding bit of treasure hunting, and *Rudbeckia laciniata* 'Golden Glow', are also good examples of old cultivars which have fallen from favour. The first is almost uncontrollably invasive, and Rudbeckia 'Golden Glow', which was sent to me by the famous (now retired) gardener, Mr Jimmy Hancock of Powis Castle is, like many nineteenth century plants, far too tall to support itself. It is hard to imagine how nature allowed such gangly plants to evolve at all (see overleaf).

Looking back I cannot understand why the fruit canes were cut back so early, particularly as several garden notes start 'So much to do. Very, very hard day's work'. It cannot have been necessary. Even the strawberries were decimated. 'Kept a few deadish plants for next year'. Was the weather really that dry? In this part of Hampshire we do get slightly less rain than most of southern England. Apparently the Isle of Wight divides and lifts onshore rain-carrying breezes, parting them carefully for eighty or so miles over the mainland. They meet again somewhere near Newbury. In a long, hot, dry summer it can be quite upsetting to see rain clouds either side on the horizon and to be left bone dry up the centre. But there is always an upside to nature; 1990 was an excellent year for collecting viable seeds, as a result of which I had a greenhouse full of seed trays the following year.

Although as I said I only water flower-beds in severely dry conditions, the grass is watered regularly with a revolving sprinkler spray made by Hozelock, a simple and excellent gadget which can either water a full circle or an arc of any desired radius. When the water pressure

Rudbeckia laciniata 'Golden Glow' with helianthus 'Miss Mellish' and *Helenium autumnale pumilium* at the back of the Hot Border in September. This summer I used the wrong gladiolus as substitutes for *Gladiolus brenchlyensis* which I have been unable to find.

Rudbeckia laciniata 'Golden Glow' – detail.

is at its best I can water the whole Tennis Lawn (that is about 1000 square metres) from four positions. On August 11th I wrote, 'No hose ban so far'. Other parts of Britain, however, had endured weeks of hose banning.

During the summer of 1990, making bonfires was an easy and terrifying experience because almost everything burnt like tinder. Even with water buckets and hose on hand I gave myself several frights. I was slow to learn.

At this stage in the garden's redevelopment I had managed to find almost all of the plants that Jekyll chose and the planned part of the garden did look good. As I worked to perfect the Jekyll bit, I realised that parts off-plan were being left a little neglected; they went in the end of year notes as projects for the following year – and do so annually, on a carry-forward basis. I think most gardeners are natural procrastinators through over-ambition.

One of the 1990 projects was to make a tennis hut. Photographs taken of the garden between about 1920 and 1940 show a beautiful five-sided wooden hut about eight feet across and fifteen high, with a shingle-tiled roof. It stood at the back of the Tennis Lawn. No

1990. Rose arbour winter.

1996. Rose arbour summer.

building is defined on Jekyll's plans, but she designed a recess into the yew hedge, which suggests that something was meant to stand there. A York stone pentagon marked the area where spectators should sit. We were given several estimates for a building that copied the photograph. The lowest was £9, 200. It seemed enormous – most figures seem enormous when a herbaceous border's worth of seeds costs a few pounds. We decided that, as Jekyll had not stipulated what should fill her yew recess, we would make a rose arbour. Five six-inch square oak posts with tapered corners and top would surround the stones. More of the heavy ship's rope that we had used on the pergola would hang from post to post, leaving the front open, and towards the back we would put a beautiful wooden bench. We consulted garden books old and new and I visited several gardens before arriving at this practical decision. The resulting structure is a fine sight. The posts were later hung with good nineteenth century climbing roses supplied by Peter Beales and within a few years the arbour has grown into a beautiful display of shape and movement which, throughout the year, makes a good focal point to and from the house. The roses are interwoven to form a gently rounded roof and sides which itself is quite a work of art. The bench is a copy of a Pyghtle Work bench, c.1912, made today by Julian Chichester. Total cost of the whole arbour was around £520.

Far left: The rose arbour that we built because we could not afford to copy the original hut. John, Ros and dogs.

Left: c.1918. The pretty tennis hut with dovecote that Charles Holme built in c.1912.

**The process of
restoring an old
yew hedge to
healthy growth
and shape**

1990. The yew hedge
cut right back to the
trunks on one side.

Another job that I classified as 'perfecting' was to restore one very overgrown twelve foot high yew hedge that stood at the end of the drive by the old greenhouse. It was so badly entangled with weeds that I could not get to the centre to pull them out and parts of the hedge looked very dead. John took the brave decision to cut back branches to within inches of the trunks on one side. This is an established way to revive and improve the shape but it is a drastic step to take because the resulting hedge is a horrible sight for years. It was evidently a job that we should have done as soon as we moved to Upton Grey, not as soon as we started opening to the public. In the centre of what had once been a nine-feet wide hedge we found old bottles, bits of broken china and a tangled mass of weeds. The job of cutting back the reachable bottom half took me three days and it took another whole day for John Smith from the village to do the top, a job that involved erecting a make-shift scaffold of planks and ladders. For the next four years the yew was a curious sight but proved to be of considerable interest to gardeners facing the same problem. By 1995 the shape had improved and by 1996 there was no trace at all of the savaging. In 2001 we intend to cut back the other side. It is important to feed a hedge after such severe treatment and not to allow it to become too dry at the roots. Each spring and autumn I give all shrubs and trees, including the yew hedges, a handful of Growmore fertiliser which I rake lightly into the earth around their roots.

AUGUST 1990

My August notes touched on a variety of non-sequential items. I got shingles – painful but did not stop me gardening – and I learnt how to clean the Honda's spark plugs which quite rejuvenated it. I also decided I needed help. My diary notes that 'I employed a frail old man from farm next door to help six hours every Tuesday. Wise? Any port? Drought continues. Huge, spectacular and terrifying bonfire of all yew bits'. From 1996 onwards we, and most gardens with a substantial amount of yew hedging, sold the clippings of *Taxus baccata*, the common yew. They go towards making a cure for some types of cancer. Limehurst is the company we use. They either cut and take the yew for free, or pay about 40p per kilo if you

1998. The yew hedge
fully regrown.

cut your own. We cut our own – that way we control the standard of cut and earn about
£140 per year from our yew sales.

SEPTEMBER 1990

This month always comes as a beautiful surprise. Roses in the Rose Lawn have a wonderful
second flowering and so do most of those plants that I have cut back earlier in the year. 'Mme
Lombard' and 'Laurette Messimy' are amazing. They are riddled with mildew but so colourful
that it barely shows. They look better now than at any time this summer. Evidently these old
roses are fairly drought tolerant'.

   With experience I have learnt to cut back several herbaceous plants throughout the
summer. In a garden like this, where plants are grouped together in drifts, it is possible to thin
back as much as one third of a group at a time, before, during and after flowering, thus greatly
extending the colour season. If done carefully there are no signs of gaps. With flowers that
grow upright and individually like hollyhocks and delphiniums I would recommend
planting a few more than needed so that you can cut about one in three plants right back to
base before they have flowered (in about midsummer) and those plants will grow again
healthily to give a glorious late autumn display of colour when most other flowers are over.
It took me several years to learn that trick from my Californian gardening friends. Most
plants will flower twice if encouraged.

   September 24. 'M. Wood comes to solid-tine all grass'. Each autumn and spring we hire a
contractor, M. Wood, and his heavy machine to solid-tine, hollow-tine or slit-tine the grass.
Aerating the lawns on this scale is essential and helps control moss. Regularly during the year
we scarify with our own scarifier but this does not have the deep-digging tines of M. Wood's
machines. 'One hundred bags of topsoil arrived from Surrey Loams (£137.00). We shall top-
dress and re-seed at weekend when John's about'.

   September 30. 'At last another proper fall of rain. Funny how, no matter how heavily I
hose-water, grass only springs to bright green with real rain. Very lonely here. John is on a
twenty day biz. trip around the world and Mark is at Aberdeen (University). I'm left with
dogs and duck. Good enough company I suppose. TV News is on. Crisis in Gulf '.

The rare rambler rose 'Euphrosyne' (1895) which I discovered in the garden years after we moved here.

OCTOBER 1990

October 8. 'Cold. White frost this morning. Chilblains soon'. This is remarkably early for a hard frost, but of course early autumn frosts do not do anything like the damage of one in late spring.

October 9. 'Bright, cool day. Mr D. (help from next-door farm at £20 for six hours so not expensive) weeds two Rose Lawn beds. He asks if he can do an extra day. Tactfully, No. I tie up pergola roses with old tights and flymow grass Wild Garden'. I have several uses for old tights in the garden. Being strong, elastic and soft they can hold even quite large plants firmly without cutting into stems but allowing some freedom of movement. I also use them as an elastic cord from which to hang things like scissors and keys. I attach the other end to the gardening pouch which hangs around my waist. Thus secured things are more accessible and they do not get lost. They are also very useful for hanging keys inside houses near the doors. They can hang loose several feet from the door – out of reach of intruders – but always reachable when you need the key to open the door. Tights do not knot like string, they are very strong and one leg of a pair stretches a very long way when pulled.

Later that week I received a reply to a letter I had sent to the Royal National Rose Society's Historic Roses Group, at St Albans. I had written to ask them if they could track down a rose called 'Kitchener'. The rose I had planted in the Wild Garden was listed as 'K of K' in catalogues so I supposed that it must be the same rose as the 'Kitchener' on Jekyll's plans (which I presumed stood for Kitchener of Khartoum). It very evidently was not. The Wild Garden roses are all ramblers or species. In its second year here 'K of K' flowered. The flowers were a deep red, hybrid tea shape with wonderful scent, but looked ridiculous in the Wild Garden. When I referred to the rose catalogues, I found 'K of K' listed as introduced in 1917 and an HT. Beautiful as it was, the rose was far too young to have been on Jekyll's 1908 plans.

1994. The Wild
Garden in winter.

The Historic Roses Group did excellent research for me, which was particularly impressive as I was not then a member. They told me that at the end of last century a rose called 'Kitchener' had briefly existed but that it had never been marketed, presumably because it failed to meet the rigorous RNRS standards. People in the horticultural world had access to such plants at the time and Jekyll obviously liked that particular rose. She used it in about five gardens that she planned around the turn of the century. In October I took beautiful 'K of K' out of the Wild Garden and moved it to an off-plan bit of the garden, replacing it with 'Euphrosyne' and 'Blush Rambler' which are correct in other parts of the Wild Garden and which are easy to grow from root cuttings.

The story of how I discovered 'Euphrosyne' is interesting because, as I said earlier, I had given up hope of ever finding that rose. In 1987 I had noted in my diary, 'I asked a group of Australian rosarians what the pretty pale pink rambler growing against the shed and against the Orchard wall might be. One told me that it looks like 'Euphrosyne', if a little pale. I must try to discover. If it is, I have found the rose that I believed extinct as I can't find it in any rose catalogues'. (I later learnt, from that valuable booklet *Combined Rose List*, published annually in Ohio, USA, that it is sold in only three nurseries in the world, so I ordered a plant from Les Roses Anciennes de André Eve, in France, and it proved to be the same rose. Oddly enough they were small but very healthy when I discovered the two neglected plants here. After a few years of pampering, feeding and pruning it developed a heavy mildew – the ingrate – but strikes root easily from cuttings so I have plenty of spares).

NOVEMBER 1990

The month was cold, bright and beautiful. The garden looked as good as it always does when it returns to bare brown earth and discipline. Mr D announced that he did not want to work over the winter months. I was surprised and grateful as there is not much to do from November onwards, but I would not dream of hiring someone only for the busy months and dumping them when there is no other work to be found.

DECEMBER 1990

Early in the month it snowed, thick, white and very deep. People in outlying places were snowed in. I hibernated towards the end of the month and read; I was enjoying Richard Bisgrove's *National Trust Book of the English Garden* because it put Gertrude Jekyll into the context of garden history and justified her importance. As usual I had not planted the hyacinth bulbs in time for Christmas flowering, so a bowl of green lumps was displayed. 'Big Christmas lunch with too many people squashed into the dining room'. Jekyll did not like Christmas much and neither do I. She is quoted as saying 'Forgive us our Christmases'.

Garden Notes end with intentions for next year. This year they went as follows: 'Did a tour of garden, making notes of work to be done in 1991. Prune box hedges in May. Prune yew in August'. For the first four years of their growth we did not cut the yew; after that time we carefully trimmed the plants into a narrow shape in order to encourage upward growth. By 1998 they had grown to their full seven feet and were pruned like a hedge, slightly narrower at the top than at the base.

'Edge Kitchen Garden with herbs. Put a pergola walk along stone path at far end of Kitchen Garden. Summer-prune apple trees'. Generally, good intentions do get done – but not necessarily the following year. 'I want to plant fruit trees along the Orchard walls, probably apricot, peach and nectarine. Cut back all weeds on the bank that edges the Roman road

The site of the Roman road which is now simply a deep-set path which lies on a hard flint and stone base.

The one thousand eight hundred year old yew tree which marked the Roman road that runs through this garden.

and make a shade-loving plant feature of that bit'. That is a job that gets started annually in early spring when I have a bit of spare time. It is usually abandoned in April and, by the time we get around to tackling it again in the autumn, we might just as well not have started – the weeds are back in force.

Ordnance Survey maps show that the Roman road from Silchester to the south coast ran right through our garden. Roman roads were marked from time to time with an evergreen tree, often yew, so that the line of the road would be visible when the countryside was covered with snow. At the top of our drive stands an ancient yew. A representative from the Tree Conservancy Council who came to look at it, estimated its age at between eighteen hundred and two thousand years, and wrote as follows:

The Manor House Yew

This yew seems to be in the process of regenerating. It is hollow, but over half the old bole remains. New growth is both flowing over the sounder dead wood, and growing out from the bole and branches. The old shell has the gnarled and warped appearance of ancient wood. The tree has heaved towards the road, perhaps in the 1987 hurricane. The site is interesting; the tree is both on an existing road and the line of a Roman Road that runs toward Southampton. The tree is situated on the left of the entrance to Upton Grey Manor, the site of arguably the best restored and most complete of Gertrude Jekyll's gardens. The tree could be an ancient waymarker, and further yews and stumps remain to be investigated on the Roman Road, particularly on the boundary fence of the local vicarage. It could also be associated with the site of the local church, which is next to the Manor.

The girth of the tree is 18′ 8′′ at the base, 18′ 4′′ at three feet from the ground, and 19′ 0′′ at four feet. It was probably once a bit larger than this, bearing in mind that it has lost part of one side. It is female.

The Nuttery in spring
with bluebells and
primroses. In the
background is a bench
made with the
coppiced hazelnut
branches.

Coppiced branches of
hazel trees (*Corylus
avellana*) and the rose
frame we made.

Chapter Seven
1991

JANUARY 1991

The year started wet and mild. '*American House and Garden* rang me to ask which campanula I grow. Perhaps we will be in the magazine? Haven't dared ask yet. Better to assume to them that we will and to myself that we won't'.

January 16. 'Today we are to be judged by Historic Gardens in order, possibly, to be upgraded from Grade II to Grade II★. Stupid timing, midwinter'. They did not upgrade us as far as I know.

January 17. 'War starts'.

January 25. 'Miserable news from Gulf'. That was about the only mention the Gulf War got. Garden notes are strictly concerned with gardening and other news hardly features. But death in the garden, death of anything, bird, beast or plant was recorded solemnly as of course were all gardening events, great or small – with monotonous regularity. 'Did wonderful helianthus 'Miss Mellish' survive the cold?' It certainly did. It had spent the winter spreading its thick white roots all over the place and came up triumphantly to prove it in the spring.

'We've put in a bid for Peter Page's stable cottage and he is probably going to accept. I could get a full-time gardener. That would be the best way to start 1991'. (Six years after paying £185,000 for the listed manor house and its Gertrude Jekyll garden we paid £250,000, about 35% more, for the small stable cottage and the half-acre garden. Those were the Margaret Thatcher boom years). I had always considered the cottage, that had once been the stables to the Manor House, an integral part of the whole, and had lovingly tended its garden. Although we had hoped to buy it from 1989 onwards, the owner wanted to find another property before he sold. Our bid was accepted by the end of the month and, with somewhat desperate haste, I put an advertisement, asking for a full-time gardener, in the magazine *The Lady*. It must have been very well worded as replies came in thick and fast for the next four weeks. Quite why I chose *The Lady* I do not know. It is not a gardening magazine. I imagine that I wanted help in the house and in the garden and thought I would get both by advertising for a married couple. I had well over a hundred replies, very few from gardeners. Most called themselves handymen. I remember being torn between employing someone who knew very little about gardening but who might learn from my scant experience, and an experienced gardener who would take over my garden and would always know better. I decided, unfortunately as it turned out, that a hard-working handyman would suit me. Meanwhile I ploughed on with gardening.

January 30. 'Tackling the Nuttery drastically. Cut trees down to small shrub size on front two rows'. Wrong; I should have coppiced them right to their base because my method made them grow like shaving brushes – masses of mini branches. Ideally hazel should be coppiced in rows once every four years, so that there is some cover for the under-planting of bluebells and always one row mature enough to provide nuts and hazel poles. (If thicker poles are required, the time between coppicing is longer). 'That makes weeding and raking at roots far easier. Hope bluebells don't mind sudden light'. They did not, but bluebells will not tolerate bright sunlight for long.

The gardener's cottage converted from the Manor House stables.

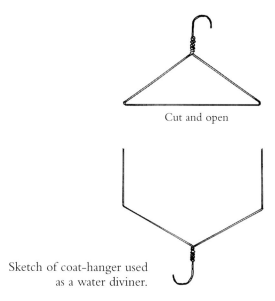

Cut and open

Sketch of coat-hanger used
as a water diviner.

FEBRUARY 1991

Three subjects dominate February notes: the regular report on how bitterly cold it is; the exhausting business of interviewing and deciding who will be the best couple to help me run house and garden and to live in the cottage; and how Roast is coping with winter on her own. As her pond was frozen solid I tried bringing her into the dog run at night because it is sheltered but I knew she hated it. It was unnatural and it smelt.

Mid-month I noted that it was the coldest February since 1987 and that I hoped the damage it was doing to bugs was worth the suffering it caused us. Most important I recorded that the collie, having had one too many blood-letting fights with terrier Ratty, 'went to live with the Hankins. I think he'll be very happy. They seem to love him'. All proved true.

Even in that freezing weather the pond level was evidently still dropping. I wondered where the leak was and where all the water was running to. A friend showed us how to divine for water using a wire coat-hanger, and I decided to try that method here.

February 18. 'I was out, trying to water divine' (in order to discover in which direction the

Upon Grey village. The village shop and pub are at the bottom of the hill.

pond was leaking) 'all fairly hopelessly; and I met a man with a metal detector in the field opposite who had just found a George III silver crown. It was black but strangely beautiful. Felt rather inadequate with my contrary wire'. Over the centuries villagers have lost or buried treasures in the area and today the fields are scanned by men with metal detectors who appear to have rather more success than I had in my search for water. Both John and I have seen people divine using metal, plastic or wood rods and we have been allowed to hold one end of the rod which jumped around uncontrollably, so I have proved the system can work but unfortunately neither of us seems to have the gift.

I began to interview applicants for the gardener-housekeeper job. After weeks of talking to various ages and types from a far too grand butler and his wife to just-left collegers, we chose a couple who seemed very good. They were younger than I; she was cheerful and they were both keen to take on the jobs of gardening and housework. I telephoned the two references they left us. The first gave a glowing report and the other reference was good enough, with the one reservation that the man had once had a drink problem which he had completely overcome. But John and I liked them so we signed a remarkably complicated contract and they moved into the cottage. For a year things went well but relations began to sour slowly and nastily after that time. Towards the end of 1992, the man had started drinking again. First he turned on his wife and then on me. Soon he stopped working altogether and I was back where I started with no help, but with garden visitor numbers growing rapidly. After two years I told him to leave and that I would try to help him find other work. Unfortunately two years is the time after which it is very hard, legally, to let anyone go for whatever reason, as he probably knew. He stayed aggressively 'put' in the cottage and I saw no prospect of getting him out. Luckily for me he was unpopular in the pub and throughout the village so he found life in Upton Grey miserable. There followed an extremely unpleasant three months, during which he took us to the industrial tribunal, but eventually he gave up the fight, took a car and left; his wife, whom we both liked, went her separate way and I learnt some useful but painful lessons. The residents of the village gave me moral support throughout the ordeal. It is good to live in a community where people support each other. Having a popular village shop and pub provides two important focal points for building a community spirit. Upton Grey is a wonderful village.

Ros with Roast the duck.

MARCH 1991

Going back to March 1991, my garden diary was filled with optimistic notes about how relieved I would be to have help both in the garden and in the house and how tidy everything, including scruffy me, was going to look. The funny thing is that I continued to do as much gardening as ever, heavy-work gardening, not just the easy bits.

The Kitchen Garden and the old garden shed where I found treasures from the 1908 garden.

Having completed the deal on buying the stable cottage and its garden we also now owned the garden shed. I had never been inside the pretty wooden building. When I investigated its contents I found a gardener's treasure trove. There were old tennis-court posts and nets, a line marker for painting white lines, terracotta pots of all sizes and some very pretty shapes, an old china sink, and rusty old garden tools, scythes, forks, hoes and buckets. Garden notes record all that and also: 'On the wall is scratched *1920* so it must have been put up when the Savill family were renting the house from Charles Holme. *Penstemon Scarlet* and *Penstemon White* were also scratched; and *King of Denmark, Colonel Holford, Paul Crampel*. Wonder what they were'. I have since discovered that 'Paul Crampel' and 'King of Denmark' are pelargonium hybrids and they are still available at specialist nurseries. I have not discovered what type of plant 'Colonel Holford' was.

March 5. This is rather a sentimental entry, one that I would have censored but for the following day's entry. 'I dug cow parsley out of Orchard (of course that means I dug **some** cow parsley out of Orchard – I'll never get rid of it all). Roast spent all afternoon with me cuddling up and eating dug-up worms'.

March 6. 'ROAST KILLED BY FOX'. John dug her a beautiful grave on the holly mound by the churchyard. Roast had become a cheerful member of the family. When artists came here to paint, which happens on occasions, she would sit beside them quietly, helping to enhance the peaceful scene and to eat up their picnic. She got on extremely well with all the dogs, the people who deliver our papers and letters, indeed all our friends and regular visitors. We mourned the loss of a real character.

March 7. That morning the *House and Garden* magazine was delivered. Now this diary note is shamelessly fickle of me. 'WONDERFUL AMERICAN HOUSE AND GARDEN ARTICLE. WE ARE PICTURED ALL OVER FRONT COVER AND BIG SPREAD INSIDE. April issue, and Roast is immortalised with dogs and mower. The most important one of us all'. Indeed she was. She was pictured marching determinedly in goose-step style (they really do stick their legs straight out in front) behind the dog-mob. It is the most glorious picture and it did prove to be the start of a very exciting new string to my gardening bow – travelling the world giving talks. That picture, needless to say, goes with me everywhere. The entire article about

'Aunt Bumps' was Edwin Lutyens's nickname for his angelic fairy godmother.

the garden was beautifully illustrated with absurdly flattering photographs and Adrian Higgins' text was excellent. About a month before publication, one of the editors had telephoned to ask more questions about our herbaceous flowers, and for the first time I had plucked up enough courage to ask her if we might appear in the magazine. 'Gee, you're not only in our magazine, you're all over the front cover,' she had said. The flattering article ran as follows. I could not have hoped for better.

Cover picture from *American House and Garden.* Photograph by kind permission of Christopher Sykes.

Almost sixty years after she died, Gertrude Jekyll continues to haunt the minds – and gardens – of designers, scholars and gardeners on both sides of the Atlantic. Her ideas of colour sequence and associations, exuberance without fussiness, and the integrity of the individual plant in a sympathetic setting have survived decades of neglect and, lately, the turn to over-used perennial species. Nowhere is she more alive today than at the Manor House at Upton Grey in Hampshire. She stalks the borders and terraces daily, reincarnated as Rosamund Wallinger.

The two are unlikely soul mates. Jekyll was the frumpy doyenne of the arts and crafts movement in gardening. Stout and serious-minded, she went about changing the late Victorian and Edwardian landscape with the same self-assurance as her young cohort, the architect Edwin Lutyens. By contrast, Wallinger is a slim attractive stockbroker's wife who cannot bring herself to gloat over the results of the seven years she has spent creating what Jekyll chronicler Jane Brown calls the finest example of a restored Jekyll garden anywhere. 'Jekyll's friends used to call her Aunt Bumps, and Ros, to me, is getting to be like Aunt Bumps,' says Gilly Drummond, a long-time friend who, as head of Hampshire Gardens Trust, helped Wallinger obtain the advice she needed to restore Upton Grey.

Even by Jekyll's standards, the range of colour and the sophistication of plant materials are unusual. The reason lies with another whose ghost also walks Upton Grey: Charles Holme, an industrialist who retired in his forties to pursue an interest in the arts and crafts movement. A year later, in 1893, he founded The Studio *magazine. At the turn of the century, he had the manor built around the shell of a sixteenth-century farmhouse. For the garden he turned, naturally, to Jekyll. (Holme is buried in the graveyard of the village church, adjoining the Wild Garden she designed for him.) The complexity of Jekyll's work at Upton Grey is a direct result of Holme's own commitment to art and his expertise as a gardener. This, in turn, has made Ros Wallinger's task more challenging – and rewarding. Her endeavours are the second half of the manor's story, for the restoration has transformed not just a garden but a human being.*

Drummond introduced Ros Wallinger to Jane Brown and, through the Gardens Trust, to the writer and plantswoman Penelope Hobhouse. While Brown gave historical perspective on the garden, Hobhouse offered advice on how to grow it again.

What has astonished Hobhouse, Brown and Drummond is not just Ros Wallinger's courage in taking on the project but the passion that has gone with it. She has visited or written to dozens of specialty nurseries in her quest to plant not just the same species dictated in Jekyll's plan but the very same old varieties. She has been helped by the resurgence of interest in long-forgotten plants, by new books on the subject, and by gardens like the famous Roseraie in l'Hay-les-Roses near Paris, whose staff gave her ten cuttings of rare rose varieties. She gathered copies of the plans for her own garden from the Jekyll collection at the University of California at Berkeley.

Now maturing, the garden is giving Wallinger an insight into Jekyll's work that few others – even scholars – can have. She lives with the garden in December, when shadows creep at the foot of the walls, and in June, when roses sparkle in the late evening sun. 'Nobody has got under the skin of the original design to the extent Ros has', Drummond observes. 'It's her own humility that has allowed her to do it'. Jane Brown, who lives nearby, comes by now and then to see how the garden is doing. In her view, Charles Holme rests peacefully in his grave, and Aunt Bumps would find a kindred spirit in his – and her – successor at the manor. 'The remarkable thing about Jekyll,' says Brown, 'was a complete lack of pretension. The whole point of the arts and crafts movement was honesty and a belief in what you were doing'.

I bought twelve copies of the magazine – all that the newsagent had.

Within a week I had bought one drake and two replacement ducks. They had a bit of Indian Runner crossed with their blue, Aylesbury blood and were not quite as beautiful as Roast but they made a good substitute and I learnt to love them. Note in diary the day I bought them simply and mercenarily says, 'John bought a compressor pump for car and machinery tyres, and for paint spraying. Appalling price; it cost £214. I went to Oakhanger and bought two ducks and a drake – a snip at £10 the lot'.

The new ducks did the usual trick of escaping to the village pond as soon as released from their box. I only managed to catch the drake and one duck this time but one of each sex was enough, as the breeding season starts in early April.

The rest of March was fairly uneventful. I was given a large jar of frog-spawn by a friend who lives on the River Wandle in London. I took it back to the pond, hoping to start a colony of frogs. Apparently if you try to introduce fully grown frogs to a pond they make determined efforts to return to their original spawning ground, so they have to be re-located at the spawn stage. Within minutes the ducks were gobbling up every last one, rather a macabre sight. Nothing survived so that was the end of tadpole prospects.

Towards the end of the month Victoria Wakefield brought the garden designer Arabella Lennox-Boyd to see the garden. She is interesting and knowledgeable. She warned me of the dangers of forming a solid 'pan' under the surface of earth if the ground is continually rotavated and never spade dug. I had not been warned of that before but it is evidently true and consequently the Kitchen Garden is both dug and rotavated annually.

At the end of March I gave my second-ever talk, this time at Farnham, for The University Women's League. It was obviously an improvement on the first talk, but I doubt that it was much good. I do know that I was terribly nervous, though garden notes only mention it in passing. For the first few years of public speaking I used the audience as practice ground, rather like I had in the days of my cooking career. Although I took it all very seriously and made desperate efforts to improve the performance I was often horribly aware of heads nodding off in the front row. Heaven knows how many slept peacefully in the dark beyond. These days the talks are better.

The day after my second talk, I had a star-studded bunch of gardening friends to lunch; Penelope Hobhouse and her husband John Malins, Jane Brown, the author of *Gardens of a Golden Afternoon*, the book that had taught me so much about Jekyll and her partnership with Lutyens, and the landscape gardener Georgia Langton with her husband David. A very nice day but one which left me writing lists of jobs to do – obviously the garden was not looking quite so perfect as I had imagined. Clearly expert gardeners can look at a garden much more objectively than an amateur. They could see faults, inconsistencies and potential as well as envisaging the garden's development through the seasons, whereas I could only see it as it was, and that, probably, through rose-tinted spectacles.

MAY 1991

May 1. 'A sunny day. It is John's birthday. I am giving him some fine presents. The first is the ten goldfish I bought last week. They are very small. I have already put them in the pond so the present will have to be given with as much verbal ornament as possible as he is unlikely to see the fish for months – if at all. The second present is golf lessons. I've decided it is wise to practise for retirement and golf is one of the few sports you can start at this age. One of my good gardening friends describes golf as the only sport you can play in middle age without feeling as though 'the bits' are dropping off you. It has crossed my mind too that it might subtly wean John off gardening. I seem to have lost authority there and he has taken to reckless strimming, weed-killing and general obliterating'.

May 2. 'Got away with most of that'.

By May 10th I had planted out all sweet corn seedlings and canna corms. Needless to say they were killed by the frost again. On May 20th Jane Brown brought Nan Blake Sinton to see the garden. At that time Nan was a key administrator at the Arnold Arboretum in Massachusetts. She must have mentioned the possibility that I might give lectures in the United States and I suppose I acknowledged that I have a wonderful core subject at Upton Grey, with plenty of material in terms of old photographs. I do not remember anything positive being said about my going to the States to give talks, so that event was quickly forgotten too. I certainly never imagined that I would soon be travelling the English-speaking world, talking about the garden and its history to packed audiences.

May 12. John and I were invited to lunch with Andrew and Briony Lawson at their house in Oxfordshire. Andrew is the photographer who had come to the garden in 1990 to take

Hollyhocks are an important summer feature at the back of the herbaceous borders. They are prone to mildew but are easily replaced with stock grown from our own seed.

photographs for Richard Bisgrove's book, *The Gardens of Gertrude Jekyll*, which was to be published later in 1991. Luckily I accepted the lunch invitation because, for several reasons, it proved to be a memorable day. At that time it was unusual for me to accept any day-time frivolities as I honestly would rather have been gardening. It was even stranger that I managed to persuade John to come with me because he felt even less at home than I did in the world of great gardeners. We arrived as bidden at 12.45 to find the small house and garden crammed with people. I have no recollection of the house, but the garden on that May spring day was exquisite and, of its kind, the prettiest I have ever seen. The whole area was probably no larger than our Tennis Lawn. Within that space paths led from light to dappled shade. Arches, walls, trellis and statuary adorned but never intruded. I remember most vividly the tulips. These ranged through tall elegant, finely petalled to robust, strong-leafed varieties and small, delicate types in a spectrum of colours. We were given a delicious lunch and were allowed to sit informally at tables dotted around the garden wherever we pleased. The garden gurus sat together and among those I recognised were Penelope Hobhouse, Esther Merton, Susan Dickinson, Robin Lane Fox and Stephen Lacey. Other guests included writers and famous names as well as some relatively unknown, but knowledgeable, gardeners from large estates. As complete unknowns, John and I were very flattered to be included. In retrospect I would have cancelled almost anything for the chance of seeing that garden.

Towards the end of the afternoon we lined up to say goodbye and thank you to the Lawsons. As we waited a man beside me asked, 'What does your husband do in the garden?' Very disloyally I dismissed my generous, bread-winning husband with the reply, 'Oh he likes playing with the machines'. I was poked in the back by a finger and turned around to see a slight man with a large moustache and big spectacles that magnified piercing eyes. 'And who gave you your garden, my dear?' It was Roy Strong. More women should remember that it is generally the hard-working husband who has bought the pampered wife her plaything.

May 20. 'Very generous friends took me to Chelsea Flower Show on the Private Day. Won't ever want to go on a public day again. If I ever get invited to go to Chelsea in my own right on that sacred Monday, I shall consider it the ultimate recognition. There was time and space to stand back and look at plants and garden designs with perspective as well as to examine closely. I felt as though all the wonders of nature's gardens had been bought together in one season and one place. Splendid'. Throughout the week the show is wonderful, but it is sheer luxury going on the private day with time to wander gently past all the magnificent displays in far less crowded conditions.

May 26. Sunday 'First Garden Open day of 1991. Dull grey day. About two hundred people'. At the beginning of notes for 1991, in Resolutions slot, I had written 'Never Open the garden on a Sunday again. Far too crowded – bedlam'. Presumably I took that decision too late to cancel the entry in 1991's *Gardens of England and Wales*, known as the 'Yellow Book'. Whilst it is nice to share our garden with as many people as possible, we have had to cut back numbers because the garden is simply not big enough to allow crowds of people to enjoy it at once.

On the following day, Monday 27th, the first group of American visitors came and I really enjoyed showing them around. From the summer of 1991 onwards the number of foreign visitors increased annually, particularly after the *House and Garden* article was published.

May 31. 'Went to tea with Lady Gordon at Littlecross, Surrey – the house where Jekyll met Lutyens at tea with Harry Mangles. Lady G is a wise and hard-working gardener. We wandered through a forest of huge rhododendrons, of which she is justly proud. They are, I suppose as old as any in Europe. I was taken to the room where the conversation and the silver kettle had reflected rhododendrons and, for me, it was a wonderful link with our past.

JUNE 1991

June 14. 'No sign of canna. They can't all be dead, please God'. Oh yes they were. Again, beware the late frost. This June I noticed that flowers of the old rose I had found growing through the yew hedge looked remarkably like the 'Blush Damask' I bought in 1986. 'Have discovered a pretty pink rose growing through one of the old patches of yew hedge and another behind the Tennis Lawn. It looks very like Blush Damask'. So I asked visiting rose experts for their opinion and to my delight they confirmed that the roses are the same but the name has changed since Jekyll's day. On Jekyll's plans for the garden she uses 'Blush Gallica' which no present day rose catalogue lists so I assumed that it was extinct. For some lucky reason I ordered 'Blush Damask' instead, hoping faintly that it might be a similar rose. It has become a great favourite of mine. This delicate rose had survived almost a century of neglect among yew and brambles. It had even put out a few brave suckers which, as it grew on its own rootstock, were true to itself. It is a strong, sweet-smelling, multi-petalled, pale pink and very beautiful rose. I cannot understand why it is so under-appreciated.

When people ask me what plants will grow on almost pure chalk, in shade or exposed places where virtually nothing else will grow I list this rose. Other plants, which are tough to the extent that they sometimes need vigorous control, are *Acanthus spinosus*, helianthus 'Miss Mellish', *Iris foetidissima*, *Sisyrinchium*, *Rosa spinossima* and another great favourite, simply because it is ancient and bizarre, *Plantago rosularis*, the rose plantain. The following plants also seem able to survive in any situation on this chalky soil are *Echinops ritro*, *Rosa virginiana*, *Eryngium oliveranum*, *Yucca filamentosa* and Japanese anemones. They are all good value plants; as far as I know they grown on any soil but all need to be kept under control.

I believe it was this summer, though I made no note of it in my garden diary, that the most valuable book I shall ever find was added to my collection. Buffy Sacher, a great friend, telephoned me from the Heywood Hill bookshop in London to report that she had found a copy of *Gertrude Jekyll. A Memoir by Francis Jekyll*. It was a first edition of the book by her nephew, with a foreword by Edwin Lutyens. Buffy told me that letters and cards pinned inside the book were written by Gertrude Jekyll herself and were addressed to the original owner of the book, a Mrs Huttenbach. Did I want it? Oh clever Buffy, I certainly did. The cost was £50. The letters alone were worth that. When the book arrived I found 'Clara T

Rose 'Blush Damask' (detail). One of my favourite roses. I found two in the garden in 1984. There are four on Jekyll's plans. She knew it as 'Blush Gallica'.

Rose 'Blush Damask'.

Huttenbach. Fiveacres, Witley, Surrey. 1936', written inside the front cover. Six letters and cards in the old familiar writing of Miss J were pinned into the book. They were dated between December 1930 and January 1931, shortly before Jekyll's death in December 1932, when health and eyesight were failing her. They all start with the date and her address, 'Munstead Wood, Godalming' and they ran as follows:

April 28 1930
Dear Mrs Huttenbach,
My good Gibbins prompts me write to you by saying he's sure you would like to see the primroses – this I do with the greatest pleasure. I am just recovering from a long illness and am not seeing many visitors but it would be a pleasure to see you for a few minutes. Perhaps to tea near 4.30 any day this week.
Yours sincerely, G. Jekyll

June 6 1930
Dear Mrs Huttenbach,
Gibbins tells me that you know of someone who seems to be just what I am looking for as an oldish house parlour-maid. I should be greatly obliged if you would let her know that I should be willing to engage her on such good recommendation and that I should be ready to receive her next week or at any early date that would suit her.
I feel sure that she would find it a happy place. I have been so long used to having good trusty maids about me – my other two have been with me for twenty years; and such a one as you mention I should greatly value. May I hear something about wages, her full name and when she would be able to come.
With much gratitude,
I am yours sincerely, G. Jekyll
You might (like) to see the Agathea within the next few days. [Agathea is now known as Felicia]

June 21 1930
Dear Mrs Huttenbach,
I am glad to tell you that I have employed Mary Platt who will come to me on July 15th. For the sake of the usual form I wrote to Miss Healy Jutt and have received from her such a charming letter and account of Mary that I know I have secured a valuable and sympathetic servant. I am very grateful and thankful to you.
Yours sincerely G. Jekyll

October 12th
Dear Mrs Huttenbach,
Please accept the little parcel of Sisyrinchium Bermudianum with many thanks for what you have sent. I did not answer you about my books. I think the one you would find most useful is 'Colour Schemes in the Flower Garden' published by Country Life.
Yours sincerely G. Jekyll

January 2 1931
Dear Mrs Huttenbach,
I was glad to have your good pictures of yourself in your garden and I am sorry to be so late in acknowledging it and your kind messages, but I am being kept with only an hour or two out of bed or my bedroom and correspondence gets into sad arrears. All good things to you.
Yours sincerely, G. Jekyll

The author Francis Jekyll, the son of Herbert, Gertrude's favourite and younger brother, was forty when his aunt died in 1932, and had spent most of his childhood at Munstead House where Herbert and Agnes brought up their three children, across the road from

Munstead Wood. Francis ran Gertrude's small plant nursery for nine years after her death and he wrote this book with great understanding of the aunt he knew so well

Mrs Huttenbach also pinned into her book a copy one of Jekyll's obituaries, several reviews of Francis's biography and Gertrude Jekyll's funeral service programme from St John the Baptist Church, Busbridge, on the front of which is printed:

Gertrude Jekyll November 29th 1843 – December 8th 1932 In Deo Confido.

[The programme includes: The extract from *Wood and Garden* which starts, 'The love of gardening is a seed that once sown never dies, but always grows and grows to an enduring and ever-increasing source of happiness.']

To be played before the Service:

Elegy – Parry
Andante from Sixth Sonata – Mendelssohn
(Mendelssohn had been a personal friend of Gertrude's parents and had briefly given her piano lessons)
St Anthony's Chorale – Haydn.
[The service included the following]:

I am the resurrection and the life St John XI, vv 25, 26
I know that my Redeemer liveth Job XIX, vv 25, 26, 27
We brought nothing into this world, and it is certain we can carry nothing out
1 Timothy VI, v 7; Job 1, 21
Psalm 103. Praise the Lord, O my soul
The Lesson (The Revelation of St John the Divine XXI, vv 1-7).
Chorale Commit thy Way to Jesus – J. S. Bach.
Collect Advent I
A prayer of St Chrysostom.
Collect. III – Lighten our darkness
Hymn 27 Abide with me; fast falls the eventide.
[On the back page is printed]:

Largo – Handel. (By her request).
Prayers at the Grave. Nunc Dimittis.

The brief announcement of Jekyll's death is pinned in to the funeral service. It ends with a practical note which John enjoyed, 'Trains: Waterloo, 1.38 arrives Godalming 2. 45; return, Godalming, 3.35, arrives Waterloo 5.41'. Life was rather slower in those days. Another newspaper cutting mentions that she left an estate of £20, 091 (net personally £14, 389), and that she was to be buried at St John the Baptist Church, Busbridge, Surrey.

I found this final addition to the book, written on page 13, in Mrs Huttenbach's hand:

Inscription by Gertrude Jekyll above her autograph in my copy of her book, *Colour Schemes for the Flower Garden* 3. 5. 30:

If my books are of use to those who love their gardens, it is because I have never written a word that was not the outcome of personal work and observation.

The quotation feels very familiar but I cannot trace it in her writings. It is good to have such a strong contact with Jekyll in our house.

Graham Stuart Thomas
and Hazel Le Rougetel.
Taken in the Royal
National Rose
Society's Gardens of
the Rose, St Albans.
Photograph by kind
permission of Ann Coghlan.

June 16. 'Coach load of visitors'. I began to realise that visitors arriving in coaches are far easier to manage. I give them a quick introductory talk then hand out plant lists and let them make their way around at their own pace. Although money taken was going to The National Gardens Scheme, I started making tea and cakes for home income. I borrowed the village hall's tea urn, filled it with water and tea-bags then brought all to what our Spoonerist teacher at cookery school had memorably called 'a full bollocking Royal', at which point the brew bubbled away in the urn for anything up to two hours until people were ready to drink it. For a has-been professional cook, I should have known better. I made disgusting tea that way. It took a disgruntled coach-load from Bournemouth to tell me that it was 'stewed, dear'. Teas are quite good nowadays.

July 17. 'Clive Nichols, photographer, came'. He took some good photographs of the garden and some typical but unflattering ones of me. It was a very hot day and I was digging away strenuously. There is a glorious photograph of me standing in the middle of the Hot Border, surrounded by deep red *Lychnis chalcedonica* and looking every bit as bright red myself. I very rarely make an effort to look good when gardening, but from time to time events like that do make me regret my laziness. Another moment that made me (temporarily) resolve to improve my appearance was when the first, and by no means the last, visitor asked me if the gardener was my son (the gardener was then thirty-four and I was forty-seven). Clive's photographs appeared in a gardening magazine later that month. Several magazines and newspapers were beginning to take an interest in the garden and from time to time we were surprised to be told an article had been published of which we were completely unaware. To my amusement, a photograph of me appeared at the head of an article in a daily newspaper that had nothing to do with this garden and no mention of why I was there or who I was.

I learnt a good tip earlier this summer which I simply noted as 'try drying peonies'. In late spring I had been to a demonstration on how to dry flowers and had left the event muddled and convinced that it was too much work for too little reward. Seeing my miserable collection of sepia-shaded Helichrysum dumped in a cup on the garden room table a group of visitors

Rose 'Mme d'Arblay'
(1835).

The making of the grass steps

The Wild Garden in December showing grass steps at the entrance and the small, newly planted trees behind.

1991. The entrance to the Wild Garden before grass steps were returned.

Making the grass steps – the simple tools we used.

The grass steps completed.

discussed the range of plants that would dry well and the techniques of drying flowers. One of them asked me if I had tried drying my peonies and I told her why I had not. Patiently she explained that these flowers are amongst the simplest. Ideally you should choose deep colours as all flowers fade. Pick them in just opening bud towards evening when they are dry but not sun-baked. Hang them in a bunch upside down in a dry dark place, the warmer the better. The next day I picked three 'Sarah Bernhardt' and three *Paeonia officinalis rubra*, took them to the cellar to hang them as instructed and forgot about them for three months (longer than necessary. I was told six weeks is the minimum). The following year I put them in a bowl for winter decoration and they looked good, particularly the deep red rubra.

AUGUST 1991

'Bamboo beginning to grow well at last'. They made a remarkably slow start, but as I have said, they were simply waiting to pounce and nowadays have to be strictly controlled.

The 'Mme Caroline Testout' should-be-shrub rose was shooting out long climbing branches and I was cutting them off regularly and viciously in order to try to make it look like a shrub. It did not work, the resulting plant looked terrible both in shape and health. I still do not have quite enough of the shrub variety to fill the Rose Lawn so continue to use both types, shrub and climber. Today I peg down the long shoots of the climbers which encourages a profusion of flowers to grow along the bowed stem. This works with several herbaceous plants, as the bending of the stem slows the flow of sap and encourages flowering shoots. Even rudbeckia and helenium respond to this surprisingly well.

SEPTEMBER 1991

'Bats in the house again. Neff has been stung in the throat by a wasp and coughs a lot. Surprised it doesn't happen more often in the rotten apple season. Vet has seen him. Dogs eat apples continuously and come inside and fart all evening. This will go on until January – ugh'.

'Digging in the Orchard, I found a pathway of beautiful old York paving stones hidden under several inches of moss and grass. Wonderful treasure trove'. By digging carefully in an old garden, one can discover hordes of exciting things. We have unearthed several small, white, clay smoker's pipes, and some very old bottles. One is made of clay and has 'Basingstoke' stamped on its side. Some are old glass bottles; these are fascinating. They have a glass marble inside. When the bottle stood upside down the marble stopped liquid flowing out, but it would move clear of the mouth when the whole was turned upright, allowing the contents to be drunk. The folds and shapes of the bottles are astonishing.

'Graham Stuart Thomas and Hazel Le Rougetel came to lunch. He identified the two very robust old climbing roses 'Lady Waterlow' and 'Madame d'Arblay' which we found when we moved here in 1984. He tells me to feed Tomorite to sickly roses'. 'Mme d'Arblay' has become very rare and, to the best of my knowledge, Peter Beales is the only rose nursery in the world that stocks it today. I wonder why; not many roses at Upton Grey have the health and beauty of the rose named after the married Fanny Burney'. Peter Beales describes 'Mme d'Arblay' as: 'Rambler. Cascading clusters of small, cupped flowers of blush pink to white. Scented and very vigorous. 1835'. I love it. It is enormous and because it is old and venerable I leave it be, covering the cherry plum tree that it scrambles through. I feel that if I cut it down to size at this age I will do more harm than good.

OCTOBER 1991

Perhaps Nan Blake Sinton had written from America suggesting I go there to give talks or perhaps I had been asked to give more in England. For whatever reason John told me I should have a professional lesson in public speaking so I booked a session of two half days at MAST, near Slough, with Sue Akester.

October 11. 'Went to MAST to learn to talk in public'. That is all the mention it got. But it was a very useful and important lesson and taught me a great deal which, although I certainly did not put it into practice immediately, set me on the right lines for better public speaking. Sue Akester, my teacher, told me to stand upright, look at and around the audience, to take pauses when necessary (very difficult when nervous), show enthusiasm, follow a disciplined line with reminder cards and to try to look cheerful. I went home and practised in front of the looking-glass and destroyed any vestige of confidence I might have had; but she was right in every respect and she is a very good teacher. I did begin to improve my performance eventually.

October 19. 'Manured all beds in the Formal Garden. We start to make grass steps at entrance to Wild Garden'. These three steps were on Jekyll's plans. They form a shallow semi-circular entrance on what had reverted to a small grass bank when we arrived in 1984. Grass steps are not a common feature in today's gardens, which is sad because with modern machines like Flymos, they are relatively easy to keep tidy and they do look beautiful. The making of them was laborious but simple. Having marked out the radii, the grass turf was carefully lifted with a flat spade, then steps are cut into the earth and made compact. This is important because over the years the steps are inclined to sink with wear. Edges to steps are held in place either with bricks or, in our case with thin, long, three-inch by quarter-inch, wooden boards pegged to batons. Then the turf is replaced and the steps are complete (see page 151).

NOVEMBER 1991

'Tree surgeon came to quote for cutting Leylandii trees down to half their height; very drastic'. The trees were about thirty-five feet high and dangerously close to a neighbour's roof. We did have them cut back. Two out of the nine trees died and the remaining seven will always be an unattractive shape after decapitation. They are off the Jekyll planned area so we have no regrets about that butchery. Leylandii do not react well to being cut back hard.

DECEMBER 1991

It was particularly cold but there were wonderful hoar-frosts and I took a photograph of the Wild Garden which looked so breathtaking that we had it made into a postcard. Trees for the Wild Garden arrived, walnut, amelanchier, lilac 'Mme Lemoine' (the Lemoine family must have been very important all-round plantsmen as several cultivars are named after them) and *Viburnum opulus* which Jekyll called 'water elder'.

Border 5 before grass edges were restored, flowers are growing over the stone path.

Edging the herbaceous borders in order to get a proper perspective of the path

Re-making the grass edges. All plants were moved back in the border and the earth strip edged with a wooden board before it was seeded with rye grass.

Chapter Eight
1992, 1993 and 1994

JANUARY 1992

Most gardeners are opinionated and brave in voicing their opinions. It pleases me that when I ask a fellow gardener what he or she thinks of a scheme they will answer frankly and put up sensible arguments in defence. This often leads to interesting discussions and does not offend because it is considered advice, not criticism. Very few people say 'I love gardening but am a hopeless gardener' though they may admit to shortcomings in a great many other interests. It seems that dealing with nature gives confidence even to the beginner. Try asking a friend what he or she thinks of your garden and you will probably get praise tempered with kindly suggestions for improvement, but ask the friend what he thinks of your dress sense or of your house decoration and he will rarely be honest. Odd. Odd too that you design a garden but decorate a house. The very words give the garden more dignity.

If people dislike a Jekyll plan it makes for a debate although her garden will not be changed. One valuable criticism led me to making changes which I discovered were Jekyll intentions but that I had overlooked. By planting to the very edge of the main herbaceous borders as instructed, the plants spilled heavily over the sides and in high summer there

Grass edges and path the following year.

was virtually no sign of the path that divided them. I do not remember precisely who, how often, or when the questions were posed so they obviously caused no offence, but one particularly repeated query about the over-planting made me return to the plans. On checking I found that Jekyll had designed the paths to be bordered on each side by an un-planted grass or stone area which gave the overall picture better composition and perspective (see plan pages 38 and 39). Over this winter I went to great lengths to lift almost all the plants, move them back in the borders by about a foot and line out a new edge with two metre wooden batons and then sow grass seed. Now the proportions are right, the beds look better, the plants healthier and the path has purpose.

I tidied the greenhouse and the garden shed when the weather was vicious, and took ivy off trees when it was bright. When the earth was not iced hard, I moved plants and weeded around the pond. 'Have decided to get five bantams so am about to convert a corner of Orchard into chicken run'. On my regular travels through the neighbouring country town of Odiham I had noticed dozens of little birds running free around the fields. One day I stopped at the farm to ask the farmer's wife if she would sell me some and, to my delight, she agreed.

FEBRUARY 1992
February 5. 'Tonight I will give the first talk after the October lessons, so I wandered fields and garden with dogs practising and muddling. First aconites are up in Wild Garden'.

February 6. 'V. mild, lovely day full of bird-song but don't recognise the birds. Ducks well. Chicken pen nearly finished. Rang the Odiham farmer about the bantams she had promised to sell me, but she keeps telling me they aren't ready yet. They are truly beautiful birds. They look like small, round, colourful chickens; but I am getting desperate so ordered *Poultry World* to see if I can find another source. Talk went OK but found I rush slides. Need more practice'.

February 22. 'Ivor Wherrel gets me a chicken shed for £20 (as shelter inside the pen). A good buy. Moss and some disease on rye grass lawn, so use Mildothane'.

February 25. 'The farmer who said she would sell me bantams is taking too long. I keep telephoning. They are never ready so I'll get chickens from Harry Hunt'. (A local farmer).

February 28. 'I have four pullets and one cockerel, foxy-brown. The breed sounds like Widenize' (Winadot as I later learnt) 'but I don't understand the Hampshire burr too well and couldn't keep saying "what?" Anyway they are in their run and happy. I will let them out when they have developed a homing instinct – in about two days'. It did not take me long to regret that change of mind. Chickens kick earth and stones everywhere and they eat valuable plants. Bantams, I was to learn in due course, are better behaved, more intelligent and great fun to have around.

MARCH 1992
March 2. 'FIRST EGG. Cockerel looks wonderful. Hens a bit tatty'.

March 9. 'Pruning Rose Lawn roses. Chickens are pecking around free range. Very soon I'll have to defend the Kitchen Garden. They kick the stones and bits all over the place, ruining my edges (and lawn mower blades). I have had to cut back several once proudly upright young dicentra where chickens have rootled and I am cutting hazel stakes to support other bent plants. The Felco secateurs are strong enough to cut cleanly through the hazel-nut branches'. My secateurs are kept in a stout pouch that hangs around my waist, together with a few indispensable gardening gadgets. These include a pair of laddered tights for tying most things, scissors for cutting anything that secateurs cannot (like string), a fork for spur-of-the-moment weeding, a penknife and, one of my favourites, a small whet-stone for sharpening any blade. You will be surprised how many things need sharpening in the garden tool kit; not only blades of scythes, secateurs, knives etc but also the base of a spade or a half-mooner. It is so very satisfying to have sharp equipment, and so simple to achieve. It is also a good and cheap present for gardening friends as the whet-stone is easily lost and a spare is useful.

March 19. 'Pond lamentably low. Ghastly green. Sowed twenty trays of seeds in greenhouse. It is effectively a cold greenhouse as small tube heater is far too small for the area'.

'Estimate for tar and gritting the drive and putting in adequate drainage comes to £11,000. Sounds big but the contractors are a very good firm and we've seen other work they have done locally'. For once we did not go for the cheap option, and are very pleased with the result. We had admired a local drive as we drove past it so we asked the owner who had done the work. 'That', he said 'was done over twenty years ago by R.M. Bleach & Co, of Liphook in Hampshire who do surface and drainage work – the two run together'. We rang Mr Bleach who told us that he was about to retire but that his son had taken on the business and that they would come and quote for the work. They impressed us and, although their quote was not the lowest, we felt comfortable with them and the job they did has proved excellent. The drive was not only gravelled and drained but edged with wood which looks attractive. Not bad really – a twenty-year-plus word of mouth recommendation. It proves two things: that if you do a good job, your business should prosper, and that good local craftsmen still pass their craft on from one generation to the next.

March 24. ' A man from Devon came to quote for re-lining the pond with what he said would be the correct clay, as the brick clay we had used in 1985 was clearly wrong'. Having noticed that several village ponds in the surrounding chalky countryside managed to hold clear fresh water, and to hold it with no visible signs of a running source, I remained determined that our pond would one day seal itself and hold the clear, clean tap water that we fed it. Most village ponds have been formed over the centuries by a mixture of subsoil, clay and the weight of cattle feet as they trod the edges, puddling the base. I saw no reason why our once naturally spring-fed pond should have lost its water-proof foundation now that a solid block of clay had been trodden into the base.

So we bit the last of our 'Hideous Waste of Money' bullets and commissioned the man from Devon to re-line the forty foot pond with Devon clay. This, being different from brick clay, is paler and less dense and evidently does hold water in Devon. He quoted £1200 for clearing the pond of existing clay and re-lining it. Again we hired the JCB to do the job of re-lining the pond and, at the same time, making deep trench-like ruts all over the top end of the Wild Garden. A huge pile of the old 'brick' clay that we had used the previous time was piled near the road to form a bank. It has proved quite a useful wind break and screen from the road. It also reminds me, when I try to dig, plant or weed it, how lucky we are to garden on light, manageable, if rather poor in nutrients, chalky soil. I hope that this will prove to be the last expensive mistake we make in the garden. Devon clay does not work either, as I was very soon to discover!

The pond after the
second unsuccessful
attempt at clay lining.

APRIL 1992

April 10. '6 a.m. Pond isn't leaking' (oh yes it was). 'Tories in' (General Election). Took photographs of daffodils in Wild Garden which I believe are the original 'Emperor', 'Empress', and possibly 'Leedsii', 'Horsfieldii' and 'Barrii', that are on Jekyll's 1908 plans. At the RHS show last week, I met Sally Kington, the Daffodil expert, and agreed to send photographs so that she can compare these with named prints in the Lindley Library'.

April 20. 'Killed 4 Lily beetles. First Asparagus picked, at least 2lb., very good. House martins back and busily rebuilding battered nests'. Lily beetles, which had only recently

The entrance to the
Wild Garden and
daffodils.

invaded Hampshire from Surrey, are resistant to most pesticides, but they are a bright shiny
red and large enough to spot from a distance so I manage to control them with a satisfying
manual squash.

MAY 1992

I was still working for Hampshire Gardens Trust, visiting people who had discovered that
theirs was a Jekyll garden, or institutions whose gardens were by Jekyll. Amport House and
Winchester College Memorial Cloister were among the gardens I advised on. I had learnt
from my own mistakes, and from a continuing study of Jekyll, just enough to be able to add
value to other restoration projects.

At home I worked on trying to control the Nuttery. Dock weeds and cow parsley were
beginning to over-run the bluebells and primulas. The only way of controlling them
practically was by hand-weeding.

May 28. 'Sunny, hot. Two hundred and three garden visitors. Sold teas and a few plants.
Think most people enjoyed themselves. Garden does look beautiful, particularly the peonies
which quite compensate for the sickly roses. I wish our plants were better labelled. The few
we have get lost in the undergrowth as soon as plants bush out'. Later I drew up a garden
guide leaflet with maps and plant lists as well as a description of the restoration and history
of the garden. I find this easier to understand than labels or lists that are unrelated to a plan.
Possibly that is because I composed it – I often see puzzled faces peering into the pages,
trying to work out my diagrams. Anyone intending to open a garden that includes
herbaceous borders should attempt a plant layout guide because labels invariably get lost in
the long run.

Like a great many things in life opening your garden to the public brings both blessings
and curses but, apart from the opportunity it offers burglars, the curses are minor. There is
a danger that if you open regularly people will turn up at any time and hope to be allowed
access; and if you specify a date nine months ahead it is well nigh impossible to cancel it
if a disaster arises. I think it was this summer (but not being a horticultural event it gets no
mention in garden notes) that the *Telegraph* newspaper published that our garden would be

Close-up of important
daffodils.

The rosarians with Professor Fineschi in Tuscany (the group includes Martin Rix, Bill Grant, Sarah Coles and Hazel Le Rougetel).

The rose 'Killarney' (HT 1890). The very rare rose which at that time only three people in the world grew.

open on a particular Saturday. At two o'clock sharp we were lunching in the garden with friends when to my surprise cars drove up and parked outside the front door. Soon the small driveway was blocked and our guests were also blocked in. A little wine and the support of amused friends who started to direct extra cars to a nearby field and to collect the inevitable entrance money made it a completely painless and rather profitable afternoon. But that evening I wrote to the *Telegraph's* editor, Andrew Hutchinson, telling him of the fiasco. A few days later a magnum of champagne arrived with many apologies. We asked the lunch bunch back to celebrate and with the considerable amount of money that I had collected from unexpected visitors I bought what proves to be one of my most treasured books, *The Work of Ernest Newton R.A.* by William Newton, published by the Architectural Press in 1925. This was another example of things that started badly turning out remarkably well.

JUNE 1992

Hazel Le Rougetel and I joined an 'Historic Roses' trip to Arezzo in Tuscany to visit the rose sanctuary of Professor Fineschi. The tour was organised by Charles Quest Ritson, a very knowledgeable rosarian and writer, though his profession was, I think, the law. He is a personal friend of the remarkable professor, who treated us with touching generosity. Professor Fineschi's collection of roses is as comprehensive as any in the world, I believe. They are planted out in date and family order with one group leading genetically to the next. For a relative beginner in the rose world this visit proved to be the best lesson I could have. It was in Arezzo that I found the last prize on my Horticultural Treasure Hunt. The Rose Lawn at Upton Grey is planted with five roses, 'Mme Caroline Testout', (shrub), Hybrid Tea, *c.*1890; 'Mme. Lombard', Tea, *c.*1878; 'Mme Laurette Messimy', China, *c.*1887; 'Mme Abel Chatenay', Hybrid Tea, *c.*1895; and the mysterious rose 'Killarney', for which, as I said earlier, I could find no source. By the second day of our visit I was beginning to believe Professor Fineschi to be omnipotent. He not only grew and showed us the rare shrub form of 'Mme Caroline Testout', the climbers 'Reine Olga de Wurtemberg', and 'Euphrosyne' (and this helped me confirm again, with confidence, that those roses I had found growing against the shed and Orchard wall at Upton Grey were indeed 'Euphrosyne'), but he could also run through their pedigrees with incredible detail naming breeder, date of introduction, species, country of origin and parentage. I told Professor Fineschi that my search for Jekyll roses was complete but for the elusive 'Killarney', and to my pure delight he took me to where he grew it, beside its parents (I think) in the area of roses introduced in about 1900. It is beautiful, similar to 'Mme Caroline Testout' but more subtle in shape and size. It has pale pink petals and holds its head well against strong green foliage, quite one of the loveliest roses I know. And remarkable Professor Fineschi sent me two rooted cuttings of that very valuable rose the following year. Astonishing generosity. I hope that I will be that magnanimous when my bud cuttings have taken and multiplied. We were a party of about ten, all except me very well known in horticultural circles. At the end of our stay the Professor gave us a short talk in halting English, describing how he had built up his collection over the years. His seven-year-old grandson joined us for the talk, sitting enraptured on the edge of his seat, evidently very proud of his grandfather – another great rosarian in the bud.

On our return I decided to make a small museum at Upton Grey, with a display of documents covering the garden's history over the century. It is housed in a room we call the Garden Room, a small loggia beside the garage which can be safely left open for public access. Over the years the display has become very comprehensive in its narrow field. It starts with photographs taken in 1900 when the house was a farmhouse, and continues to today, covering almost every decade through dereliction to restoration. I also have old copies of *The Studio*; information about Charles Holme, Jekyll and Newton, and media articles. Copies of Jekyll's plans are included, together with printed lists of all our plants. I wrote a short garden guide in leaflet form which I mentioned earlier, collating most of the information. Visitors can now judge Jekyll more objectively, knowing what her plans for the garden had been and what stage of development we have reached.

June 26. 'One Aylesbury duck has built a nest and sits on eleven eggs right in the middle of the Kitchen Garden. For some reason she has decided that this area, being closer to the house than the pond, is safer'. For the next twenty-five days I watched over those eggs with every bit as much excitement as a grandmother watches for her first grandchild.

The chickens never did earn my love although they amused me. The cockerel, who was extremely protective of his ugly wives, made several assaults at my rubber boots (I quickly learnt not to go near him in shoes). The chickens had a large pen and were frequently allowed out into the garden on what became known as 'probation'. They always failed to honour conditions, annihilating whichever vegetables took their fancy and they followed that pillage with their customary scratch, which involved flinging stones and mud all over the grass edges. Late one night I collected the chickens from their sleeping perches and returned them to the local farmer. It seemed that smaller versions of a chicken would do less damage, both in appetite and kicking power so later that summer I bought three Pekin bantams, small round bundles with ludicrous tufts of feathers that covered their feet like outsize carpet-slippers (seriously inhibiting earth-scratching as it happens). They lay eggs, but only during the breeding season, and then do so in quite unfindable places so that eating any eggs eventually found is a risky business. I bought the two hens and one cockerel Pekin bantams from Kim Courtauld and was given a further three Pekins the following year by Prue Lane Fox. Bantams are undemanding and independent birds. As soon as night falls they roost up a suitable tree, one that is evergreen, tall, sheltered and has branches strong enough to support a small colony of birds. I love these little birds and their amusing, engaging habits. Every morning I am greeted by the group. It seems they have been watching the waking household since dawn because, no matter which door I emerge from, they rush towards me in an ungainly fluster of feathers, half running, half jumping, like an aeroplane that is trying to take off but is too overloaded.

The bantams.

Double-digging the
herbaceous borders.

The job finished.

Gypsophila paniculata,
which grows where
oriental poppies have
died back.

OCTOBER 1992

It was seven years since the main herbaceous borders had been double dug and planted. By autumn 1992 they needed the thorough reconditioning which requires removing very nearly all plants and again double-digging loads of well rotted compost and manure into the beds. The exhausting work on the main herbaceous borders is meticulously logged. 'Struggling on with Hot Border. Still on first ten feet (of sixty). Have marked all planting areas with poles and boards before I clear plants out; then dig in a bucketful of good compost per square foot; divide plants which have over-grown and throw extra bits over back of hedge onto make-shift compost heap! With very few exceptions all plants have multiplied and badly need dividing. Day lilies, kniphofia and meadowsweet are a nightmare to uproot; so is *Gypsophila paniculata* – I can't believe that such a frail plant should have such huge roots. Eventually I replant the whole bed with healthy stock. Each ten foot strip takes about a day'. This ritual of completely overhauling each border takes place about every seven years.

Four days later and still on the same job. 'Just hit a wasp nest in compost heap. Suspected it was there as stung last week. This time at least seven stings (I trod in it). Leg like balloon and VERY itchy all over. Can't resist using compost tho', so bravely 'puff' wasps to death wearing several layers of protection (used excellent Rentokil Wasp-Nest Killer in puffer pack)'. A few days later I dug down to the surprisingly beautiful abandoned wasp nest. It consisted of delicate layers of fine grey material and was built as accurately as a perfect molecule.

I think our gardener was beginning to come off the rails about this time. I did most of the work myself but he helped a bit.

During the summer and autumn of 1992, I took transparency photographs of all parts of the garden. I knew very well that my talk depended heavily on the slides that illustrate it and, being rather a woeful photographer, I worked on the principle that, if one in five shots was successful, I should take a large surplus. I have a Pentax camera which can be used

Wall and herbaceous border in flower.

automatically or manually, and a tripod. A good photographer needs no more for adequate results. But I never seem to allow enough time to do the job properly; setting up tripod, attaching camera and adjusting settings takes time, and nature keeps interrupting with wind flurries or passing clouds. Photography is a project I have still to tackle.

The expensively relined pond soon turned from khaki green to cloudy white and remained in that condition for the following eighteen months. It continued to leak at the same rate as before. Very evidently china clay is too fine to use as a waterproof lining. It simply hangs in suspension in the water and, as ducks are notorious for diving and foraging through the bed of the pond, the clay stood no chance at all of settling.

In October *Country Life* magazine featured an article about grass tennis courts in private gardens. I had given them a fairly comprehensive interview which covered the initial preparation of the subsoil, through weed-clearing, stone removal, top-dressing, heeling in, and sowing with the precise mixture of grass seed that constitutes a good tennis lawn. I went on to describe annual up-keep and costs of all grass in the Formal Garden and was surprised to find quite how much we did spend annually. It came to about £500 a year without including labour costs. As a result of that article I was invited to lunch at The All England Tennis Club at Wimbledon, a rather greater honour, I thought, than being invited to watch the finals of a match. Basil Hutchins, my host, introduced me to Mr Seward, head groundsman. Together we had a happy day discussing the very fine art of good grass-keeping. I learnt a great deal and appreciate how well their grass is maintained under such demanding conditions.

The rambler roses on supports in the Wild Garden.

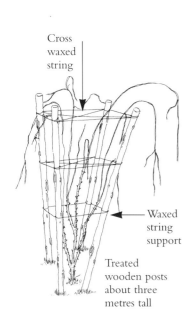

Cross waxed string

Waxed string support

Treated wooden posts about three metres tall

Diagram of the rose supports.

As the year drew to a close I had a letter from Nan Blake Sinton in Massachusetts asking if I would join her travelling circus of garden lecturers to give a series of talks for *Horticulture* magazine on the east coast of America the following April. I always say yes first and think better of the proposition later, so I agreed. It gave me a daunting goal but it is only by aiming at goals that you have any hope of scoring. I was not confident, but I did terribly want to tell the world about Jekyll and this piece of paradise.

My confidence was certainly boosted with the publication of Richard Bisgrove's book *The Gardens of Gertrude Jekyll*, which I mentioned earlier. I believe that this book explains Jekyll's garden art better than any other. Not only is our garden included in several chapters, it is featured with the very flattering photographs which Andrew Lawson had taken in 1990 and the text is the biggest compliment to our labours that we are ever likely to be paid. How do photographers extract such beauty from an ordinary garden scene? I am continually surprised by the ingenious angles that different people decide to photograph from or towards and by what a strange kaleidoscope a garden can make. Look through a lens in April and see a picture of yellows and gentle purple-tinted blues with plenty of earth and stone to make strong back-ground structure. Look again at the same view throughout the year and colours, shapes, shades and perspectives change quite dramatically. The effect that colours have on each other can shorten or lengthen perspectives. A colour seen from a distance also changes; a fact Jekyll was well aware of and that is why blues and greys seen beyond reds seem to have greater distance. Jekyll tells a story that explains this impression. If you look at a green hedge and beyond that to a green field you may believe that both greens are equally strong but if you take a leaf from the hedge and cut a hole in the centre and look through that to the distant field, the green in the background will appear blueish and paler through the atmosphere. Conversely you can trick the brain into seeing shorter perspectives by inverting the colours and looking through a cool (blue) colour towards a strong hot colour (red). This and many other scientific and interesting facts about colour are clearly explained in Andrew Lawson's excellent, *The Gardener's Book of Colour*.

Richard Bisgrove's book was one of several publications that were beginning to refer to the garden. The penalty for flattering publicity is paid when the garden ornaments that featured so prominently in publications disappear overnight. We are now ingeniously 'alarmed' but in the innocent early 1990s, it was a simple job for strong men to creep past snoring dogs and clear the garden of leaden cherubs, sun dial and wrought iron gates. This invasion of our sacred privacy had a strange effect on me. It elicits pure rage, a completely uncontrollable desire to kill, all of which is expressed by my jumping up and down on the spot and calling on the gods to obliterate the felons. Living alongside the churchyard and its sleeping souls, I have no doubt that my prayers are heard and that horrible things happen to those who do horrible things to us.

The winter evenings of 1992/3 were largely spent practising slides and notes for the coming American tour, a performance that is as excruciating to recall as, I believe, it must have been to watch. John was my audience and pretended not to read a newspaper as I blundered through the rehearsals.

During those cold winter days I continued to trim and tidy the garden. One annual ritual that I always perform between December and February is to spread 'Casoron G' granules under all mature shrubs, hedges and trees whose roots grow in bare earth. Casoron G has the very useful property of repressing germination and growth of all but the most persistent weeds, without damaging mature shrubs, so making the summer job of hoeing and weeding at the base of those plants relatively easy. It is, however, a chemical, so I may one day abandon the practice if I become completely organic.

December was a very wet month and there were floods over most of Britain. As usual one of the best things about that Christmas was the feeling of relief derived from giving all the dreadful left-over, lumpy Christmas pudding and mince pies to the ravenous ducks. I draw the line at giving them turkey. Weather turned cold and the pond froze over, so I carried bowls of warm water out to the birds several times daily whilst wondering how they survive at all when the pond, their haven of safety, is a skating rink, and the source of all drink is a block of ice. The fox terrier annually performs her strange ice-dance at this time of year. She treads very carefully around the edge of the pond, establishing the strength of the ice, then trots bravely towards the centre where she proceeds to jump up and down on the hard surface as though trying to break through to catch invisible fish. It is a very funny sight, and judging by films I have seen of Arctic foxes doing much the same thing, it is the perverse nature of such animals to perform this ritual. On December 30th this year she fell in. Diary notes 'v. v. cold overnight. Ratty went on to the pond to do her jumping cabaret for me but, mid-pond, she went through the ice (incredibly). I tried to scramble out to rescue her but fell over and got covered with sticky clay base. Ploughed on frozen. We're both OK now'. She still does it – has not learnt. I have. I certainly do not encourage it any more, though I miss the cabaret.

1993

The year started with serious work on controlling the beautiful rambling roses of the Wild Garden. 'The Garland', 'Dundee Rambler', 'Blush Rambler', 'Euphrosyne' and 'Jersey Beauty' had grown to fully fifteen feet and, as is the habit of ramblers, grew thickly from their base. The effect in late June of this glorious heap of untrained flowers on rich green bending stems is like looking down on a full, lacy, stiff petticoat that has been left untidily on the floor. Jekyll's roses were often allowed to grow thus in beautiful heaps but it is simply not practical in these days of Do It Yourself Gardening. I could neither feed nor weed the plants and when roses dropped their flowers and leaves at the end of the summer they left an ugly patch of sheltered nettles and dock-leaves in the wake of faded glory. From a very good rosarian in Hampshire, Peter Wake, I learnt to construct a device that was to answer all problems and yet allow ramblers to grow freely and healthily. Each rose is now surrounded by three or four (according to the size of the rose) sturdy round posts about eight feet high. At intervals of about three feet up the posts, heavy-duty waxed string is wound both around and across the posts, so forming a strong support for the rose, whose branches are then pulled through and out of the framework to form a natural shape, but one that does not quite reach the ground. Now feeding, weeding and general maintenance are relatively simple jobs.

Detail of rose supports.

165

Some roses hold their flowers through cold December and well into the New Year. I find it surprising that the late January defiers of nature are quite so admired by gardeners. Personally I prefer the sight of well-pruned roses to those whose faded flowers look rather incongruous mid-winter. It reminds me of an old woman who continues to dress in the inappropriate frills of youth – an attempt to defy age but which succeeds only in mocking the wearer.

At some time in January 1993 I bought a projector and screen. Knowing that I had to make a serious effort for the coming American talk tour, I had slide copies made of the dozens of photographs taken when the garden was an over-grown jungle, and during its restoration, as well as photographs of Jekyll herself and of her plans for the garden. It made up a good prompt list for my talk and quite frankly the pictures themselves told a good story without much chat from me.

MARCH 1993

As a result of my letter to the Royal Horticultural Society asking if any of our daffodils might be 1908 originals, Sally Kington came to Upton Grey in early March 1993 and took some flowers back to London for identification. On the 25th March I went to meet Sally and Brent Elliott at The Lindley Library in Vincent Square and had a fascinating morning looking through beautifully illustrated books on daffodils. I claim with some confidence that two old cultivars are still here, 'Emperor' and 'Empress'. The others seem to be lost – perhaps they were never planted by Charles Holme. Still, two relatively unusual daffodils surviving all those years of neglect is very rewarding. Incidentally, the Lindley Library has the greatest collection of botanical books that I have ever seen.

March 30. I took off on what was to become an annual event, my first American talk tour. The three other speakers were to be Judith Tankard, Fenja Gunn and Patrick Chasse. Judith has written several books and articles about Jekyll and had visited us at Upton Grey. Fenja had recently published a very well researched book called *Lost Gardens of Gertrude Jekyll*, and Patrick is a writer and garden designer. I was very, very nervous, completely lacking in confidence and, in that tense state, felt quite isolated from the real world. I had been warned by Nan Blake Sinton, who was organising the trip, that two things were vital to survival as a speaker. First, never be late for a flight because all tickets are bought by the hosts at the lowest possible rate and are therefore not exchangeable, and second, at no time be separated from the all-important slides; they must travel as hand-baggage at all times. I have since swapped tales with less conscientious travellers about the nerve-wracking consequences of becoming careless through over-confidence and have made a few dreadful blunders myself. In Kansas I went on a pre-talk jog (following the custom of the country) and got so lost that I had to hail a passing police car to drive me back to base. That in itself was difficult as I did not know the address of 'base'. The policeman rang through to headquarters, 'I'm taking a dame on board' he announced before trying to work out where I wanted to go from the surname of the people I was staying with, Dickey. Having fined it down to a short-list of three he switched on sirens and flashing lights and delivered me back to bewildered Carol Dickey, a little late and very flustered, but the incident made the start to my talk amusing. In Castle Hill near Boston, a truly magnificent arts and crafts house with spectacular views down to the cold grey sweep of the Atlantic ocean, I wandered off in search of peace in order to practise my lines, and quite forgot the time. A distraught woman eventually found me at the top of the house in a maid's room. 'Thank goodness I've found you. You were meant to start speaking ten minutes ago'. I scrambled back to the auditorium where the patient audience was

John Lindley
1799-1865, founder
of the Lindley Library.

comfortingly forgiving. 'She's still on English time' said a sympathetic soul near the front.

Over the following ten days we gave talks at Cleveland Botanic Gardens, Winterthur in Pennsylvania, Wave Hill just outside New York, the memorable Castle Hill near Boston and at Hamilton Botanic Gardens in Ontario.

After travelling several hundred miles with Judith, Nan, Patrick and Fenja, and the last talk over, we drove back to New York City, a merry little band of performers who had been through momentous times together to emerge better people for the buffeting and ordeals. We celebrated survival with a happy last supper in New York. For a fleeting moment I felt as I had when the animals and I had appeared on the front cover of *American House and Garden*, ephemerally famous. I was not. I returned, as obscure as ever, to England, to the garden which had done so much for me, to the birds and beasts who were not remotely impressed by traveller's tales, and to the role of working gardener.

The first day home, April 25th a Sunday, I wrote ecstatically in garden diary, oblivious of what was to dawn on me the following day: 'Home. Garden looks wonderful, green and lush. All very healthy and amazing growth. First laburnum flowers starting'. Grouped naturally as they are in the Wild Garden, the laburnums do not look contrived. They echo the yellow of the daffodils below and when flowers are over, their frond-leafed branches droop gently towards the grass bank and rambling roses. 'First oriental poppies opening and asparagus is already feeding the ducks. Peonies are their full height but still in tight bud. Dicentra in flower. I feel so energetic and very happy to be back. All five ducks still around and one bantam sits on eggs. Dogs well, though surprised to see me. I've never been away longer than eight days before. Car battery flat. Weather damp. Did lots of weeding. Daffodils almost over. Pond still leaks. *Plus ça change*'. There was a price to pay for the idyllic life.

The next day, Monday, I found one unpleasant change at home. The gardener had been

In Winterthur Gardens, Pennsylvania, USA. Left to right: Patrick Chasse, Judith Tankard, Tom Buchter, RW and Nan Sinton.

drinking, quarrelling with his wife and doing precious little garden upkeep. I got down to heavy gardening with gritted teeth. The garden open season started and the season's happy visitors began to arrive. I performed my habitual juggling act of welcome, slide-show, teas, cake-making and gardening and, on a sunny day, I continued to enjoy the garden. On a bleak day, however, I had verbal battles with the ghastly gardener (WHEN he showed his head above the parapet) and miserable moods took over. I remember one dark afternoon when I sat in pouring rain under a very inadequate umbrella taking entrance money from equally gloomy-faced visitors. After two hours I had netted about nine pounds from six visitors and decided to indulge myself in a quick cry. I don't remember if they were tears of rage or sorrow, but was well into it with nose and eyes running when Charles Quest Ritson of the Italian rose holiday in June 1992 appeared, wrapped to his brows in water-proof clothing. It completely cheered me. Charles is not a sentimental person; we discussed safe obliteration of alien bodies (in other words how to get rid of the gardener) and by the end of the afternoon I was fired with determination to overcome all problems. However, getting rid of someone who has worked for you for over two years is not easy, even with complete justice on our side and the full support of the village. We were taken to an industrial tribunal. He claimed constructive dismissal which legally means that, although he had handed in his notice, it was because I had made life here so miserable that he was forced to leave. It seemed to us that he had a very flimsy case but both John and I had a wretched time preparing for what looked like becoming weeks of wrangling.

Garden notes became a little emotional during the early summer of 1993. Sickly Sentiment, I called it, and continued to write in the sickly, rather florid mood.

'Full Moon. Foul Mood. Could be worse, I suppose. There is a magic about this house, the garden that clothes it, and the restoration of it all from near dereliction to close renascence.'

Earlier in the year I had been asked to join Penelope Hobhouse in Connecticut to give a talk at the Glebe House Museum. I flew to the United States in July, had a wonderful time seeing Connecticut which immediately became another place on my list of 'where I would like to live', and gave a slightly better talk to an encouraging audience. Like most Americans that I talk to, they arrived looking far better dressed than I. As usual I felt scruffy and more like their gardener than their lecturer but appearances can be deceptive. These well-dressed beauties are often knowledgeable gardeners with a great deal of practical experience which they are happy to share. We sometimes end talks with open discussions about, for instance, when and what to feed plants or when and what to cut. Americans are very imaginative shapers of plants, partly, I suppose, because many of them garden in a small area so have to control the growth of plants in order to let in light and rainfall. They 'topiary' an astonishing range of plants from the obvious yew and box to rosemary, geraniums, in fact it seems to me almost any shrub, and with this careful control they can raise or lower the contours of a border making interesting shape in a relatively small space. The word derives from the Latin *topiarius* which loosely meant landscape gardener, so perhaps all gardeners are topiarists. When I am asked what my favourite gardening present is I divide it into two answers: giving and receiving. As a receiver I love really good quality (and expensive) secateurs. As a giver I meanly choose the indispensable small knife-sharpener or whet-stone that I carry everywhere in the garden. My American audiences ask questions about our annual rainfall, our lowest and highest seasonal temperatures, and what sort of grass seed we use in which parts of the garden. They are interested in garden machinery and the running costs of a five-acre garden. They take an interest in garden history, particularly English garden history.

I spend most of my spare time between giving talks in America, looking at their gardens. I admit that those I am shown tend to be the best in their field so I cannot judge the whole spectrum very accurately. My instant impressions are that American gardens are quite small, well designed and have plenty of structure. A large proportion of gardeners turn to professional designers for advice. Very few people employ a full-time gardener and those gardeners are often handymen rather than horticulturists; consequently gardens are designed to be labour-saving where practical. I am surprised by how few Americans grow plants from seed. The nurseries probably do a thriving business, and deservedly so, because those I have seen sell an impressive and very extensive range of plant material. Laudably their aspirations seem to be more horticultural than commercial. One thing I find amusing and very impressive is how confidently nearly all American gardeners grow plants from cuttings. They take it for granted that a stick will take root and they say it with innocent matter-of-fact honesty. I always enjoy these working holidays. The Connecticut trip was a good break from garden troubles at home. There's nothing like a good fright (which all talks give me) to take the mind off woes.

Back home in Upton Grey I realised that nothing lasts forever. After about three months of unpleasantness the gardener backed off and withdrew his allegations about constructive dismissal and his right to remain in our cottage. John and I were left bruised, shocked and short of one car (which he kept) but, by some strange compelling fate, not quite bloodied enough to give up completely. We knew that, if we wanted to continue opening to the public and enjoying all the new facets of the garden world that were opening up to us, we would have to employ a full-time gardener. So we picked ourselves up, cleaned out the pretty cottage, and advertised again for a full-time gardener. This time the advertisement was carefully worded to emphasise that a qualified gardener was needed and I did not ask for help with house-work.

I advertised in the RHS Journal, *The Garden*. By fortunate coincidence an advertisement, asking for a gardening job appeared in the same issue. It was placed by a fully qualified gardener working in Toronto in Canada who, having recently married an English girl, wanted to return to England and start a family. I answered his advertisement, convinced that we would neither be able to afford such a gardener, nor would the advertiser want such a parochial job. I had about sixty replies to my advertisement. Phil Brailsford tells me he had about twelve to his. Odd, but jobs were at a premium, I suppose.

Because he was temporarily in England, we arranged to meet immediately. I liked Phil; Phil liked the cottage, and on the first of October 1993 John, Phil, his wife Sally and I all took the brave step of joining together to keep Miss Jekyll's plot going. I am well aware that an experienced gardener should want to express his talents and his love of certain plants in the garden he takes on. That is not possible here. We are locked into Jekyll and her 1908 plans; it is a situation which suits me well, but which must be inhibiting for Phil whose own garden is very small and has now become a play-area for their young children. Phil is patient. He does not complain. He and Sally grow beautiful children instead of plants.

Over the winter of 1993/4 we planned projects. It was good to have someone to share ideas and enthusiasm with. If Phil and I didn't agree on a scheme I would voice disapproval immediately but Phil would do so more patiently; somehow we managed to persuade each other into changing minds in fair proportions. There are obviously no major garden changes to be made in Jekyll's garden. Our projects are simply perfecting bits, but those are sometimes very big perfectings. A prime example, one of our most ambitious projects is trying to repair

The old greenhouse in a derelict state. Wood was rotten and most of the glass had fallen out.

The old greenhouse partly restored. We made new window frames and added two posts to support the sagging roof but we did not dare replace the glass because we thought the whole thing might collapse!

The rebuilding of the last drystone wall and its importance

the beautiful Edwardian greenhouse that has stood close to the stables/cottage since early this century. It requires a great deal of work on the wooden structure, the badly warped windows, the metal vent-winding mechanisms and the old stoves. It is virtually a case of rebuilding so we only work on it in less busy winter months and we are still at it.

In 1993 there was one outstanding feature of Jekyll's plans that we had left uncompleted, simply because Charles Holme had never built it. A small drystone wall had been planned to stand between the Tennis Lawn and Bowling Lawns. 'Thrown out' was written across her amended 1909 plans. Brave of Charles Holme to defy Miss Jekyll, and wrong, because it gives a beautiful balance to the garden architecturally! The twelve-inch high wall replaces a very small grass bank which, like most grass banks, Jekyll would have disliked and which we proved, by scuffing it to moss every time we tried to mow it, that the wise gardener was correct in changing. The terracing is far better proportioned now. In 1986 I had noted the importance of that area of grass when looking back towards the house from beyond the Tennis Lawn; but with hindsight it was a little too massive. The small wall subtly breaks the green expanse and now terraces and grass display the house perfectly. From the rose arbour seat beside the Tennis Lawn I have my favourite view of the house. This is where I take garden visitors to show them the importance of complementing architecture with planting and landscaping.

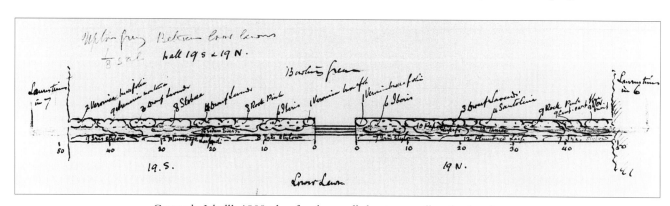

Gertrude Jekyll's 1909 plan for the small drystone wall and other features.

1991. The Tennis and Bowling Lawns before building the small wall.

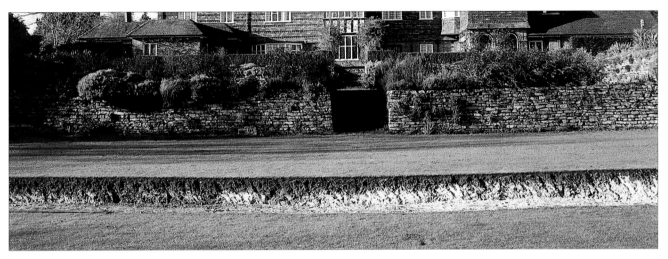

1993. Work on the small wall started. This shows the high chalk level and explains why we have to add compost and manure to the earth regularly.

The small wall completed. The steps are shallow and typically Jekyll.

In the spring of 1994 we commissioned Anthony Archer-Wills to line the pond for the final time, we hope, in our lifetimes. Anthony and his team of pond experts came to dig out the pond then lined it with heavy Bitumastic sheeting and replaced the surrounding earth and stones, leaving no suggestion that the pond is not natural. They put a small circulating water pump above and to one side so that water trickles down the stones in the very way that the original spring once ran. It all looks beautiful despite the fact that diving ducks continue to muddy the water.

Thanks to Phil's industry the Kitchen Garden, which is on Jekyll's plans but not specifically planted, is now formally laid out and it makes an interesting addition to the garden. We started work on it in May and continued, between other garden duties, until the end of 1995. It was a fairly major project which required a great deal of construction as well as replanting. Visitors enjoy looking at kitchen gardens because they are areas most people can relate to and borrow ideas from. It is well known that vegetables can make beautiful, sometimes colourful, and often structural plants. Certainly the maize that grows in the herbaceous borders here fulfils a useful structural role in late summer when most other plants are wilting and collapsing. Box and yew hedging now give direction to walks around the Kitchen Garden and we have built a rose-hung pergola at each end to add summer colour. Along one side we now have a rope walk, which serves a double purpose. It makes the walk up the other side of the Kitchen Garden interesting instead of repetitive and to some extent it serves as a screen to hide the rather messy area where our bantams roost and ducks are penned during the fox weeks. The posts are hung with the beautifully plaited ship's rope that we use in other parts of the garden and are planted with roses which Jekyll is either known to have used or which were available to her. Some of our own grafted rose buddings and rooted rose cuttings are also planted here and I am watching with interest to see which of the two types will make stronger plants. I am told that roses which are grown on their own roots develop into healthier plants but I have yet to prove this because, as far as I can judge, the types of roses which take root readily are healthier cultivars in the first place. Most of the plants in the Kitchen Garden are reserve stock for Jekyll's borders, that is divisions of herbaceous material and plants grown from our own seed. A smaller area is reserved for vegetables for the household or birds – whichever gets to them first.

1988. The pond.

1996. The pond restored for the last time. We eventually accepted that clay on chalk would not hold water here.

Looking down the Kitchen Garden to the pergola with the rose walk to the left.

1994
JANUARY FEBRUARY AND MARCH

January 3. 'We have bought a basic, but perfectly adequate, propane gas heater for the small greenhouse and we have a simple cable-heated surface of about four square feet on which to grow seedlings. Phil installed it'. We set our thermostat to a minimum of 5 degrees centigrade. That revolutionised life in the greenhouse. Since then we have been able to grow nearly all the plants we need either from seeds or cuttings. With the exception of vegetable seeds we buy very little extra material nowadays. Occasionally I buy trade seeds of the annuals like snapdragons and variegated corn because, if I use my own seeds year after year, I produce progressively weaker plants. I am not sure if this is due to in-breeding or because our soil is poor. One of my favourite sources of vegetable seeds is the Henry Doubleday Research Association at Ryton, known as HYDRA. They supply seeds of old or unusual vegetables in an attempt to keep sources of uncommercial genetic plant material alive. The Purple Podded Pea is a great favourite with visitors here as it is with me and, by coincidence, it was with Jekyll. She wrote an 'Ode to the purple podded pea' to prove it.

It was our intention, initially, to grow extra stock to sell. We always have a surplus of some plants, but we soon found that the business of potting up, buying in the compost and actually running the 'plants for sale' stand on garden open days is simply not financially viable – so we now give away or compost surplus stock.

One very happy change in garden notes is that I began to report more of what Phil had done and progressively less of what I had done in the garden – particularly during the winter months.

February 18. 'Bantam Cockerel quickly and mysteriously died this morning. Is it poison? I am now left with two black hen bantams. One sits on his body and looks ill'. Next day. 'Overnight second black bantam died. Sad. Surviving black bantam, Mrs B, lonely, follows me. I always loved her best anyway. Ordered three more today. Spent a long time talking to Mrs B. She is melancholy. Ducks are being penned in at night now (fox season) but are reluctant to go in. Irritating'.

'New bantams arrive. Present from Prue Lane Fox. All get on well. Mrs B still jumps into my arms and tolerates a cuddle in return for corn'.

This spring must have been very wet as I often remarked that 'it hasn't stopped raining since Phil arrived'. Between October 1993 and March 1994 the water tables in this area at last began to rise.

APRIL 1994

April 12. 'Phil and Sally's first baby born last week. An enormous excitement to everybody and rather puts into perspective my joy at the birth of dozens of birds at one time. All are well and beautiful baby is to be called Christopher. Luckily no-one has asked me to hold the baby yet. Always a self-conscious and inane remark-making time, I find'.

Fertility time in the garden starts in April and various bantams take turns to disappear. They lay eggs in the most unfindable but surprisingly practical places. I waste hours egg-hunting, spying on the hens when they have left the nest for a brief feed, but they return to the nest circuitously and are well aware they are being watched.

As April ended, the house martins returned to their rather sparrow-battered nests and the summer visitors started to return to the continually improving Jekyll garden. I began casting a fly over each group of garden visitors from abroad telling them how much I should enjoy giving garden talks in their part of the world. So far I have been lucky enough to elicit invitations every year. They have always been to an English-speaking country and nearly always to the United States.

With Phil taking over so much garden work, 1994 became a year for raising general standards of tidiness, for sorting out off-plan areas, and the garden thrived under so much care. An added bonus was that John and I had time to spend doing frivolous things. Having taken up golf in a rather half-hearted way in 1991 we now began to play with the determination that only someone of middle age (with physical fitness running out) can do. We had progressed from boring practice on the driving range to actually becoming members of a club and to playing with friends. In fine weather it is an enjoyment which closely rivals gardening, but will never overtake it.

Phil Brailsford with his wife, Sally, and Christopher and Emma. After Phil's arrival my work in the garden turned from labour to pleasure.

House martins flying
over the Wild Garden.

MAY 1994

I asked Phil's wife, Sally, if she would do the afternoon teas for me on days we were to open
for the National Gardens Scheme. There were to be sixteen that year. It seemed a good idea
as Sally would keep the money and visitors would enjoy their outing. But I had not thought
it through; it was not a success because, if the weather was fine, she was worked off her feet
and if it rained she was left with dozens of uneaten cakes and pots of tea. The first open day
was such a day. 'Poured. Poor Sally made tea and cakes for dozens (on my advice)... felt rather
a fool as well as responsible. Birds enjoyed them though, and so did I'.

In late May we had our first coach-load of Japanese visitors. I like meeting them. They
are serious gardeners and admire the elements of English gardens just as Charles Holme had
admired the art and craft of Japan and her gardens, so I feel we have common ground. They
came on a wet day but clearly enjoyed themselves as we have had groups from Japan
annually since.

Looking at my notes this must have been the wettest start to a year for decades. I only
remark (in large capitals) when it does NOT rain, and I note daily the lack of progress in the
egg-hatching world of both ducks and bantams. Twenty-one and twenty-six days are a
remarkably long time to spend waiting for a great event. It makes human incubation of nine
months seem unbearable suspense.

JUNE 1994

Since I was eighteen, I had dutifully gone to Royal Ascot races each June and, because it is
a special event, one which I should be grateful to attend at all, it had occurred to me neither
to admit I do not enjoy it, nor to refuse to go. In 1993 I grew up, faced reality and decided
that this would be my last time. I wrote the obituary at the end of Ascot week in 1994, in
celebration of what I was missing, as follows:

June 15. 'This is nearly mid-summer though we've only had about five days of good
weather all year and today has been very, very, hot. It is Ascot week. Having renounced it, I
can now forget the inane remarks, the permanent smile, the blistered feet and the
aerodynamically unsound head-dress. I shan't miss the event. I'll stick to things I enjoy.

Gardening is rewarding, playing bridge with a few friends is fun, golf is exciting – really it is – and a little bit of champagne is far better than a lot'.

During that Ascot week, the duck hatched seven eggs so I was happily distracted watching over the babies until they grew big enough to waddle up to the pond. The following week, Ratty, the fox terrier came trotting up to me with a dead duckling in her mouth. It occurred to me that it was unusual for a terrier to bring the bounty home – and stupid. I was furious and laid about her with a piece of lightly rolled newspaper. It makes a lot of noise but does not hurt. She seemed a bit bemused. Two days later I saw the bantam cockerel attack a duckling. With a couple of quick pecks to the back of its neck he killed it in seconds. That may well have been the fate of the first duck. It was my fault, because I had kept them close to the bantam roosting area for their first few days. It was bantam territory and the ducklings represented a threat to the cockerel and his wives. Mother duck appeared to be oblivious of the danger and of her loss. Her offspring were very soon big enough to escape the cockerel and we lost no more for the time being.

From mid-June until the end of July we had almost no rain. It may have been my imagination but, for the following few weeks, I kept remarking how flowers were wilting. If true, it was probably because the exceptionally wet start to the year encouraged plants to keep their roots too close to the surface of the earth, producing the same results as watering in a drought. It seemed that the only practical solution was to cut back plants and prop them up where necessary.

JULY 1994

By the end of the month we had four ducklings, a drake and two ducks as well as seven bantams. Several of my rose cuttings from the year before had taken root. We had had about twelve hundred visitors and – the inevitable downside to life, just to remind us that nothing is quite perfect – there had been a third attempt to steal the leaden cherubs that stood at the entrance to the Wild Garden. Something, perhaps the alarm lights, which come on after dark if movement or heat triggers the sensors, had disturbed the vandals and they had fled empty-handed, leaving a mangled piece of lead and a broken pillar. For the following months I did a lot of research into effective alarm systems. We evidently needed an alarm which emits a loud sound when activated, because lights may serve to aid the burglar. Eventually I found a system which, five years later, I still believe to be the best. It is a screeching alarm, made by Simba Security. It works by vibration only, so is not set off by movement of prowling animals and birds. It is simple, relatively inexpensive, and effective. It has subsequently prevented two thefts. As long as there is someone around to react to the sirens, if only by opening a window, but better still by telephoning the police, it works as well as anything we have managed to find.

LATE SUMMER 1994

In August we were photographed for an English Heritage publication to be called *100 English Gardens*. At the time I thought no more of it, knowing there must be gardens more beautiful than ours the length and breadth of England. To my delight when the book was published in 1995 we were included. Patrick Taylor is the author. It is a well presented and splendid book. I suppose our garden is included because it is historically interesting, beautiful in its season, and it is such a typically English garden that it could have been planted at any time over the past one hundred and fifty years. It transcends time, fashion and style and perhaps that is Jekyll's greatest art; it has a certain immortality. Evidently the garden was becoming acknowledged as a useful reference point and living museum of nineteenth century plants for students of Jekyll. *Eryngium oliverianum* proves a favourite with many. It is not particularly rare but is neglected by modern gardeners. In September 1998 I was sent a copy of an article printed in the American magazine *Traditional Home* that was headed 'Sea Holly Aristocrats'. It included the following sentence:

> *On a mid-summer pilgrimage to English gardens, my camera's eye was drawn to the purple-veined vivid blue of* E. x oliverianum *at Manor House, Upton Grey. Upton Grey is a 1908 Gertrude Jekyll garden that is alive and well in the hands – nicely callused – of the present owner, Rosamund Wallinger.*

The summer of 1994 ended hot and dry. Mrs B, favourite bantam, trustingly laid nine eggs right outside the garage door – a vulnerable and totally unprivate place. Sadly, perhaps because she had become too human orientated, she tired of sitting on her dull nest and abandoned the eggs after a few days. One black bantam did sit through the incubation period and produced seven bumble-bee-like balls of fluff, both black and buff. I don't know who was prouder, she or I. Because standards in the garden had risen to undreamed-of heights with Phil's industry, we decided to confine the ducks to the Wild Garden for the summer months. They are ravenous eaters of all young green shoots and of most vegetables, particularly tomatoes and asparagus. Much as I love them, they make a considerable mess.

In late August, John and I drove to France for our usual five-day holiday. There was a good feeling of longing to get home and knowing that all would be well on my return. A feeling I had never had when our previous gardener was left in charge.

NOVEMBER 1994

'This is normally lethargy month because the days get shorter and colder and the garden is less demanding. But this week is exceptionally warm; everything is out of kilter and so am I. I spent several happy minutes squashing large colonies of greenfly that have reappeared on young rose tips. An hour later hands are a curious olive green yellow. 'Now is the time to clear the garden, to chop down herbaceous plants, to tidy the compost heaps and to burn wood, twigs and conkers. I won't prune back roses, rosemary, olearias etc. , because they may start to grow, and young shoots will perish when cold weather comes. I shall do shrubs in early spring. Weeding is an extravagant business at this time of year because the soil is damp and it clings to roots. Valuable top-soil follows the weeds into the barrow and I am loath to lose it'.

Phil and Sally and baby had a late two-week holiday. I realised how lucky we were to have them here and looked forward to their return.

DECEMBER 1994

The invitation I had hoped for arrived. I was invited to go back to the United States to give talks about Jekyll and the garden's restoration the following spring. The talks were becoming quite good – more fluent and polished. But as I always stick to the same broad subject, give or take a few variations, this is not a proud boast.

December 30. 'Ambition for 1995 is to get a STAR in Good Gardens Guide'. So ends the year, contented and happy; the garden looking more complete each year.

Chapter Nine
1995-1998

SPRING 1995

This was the wettest January since 1948, and 1948 was the wettest on record. Europe was flooded in parts.

Between February 17th and 28th I travelled to California and to Portland in Oregon where I gave more talks. Perhaps for the first time, I truly enjoyed them and found they flowed well. I felt an affinity with the audience, and the number asleep in the front row seemed to be dropping. They were no longer the daunting black silhouettes in an unknown crowd; I found that I was talking to kindred spirits with interests and ambitions in common. There is no doubt too that the subject of my talks had broadened considerably. Whereas the first talks had only been about the garden's restoration and the physical side of that work, I now included a short biography of Jekyll, her place in garden history and a comparison with other important gardeners.

I returned to find all in good order and got down to gardening again. Weeding is a priority at this time of year because from February onwards, when ground is not frozen, you feel you can keep on top of weeds by attacking early, and of course it stops them spreading both above and below ground. I was told that early March is a good time to divide peonies, but I have my doubts. It seems a little late in this part of England because the early varieties have already put out inches of growth. As an experiment I divided two of mine and monitored results. I divided two more the following year but one month earlier and decided that February was a better time for the early flowering peonies. I certainly feel that ten-year-old plants need dividing, because those rhizomes I dug up were enormous and appeared to include several dead parts.

SUMMER 1995

August 12. 'It is Upton Grey Flower Show today – the annual village event which really is village orientated, unlike the village fete which attracts people from several surrounding villages. This must be one of the few years this century that the Flower Show follows harvest. Through the year fields have turned from bare earth to the vivid green of young corn, then yellow, gold, brown and now the light brown, faded colour of stubble. The elder shrubs are covered in fruit, and blackberries in the hedgerows are sweet enough to eat. Earth is dust-dry – a light powder drifts in the breeze. Joyous cries from the Flower Show children ring through the village. The tent is filled with vegetables, flower arrangements, photographs, all neatly arranged in the hope of prizes. Outside the dry field is packed with game stands, a coconut shy, sack races, bash-the-hammer-to-raise-the-ball, and other tests of strength like tossing a hay bale with a rake. The same people tend to win these games from year to year, until one generation concedes muscle power to the next.

The house martins are too hot to scan the air for midges. Where do they go in this searing heat.

Delphiniums in the Hot Border. These are one of the few plant types of which I lost old cultivars and with which I have carelessly allowed new hybrids to pollinate (see page 180).

Hollyhocks in the cottage garden beds. These are used for seed head supplies.

From left to right: In New Zealand, with Annie Leonard, Sally Allison and Bev McConnell.

I believe they do not like to perch so perhaps they are back inside their shady nests under roof eaves. I know the bantams are miserable. Heat and fierce sun have them sheltering under the box hedges, the babies make dust bowls and lie exhausted. I can touch them easily. They don't have the energy to move on. The older birds are more weatherproof. The ducks simply stay on the pond, cool but murky green and so are they. I went out to garden but got diverted to shady bits, eating barely ripe plums and apples, whilst moving the hoe from one young walnut tree to another, all at a snail's pace. This is a good time to watch life. 'One may learn from nature these great lessons, the importance of moderation, of reserve, of simplicity of intention… but the lesson I have thoroughly learnt and wish to pass on is to know the enduring happiness that the love of gardening gives'. Jekyll's words often fill my head when I am pottering.

It is curious that, with drought, the greenfly almost disappear and it is astonishing that a completely wilted plant can recover fully and vigorously within an hour of watering and yet, as we have all observed, no artificial watering has the dramatic emerald-greening effect on yellow grass that rainfall has. How cleverly the clone weeds grow beside their look-alike plants, hoping to confuse the gardener. There is the potato-type weed, the carrot-type weed, the tiarella-type and the geranium-type. For years I have nurtured the little bittercress weed thinking it was its close relation *Cardamine pratensis* which Jekyll planted in the drystone walls. Now I dislike that intruder all the more for having fooled me – sour grapes I suppose. Wasps sting without provocation. I hunt their nests with killer powder in hand. Revenge is satisfying; but I am told the wasp grubs are beneficial aphid-eating creatures. The more I look, the more I see 'sermons in stones, books in babbling brooks and good in everything'. Come to think of it, has anyone a good word for horse flies? Their short, vicious season seems to be around August and my body is an enraged monument to their dull bites. Where do they hide for the rest of the year. Days are hot, and dry. I start to look forward to winter. How strangely slowly a hot summer's day drags by'. Presumably the heat had driven me inside early so I wrote a far longer diary entry than usual.

AUTUMN 1995

September 3. 'This has been declared the driest summer since the 1740s. Odd, as it started with so much rain. This is sepia weather. The countryside is pale brown, crisp and rather sinister. Birds are active until about 11 a.m. then disappear to hidden sheltered places. The over-night dews that once greyed the grass tops until mid-morning have almost disappeared by seven. I expect to see horrendous mutations of insects and things as they adapt to this strange new world. Some of my second flowering plants survive well though. Delphiniums are fine if cut right down. The composite flowers recover from almost any amount of cutting back. Roses seem to need differing personal treatment and that muddles me. I look at each plant and then decide how to treat it. After a bad start to the day with a minor car crash, I come home to dogs and birds and garden and comforting sameness. All the creatures are oblivious of everything except my importance as a source of food and water, and so a wonderful welcome. Very cheering'.

NOVEMBER 1995

November 2. I flew to New Zealand to give talks both on North and South Islands. Their important rosarian Sally Allison arranged for me to talk to several rose societies about Jekyll roses at Upton Grey and, whilst I was there, she showed me some of their best gardens. I came away believing that it has the most beautiful scenery and best climate in the world and that I would happily live there if I were twenty years younger. Of all the people I have met, New Zealanders seem the most hard-working, resilient, practical, and in a particular way, wise people. Talking to knowledgeable gardeners there was rather nerve-wracking and, because I had given lectures in so many parts of the English-speaking world by then, my nerves came as quite a surprise to me but I was well aware that my audience knew more about the subject of gardening than I. Because their climate varies from semi-tropical in the North Island, to cool and damp in the South Island, their knowledge is broad and so, of course, is their range of plant material. New Zealanders are not cosseted people as the British are. They fight hard for what they have and take the knocks of nature with fierce resilience. They made me feel quite ashamed of our rather whinging and greedy 'It's my right' society. The hardships of emigrating to a new, remote and cruel country are almost within living memory. I read some harrowing accounts of the first mid-nineteenth century settlers, of their battles against nature and the warring Maoris, who no doubt felt equally threatened.

In Christchurch, South Island, an old woman of ninety-nine told me of the grandmother she remembered well and of her remarkable adventure. The grandmother, then a young widow with two small children, had left England in 1862. She had intended to travel to Canada in the hope of setting up a new life in a country less harsh than Victorian England. At Tilbury dockside she was told that a ship was shortly leaving for a country called New Zealand where she would find better prospects for a young family. So she took this advice and there and then bought a passage to Christchurch where she arrived a few months later, one of the first settlers. Presumably she married again and made a success of her new life. The old woman remembered her grandmother with pride.

I returned to England at the end of November, tired, exhilarated and happy, braced for the annual crop of chilblains, and sore nose but inspired with an unseasonable urge to garden. Phil and I completed the work we had started on the Kitchen Garden.

DECEMBER 1995

'Today we finished putting up the new rose walk. It is designed to look like one side of a pergola with plants trained to climb up posts and along ropes. It was hard work and quite expensive but it is an infinitely more rewarding sight than a cheap, skimpy construction. It is seventy feet long; the planted side faces the Kitchen Garden and gives that area a designed and enclosed look. The eight posts stand at ten-foot intervals. They are five-inch square, treated oak, nine-and-a-half feet tall and cost £17.00 each. This height allows two foot three inches to stand in the earth and seven foot three inches above ground. The top three inches are shaped to a diamond cone to allow water to run off and then treated again, this time with clear Cuprinol. At the top of each post we put a brass rope-holder, a circle which divides in half and is re-fixed with screws when the rope is in place. As I mentioned when describing the Jekyll pergola, the rope is the size of my biceps and very heavy. Any ship's chandlers sells it second-hand for about 75p per foot. Whether it is real hemp rope or modern fibre matters not at all. The synthetic fibre ropes look exactly the same when old and oiled but are lighter and easier to handle. The important and beautiful feature is that these ropes are plaited – they

The rope walk in the Kitchen Garden with rose 'Paul Transon' (1901). I bought this rope from a ship's chandler in Southampton (detail below).

are almost works of art in themselves and they look as effective bare as rose-covered. All three pergolas, our rose arbour and the rose walk are composed along those lines'.

In July 1995 I had written to Geoff Hamilton, the presenter of BBC Television's 'Gardeners World', telling him about the garden, of our pride in it and of its uniqueness. At that time Geoff was making plans for a series of programmes to be called 'Paradise Gardens'. By a quirk of fate a group of Americans who had visited this garden met Geoff's researcher while she was looking for material among gardens in the south of England. They suggested that the Manor House at Upton Grey should be included in the Paradise series. A researcher was duly sent to appraise the garden. She came, to my concern, in early August, a time of year when this garden is not at its best. That year it was well on its way to the pantomime dame phase. It was over-blown, smudged and a little gaudy. Still, birds and dogs behaved impeccably and we were happy to be told that we were considered a possible Paradise subject. None of that was recorded in my garden diary. It all seemed a 'Fat Chance' effort which I expected would be rejected.

At much the same time my godson's wife, Clare Wilks, was also being considered for appearance in the planned series, and, by further curious coincidence, I had asked Clare to make us a living willow arbour here. Clare is an academic artist who is one of the world's best creators of woven-willow sculpture. She makes abstract shapes, as well as practical garden furniture, from several different kinds of willow. In the biography of his aunt, Francis Jekyll quotes Gertrude's attempt, as a child, to build her own willow hut. Her beloved brothers had been dispatched to boarding school, leaving her alone to amuse herself.

'…I made my hut. I did not know anything about building then, so it was simply made of supple willow stems bent over and tied, with other sticks of willow and hazel wattled in'.

Geoff intended to show his viewers both the beauty of Clare's work and how they might

Right: Clare Wilks at work on the arbour in 1995.

Far right: Detail of the woven arbour (by 1998 the woven seat had shredded so we used hazel sticks).

The willow arbour in winter. The barks of various willow showing different colours.

The willow arbour in summer. The upright living structure will last for years.

make their own woven masterpiece, so Clare was asked to allow filming of her work in progress at Upton Grey. We chose a spot in the Wild Garden which is empty on Jekyll's plans. It lies alongside the church wall in a corner which is shaded by a large copper beech. The arbour stands at the apex of two drifts of Jekyll's original daffodils, 'Emperor' and 'Empress'. Over the past few years it has established a focal point at the end of the garden and is now a very popular feature.

Clare arrived in early December 1995, weighed down by bundles of brightly barked willow sticks and muffled to her ears against the elements. She spent about four days, winding and weaving the coloured twigs to form a large arbour with plaited seat. Geoff and his team of Ray Hough, Maggie Kosowicz and camera crew came to film her as it grew. Days were dark and cold, snow lay on the ground but Clare worked on undaunted. From time to time we all met indoors for hot lunch and drinks, tales of the world of filming and gardening and for chuckles at life. Geoff had suffered a mild heart-attack some months earlier but was now in fine spirits, composing his interviews and comments in a small notebook as things happened – very spontaneously, very warmly. This mood came through to Clare and me and made our potentially nervous replies feel natural and easy. By Christmas 1995, the arbour was completed and filming finished. Geoff arranged to return to film the garden for his Paradise series in June 1996 and again in August. These were scheduled to be broadcast in January 1997.

1996

Earlier this year Garden Club of America members and other visitors to the garden had invited me to give talks in the United States. Over the busy months that followed my recollection of who arrived when and who had suggested what, are all blurred into one rather tired picture, but I remembered Virginia Sappington and her band of gardeners as being clever, amusing individuals whose company I had enjoyed; and probably remembered them all the better because, as they left the garden one hot July afternoon, I had marvelled at their feat of cramming six gardeners, plus tour leader and an enormous supply of luggage, into a remarkably small van.

June 1998. John with bantams.

It was quite a conjuring trick. Virginia wrote to me on her return to the United States and subsequently arranged three talk venues. I accepted a further three invitations to go to Kenwood in Virginia, to the Huntington Museum in California and to Kansas City, Missouri.

For the first few weeks of 1996, I did serious work on polishing my talk subjects. I went back to MAST to have all vestiges of self-satisfaction removed – and learnt several more good tips, for example, 'Don't rush'. 'Try to anticipate the next slide and introduce it before it appears'. 'Wait from time to time, to allow a point or visual image to have impact'. 'Don't flay the arms around'. 'Face the audience and try to smile or at least look relaxed'. 'Speak up'. 'Don't drop the voice'. 'Behave naturally' – all easier said than done.

I have developed packing for these occasions into a fairly fine art. The list of essentials never changes: carousel of slides, notes, laser pointer, clock, pencil and paper, as few clothes as possible, smart but comfortable shoes, drip dry shirts and a sponge-bag. Passport, ticket and money complete the traveller's package. I pack several days before I set off, so that I have time to remember essential things. The trip went well, the quality of my talks had improved and I saw yet more of the big and beautiful United States.

I returned home on May 1st, John's birthday, to find the greenhouse full of seedlings – between sixty and seventy trays of small green shoots, carefully labelled and nursed by Phil - enough to fill the Kitchen Garden several times over with summer flowers. How strange it is to leave a colourless winter England, whose landscape is a monotone sepia seen through grey, blurring mists, and to return a few weeks later in bright, vital spring to see crocus and daffodils in flower and rich, green, young crops in the fields. The season moves so quickly from bleak to beautiful. The air is light and sharp and dawn birdsong wakes the sleeping world.

Whilst I was away there had been a spate of outdoor burglaries carried out by a gang of itinerant garden machinery thieves who were working their way around Basingstoke with remarkable audacity. Apparently they drove across open fields and countryside, in a plain white van whose number plate probably changed weekly and they chose any convenient access point into a garden. They broke into our garage, cutting through the lock. Evidently they had picked their way through most of the village before reaching us, so either sunrise or some noise worried them and they left us without taking anything. After that warning we attached the Simba screeching device to all outside doors and now feel like Fort Knox, if a little less valuable.

Oblivious of the drama bantams and ducks started to lay eggs but they abandoned their nests soon after laying, when the weather suddenly turned cold again. In 1996 late frosts persisted well into May, delaying the flowering of all but the sturdiest plants and tip-killing those intrepid enough to flower early. On a very cold day, my funny, fierce, toe-pecking little grey bantam cockerel died. He had been ill the day before but I felt that the cold weather might numb him into a peaceful, natural death. I didn't feel it necessary to wring his neck though I knew he was sick. I cried and buried him in the dustbin so that animals would not dig him up. No worse than incineration I felt as I jammed his stiff little body into the plastic-bag shroud. How very light a bird is. He had looked so chubby in his ruffled feathers. He left a small clone, a cockerel chick from 1995's hatch. Clone must have been delighted to find himself King Rooster and he stepped into the traces of his dead father so cleverly that within weeks he had become 'best bantam', similar in spirit and in body.

MAY 1996
Catalyst Television contacted me again early in May to make an appointment for Geoff

Hamilton and team to film the garden in June. That spurred the urge to garden. We worked from dawn to dusk, entertaining visitors, tending plants and hoping that in mid-June the garden would look its best, that the flowers of May would cling on to life whilst those of June would bloom early, that weeds would be under control, grass green and herbaceous borders bright and upright. It is a ridiculous hope but all gardeners set unnatural goals for their big events. 1996 was one of the very few years that made it a tangible goal because spring had started late and a hot summer followed fast. Originally Geoff had intended to call the television series 'Hidden Gardens' but the previous year he decided to change the title of the project to 'Paradise Gardens'. It struck me as a great compliment to Gertrude Jekyll that, almost one hundred years after she planned the garden for Charles Holme, it should be included in a television programme which acknowledged it worthy of ranking with the exclusive few gardens that Geoff Hamilton considered a paradise. As Geoff had told me, it was not because it is an historic garden designed by a great gardener that it was to be included; it was because of its sheer beauty. Clever, timeless Miss Jekyll.

I kept up garden diary notes with the usual tedious remarks about weather, state of things and projects. In early May I wrote 'Running out of puff on Minimum Opus'. The previous year Geraldine Andrews had made an appointment to photograph the garden for a book to be published by Garden Art Press. I was very flattered when she asked me to write about the garden. With nothing to lose I started. The manuscript is dotted with moans of 'Blimey, this is hard work'. And so it was.

May 8. 'Five rose seedlings have germinated. All seedlings look depressingly like *Rosa canina*, seven-leafed and very thorny – still, can't judge before they flower'. I had kept rose seeds every year and planted them with optimism, but until 1996 had managed either to forget where I had planted them or to water them over the several months that they take to germinate. I would like to know if roses growing on laxa rootstock put out seeds of that rootstock even though they are produced on the cultivar flower head. It seems unlikely but I have never grown a true seedling from my cultivar roses.

I think it was this summer that I committed one of those excruciating blunders that still makes me blush but I made no mention of it in notes needless to say. It was particularly memorable because by 1996 I had done just enough gardening to give myself what we call *idées au dessus de ma gare*. I was at the ugly stage between knowing a little but not enough to accept inevitable areas (in my case acres) of ignorance. A fool thinks himself a wise man but a wise man knows himself to be a fool. I fitted the first category. Jamie Compton, a knowledgeable gardener and writer, brought a group of Americans to Upton Grey and as we walked past pretty *Anemone sylvestris* I asked him 'Who is the remarkable Mr Sylvester who lends his name to so many plants?' 'Sylvester' replied Jamie with a smile, 'means of the woods'. Oh dear, oh dear, if only I had thought first: *sylva, sylvarius, sylvaticus*, what a cretin. Knowing looks passed from eye to eye amongst the gardening group as I blushed *Fuchsia magellanica* puce.

May 20. 'A ghastly day. The type that makes me resolve never to open the garden again. A coach-load of old people arrived at 1.45 p.m. although they weren't due until 2.30. It had been raining all day and was horribly cold. After they disembarked, slowly, walking sticks flailing, the impatient coach driver slammed his door shut and announced that he would be back to collect them at 5 p.m. I told them that it would take them a maximum of one hour to look at the garden and that over three hours would be as exhausting for them as for me. But the merciless man drove off to fit in an afternoon of school runs and he had no intention of returning a minute before time. After a cursory tour of the garden in pouring rain, which

June in the Formal
Garden.

left them looking as bedraggled as soaked bantams, the pathetic bodies sheltered in the
garage. I gave them tea and showed them the slides – very slowly. But it was the worst garden
open day of my chequered career and I won't allow it to happen again. God I'm tired and
it's only seven o'clock. John isn't even home yet'.

Days like that leave me wondering why gardening is so popular. Both the British and the
Americans rank it among their five favourite hobbies and, judging by visits to this garden by
northern Europeans, South Africans, Australians, New Zealanders and the Japanese, so does
most of the affluent world. Gardening books are overtaking cookery books in sales, yet
gardening is hard work in sometimes horrible conditions, while cooking is gratifying and
delicious most of the time. Cooking, whilst being rewarding and a hobby that can please
numbers of people, is essentially ephemeral, whereas gardening is so long-term that you may
practise it knowing you will not live to see the end results. Gardening often provides the

materials for cooking. Both subjects, if taken seriously, can become an art. Both can be demanding intellectually and physically. Both subjects, perhaps like most art, attract the aesthete or the effete. Cooking makes you fat. Gardening makes you thin. Perhaps gardeners and cooks are masochists.

May 27. 'Catalyst TV telephoned to ask if they could change the scheduled date to film the garden from June 16th to June 25th. I felt peculiarly determined that they should not. As I have remarked in earlier diary notes the summer of 1996 was delayed by late frosts which had tricked nature into a slow start. This was followed by days of warm sunshine which accelerated flowering of all the late starters. Bearded irises, peonies, roses and hummocks of herbaceous plants were about to flower gloriously and at once. I reckoned that, in about two weeks, early and mid-summer flowers would bloom almost simultaneously and I did not want to risk missing such perfect timing. So we compromised on one day later, June 17th.

Geoff Hamilton was the first to arrive that day. He climbed out of a green Range Rover, said a quick hello and disappeared into the garden to plan and think, as he described it. Birds, dogs and I left him in peace. As he had driven down from a flower show in the north of England the night before, he had evidently not been giving Upton Grey's garden his undivided attention and, for the second time, I noticed that he came to the situation with clear head, made spontaneous notes, and then and there composed a programme around those notes. Perhaps all good television presenters work like that. If so, my respect is extended to them all because a great deal is planned and polished in a very short time.

The rest of the team arrived at about 10 a. m. and we assembled for coffee in the kitchen. Even for an event as apparently simple as the filming of a small garden for a fifteen-minute slot in a series, a remarkable number of staff and amount of time are allocated. There was a team of six. I had asked them to film the garden from the air, preferably from a hot air balloon, because so few gardens are filmed with good overall views and perspective, but they said their budget would not run to that. I can see why. The band of six spent the morning wandering around the garden, filming parts and choosing locations for interviews. I asked Geoff to

Glorious June in the Formal Garden as Geoff Hamilton saw it.

Phil in the Kitchen Garden working among campanulas. Here we keep plants for division and seed heads.

include Phil because he had done so much to turn my labour in the paradise garden to pleasure. He composed his introduction to the programme with a few scribbles into a worn notebook, had a quick word with me about how he saw this particular part of the programme being presented and then started to film the introduction to Upton Grey.

At 11. 30 a group of Californian gardeners arrived, led by Bill Grant, a very knowledgeable American rosarian. They were the only visitors I allowed that day as they had booked the date almost a year earlier, so I warned them about the BBC filming but we felt no need to change the visit. By about midday the team was ready to start filming. Geoff took a seat on a stone bench above the Rose Lawn. With a command from someone of 'Silence. Three, two, one. Shooting', the cameras started to roll. He stood up and walked towards the camera, past beds of full, beautiful, pink peonies, talking happily to man and machine about this particular piece of paradise. The garden looked wonderful, the sun shone; I did not think we could possibly have chosen a more perfect summer's day and I felt immensely proud. Geoff introduced the garden with touching generosity. 'If there was some way that I could choose my own eternal paradise this would be it… we're in Hampshire, at the home of Rosamund Wallinger'.

About an hour later we lunched together on the terrace and talked about anything but our garden. Towards the end of lunch Geoff told us, rather wistfully, that his perfect day was spent simply gardening in peace at his home in Barnsdale. The world of television and fame seems so glamorous but the staple things of life are often the best. After lunch I was told what my role was to be. I listened in a stupor, deciding that this was a guaranteed way to get a wooden act out of any new performer. Geoff or the producer Ray (suddenly everyone seemed demanding and threatening) asked me to do some pruning work in the Rose Lawn. Relatively little useful pruning is done in early June and very little dead-heading, but throughout the summer *Stachys lanata*, the old tall-growing variety, needs rigorous cutting back. It is a job I enjoy about as much as I do making the bed or cleaning the kitchen floor. It is done so regularly that it becomes an unrewarding chore. Evidently the large blue plastic tarpaulin sheet that collects clippings and saves time spent emptying buckets, was going to spoil the green-grey-pink cottage-garden appearance of the Rose Lawn, so I got down on my knees with discreet bucket and cutters and started work. Cameras began to whirr, but they kept stopping for background noises, aircraft, barking dogs, gusts of wind – almost anything. My knees were getting brown with crawling from plant to plant. The bucket was full to the brim and the stachys looked patchily bald. At last Geoff started to walk towards me. With a question whose reply was presumably going to elicit an introduction both to me and to the garden, he started the interview.

'Hello Ros. You are lucky to own this beautiful garden'. Obviously he expected a better, more enlightening response than the one I gave. I leapt rather clumsily to my pins-and-needled feet and said 'We certainly are…' I could think of nothing further to say. I had expected the sort of question-and-answer interview that is conducted in courts of law. 'Oh dear,' said Geoff patiently but obviously disappointed by the curt reply, 'let's start again'. Then quietly to me, 'we need a bit more than that'. I knelt at the roots of my ravaged stachys and composed myself. As the feet of the presenter approached for a second time I pulled myself and nerves together and honestly rose to the occasion. Together we wandered around the garden, discussing elements of the art of gardening, the use of colour and, briefly, very briefly, thanking Gertrude Jekyll for her legacy – an artist's garden. The filming over, we bade the team goodbye and resumed the usual work of gardening while the sun set over orange-purple fields to the confident crowing of young cockerels.

Geoff and his team drove off leaving John and me bemused by the experience and hoping that all had gone well enough for inclusion in the series – and strangely happy. One hundred years after Jekyll had drawn plans for Charles Holme's garden, the gardening world might be about to acknowledge her as a paradise maker.

The following month Geoff Hamilton died of a heart-attack whilst taking part in a charity cycle race. For very many reasons I was unusually saddened. I had liked him, almost known him, and of course in the cruel way of self-interest, it did occur to me that this series would probably be binned. The gardening season continued, visitors came and went. Teas and cakes were distributed, days grew shorter and I grew wearier and older but happier.

In September, a depleted team returned to film a strange finale to the Upton Grey piece. From the pond in the Wild Garden I wandered back toward the house, ducks, dogs and bantams in pursuit, heading for rest and roost as the sun fell below the horizon. We seemed like old friends who had lost their leader, making a small tribute to Geoff.

Autumn paled into winter. The crimson and gold of herbaceous borders withered away and leaves dropped wetly from bending branches. It was not a glorious autumn. Summer had put on such a dramatic performance that the season's end was subtle and slow. December was cold and forbidding and I longed for my next break, the talk trip to America that was to start on January 13th and to run until the 25th. I was to give talks on the west coast of America from San Francisco to Los Angeles, with a single new venue on the return journey, in Philadelphia. For the first time I decided to fly out Club Class on John's Air Miles and to charge the garden clubs sufficient to cover the flights. Somehow flying out Club Class gives me a sense of (quite unjustified) importance. I doubt that I will ever experience the inflating glory of going First Class.

Three weeks before I flew to the States, Maggie Kosowicz wrote from Catalyst TV telling me of the 'Paradise Gardens' schedule. The first programme of the series was to be broadcast on January 14th, Clare and her arbour would appear on January 21st and our slot was to appear under the title 'A Festival of Colour', on January 28th. That meant that I would miss programmes one and two but be back for ours.

I left Heathrow on January 13th determined to show the New World how beautiful an English garden can be, how truly impressive GJ had been in the art and craft of gardening and what a great debt we owe America for preserving her plans and albums. I also plucked up courage enough to claim that this is, of its type – a very important proviso – one of the world's most beautiful gardens. So happy and adventure-packed, in rather a mundane horticultural way, were the following two weeks, that I quite forgot about the television programme and became absorbed in another look at America, Americans and their gardening lives.

Two weeks later I returned to England full of more adrenaline than I had accumulated on any holiday and, as always, longing to get back to Upton Grey. How innocent and comforting the countryside of England looks from the air. Patchwork-quilt fields, edged in furry hedges lead from the channel towards roads, motorways and then the exciting great spread of London's glow that literally fills the horizon. We seemed to fly through centuries in seconds, to land in the vibrant bustle of a great airport.

Little had changed at home. Mrs B still jumped into my hand for corn, and old Biffo and Ratty were still around to give a stiff but heartfelt welcome, whilst young Neff always wags his entire body in confident acceptance of my safe return. I arrived home the evening of Saturday January 25th. On Sunday I gardened and sorted out life, letters and requests for garden visits. I did more of the same until Tuesday evening at 9 pm, then John and I sat in

Herbaceous borders
in summer and
winter, showing
the annual life,
death and life cycle.

front of the blank television screen, switched it on with some anxiety, and waited.

'Paradise Gardens' opened with Geoff Hamilton's twin brother speaking Geoff's introductory script as hands typed into a computer. Geoff had written a great deal of the script before his death. The programme went on to show an interesting interview with Miriam Rothschild and shots of her wild garden in Buckinghamshire. Miss Rothschild was old, wry, wise and witty, secure in her knowledge of wild plants and confident in her contribution to their preservation. After about fifteen minutes the cameras returned to Geoff and then to our garden. The excitement of seeing Upton Grey appear on the national network and looking truly beautiful was exhilarating. The first shot was of Geoff sitting as I remembered him, in the *Viburnum tinus* arbour. He rose to his feet and introduced the garden as though it was **the** paradise garden and his very idea of paradise. The whole programme was so much better than we could have hoped for; it had evidently been well edited and the result was flattering both to us and to Jekyll. The impression that he had felt utterly at peace in our garden came through strongly. We went to bed very happy.

So now the 1908 garden has been recorded on television film three times, in photographs dozens of times for various publications and through the lenses of excellent cameramen. It

Lilies and hydrangea on the top terrace. One of the many crafts Jekyll mastered was making terracotta pots. She often filled her Munstead Wood pots with hydrangeas.

has been both filmed and photographed regularly by me since the start of its restoration. As long as no future generation builds houses or swimming pools in the garden it could return to virtual dereliction when we die and be restored to the Jekyll plans again at a future date. The original plans will always be held safely for posterity. It would be very sad if the house were greatly altered because the garden design and the architecture so compliment each other. I hope Charles Holme's contribution to the Arts and Crafts Movement will survive to serve as a visual example of that movement. We shall continue to dig, toil and care for this bit of nature. It is hard work but satisfying… and far easier than writing.

Far left: Mrs B and friends on the steps that lead to the Rose Lawn.

Left: The grey cockerel.

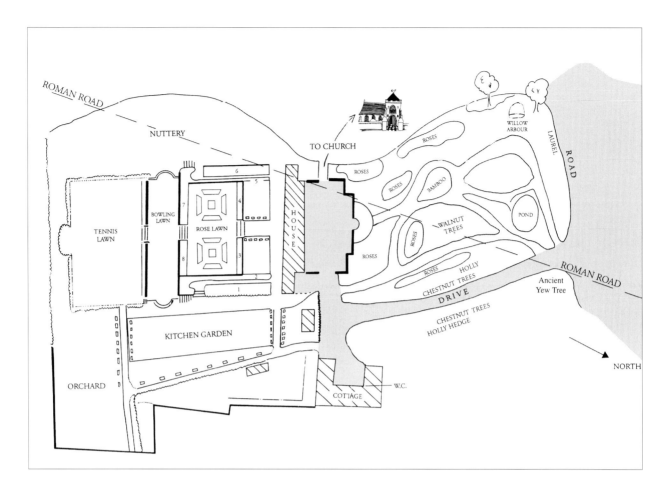

Chapter Ten

The Jekyll Legacy

Plan of the garden at
the Manor House,
Upton Grey showing
Gertrude Jekyll's 1908
layout.

Plan of the garden at the Manor House, Upton Grey showing Gertrude Jekyll's 1908 layout.

It is remarkable that, for nearly fifty years after her death, Jekyll was virtually forgotten by all but garden historians. The austerity that followed the Second World War and the fact that garden art is ephemeral are largely responsible but fortunately, since the 1980s, Jekyll's popularity has enjoyed a gradual revival. Today, over one hundred and fifty years after her birth, her doctrine is still relevant and practical. When the Garden History Society visited Upton Grey in the summer of 1996 they reported that one of the surprising things about this garden is its timelessness. It is still a quintessential English Garden. As any good gardener knows, this does not mean we should be stuck in a garden time warp. Modern gardens can be sophisticated, beautiful, exciting and great art. I believe that contemporary designers owe something to Jekyll's art but that they have developed her doctrines and moved on. In 1984 Penelope Hobhouse asked me if I would tire of living within the restrictions of Jekyll's plans. I have not, but I can understand why such a talented gardener would not be able to. I am a copier and this garden is a reproduction of Jekyll's art, not my art.

One of the most satisfying things about gardening here is that Upton Grey provides visual evidence of most of Jekyll's talents in one small garden and it has plenty of variety. Perhaps Charles Holme's instruction to her was, 'Give me a Jekyll garden with something of all you love; an example of each of your tenets'. I am biased, but I can find almost every element of garden art at Upton Grey. If we walk through the garden and consider its features, I shall try to justify that extravagant claim. We will start to the north-west of the house in the Wild Garden.

The entrance to the Wild
Garden with its wrought iron
gates and leaden cherubs.
Bergenia and hellebores grow
at the foot of the wall.

The grass steps at the
entrance to the Wild Garden.

193

Cistus laurifolius grows beside *Rosa arvensis* and rose 'Jersey Beauty'. Jekyll groups together different plants with very similar flowers.

Upton Grey has Jekyll's only fully restored Wild Garden. It covers less than two acres and is approached from the house by grass steps. These make a beautiful formal but natural entrance. Three shallow treads of fifteen inches with a three-inch rise form a gentle green semi-circle that leads to the mown grass path. This winds through uncut grasses, filled, in spring and early summer, with wild flowers of the primula family, wood anemones, fritillaria, violets and many others. The long grasses ripple in the breeze and change colour seasonally from fresh young green to fading buff-yellow and palest purple as winter approaches. Their seed-heads, when examined closely, are as fine a work of art as any of nature's triumphs. Perhaps the flowery meads of medieval gardens were a little like this. The grass path divides from time to time and travels left through mounds of white and pale pink rambling roses on towards unkempt bushes of single-flowered species roses. Here the single, rose-like flowers of *Cistus laurifolius* look so like their neighbours the rose 'Jersey Beauty' and *Rosa arvensis*, a

Rosa virginiana (a species rose which Jekyll knew as *Rosa lucida*) whose stems and hips turn red in winter.

Rambler roses 'The Garland' (1835) and 'Dundee Rambler' (1850).

species rose. In winter months *Rosa arvensis* has near black stems and hips, while *Rosa virginiana* is bright with scarlet hips and red stems. The species roses lead on to a small woodland area of birch and walnut, past bamboo and a surprising group of tree lupins planted beneath three laburnum trees which flower like a reflection of their neighbours, yellow panicles dropping down towards the upright yellow flowers of the lupins. Beyond

The pond with *Iris pseudocorus* in foreground.

these, a glorious stand of kniphofia lines the mown path that leads to the pond. I love that sudden flamboyant display of stiff red heads that lead like an affectionate joke to the tranquil pond where plants that are predominantly green and natural grow. (In a perfectly innocent way I have always described the stand of kniphofia that leads to the pond as an 'erection' of kniphofia. When I presented the incredibly patient editor of my reams of garden notes with the description, he wrote 'hmmmmm?' in the margin, and looking at the rather phallic flower heads I now see why. Suddenly editor, who until then I had imagined as a wheel-chair bound octogenarian with time on this hands and a surfeit of brains in his head, leapt to humorous life. It was some time before I met him and saw how wrong the image had been).

Ferns, water irises, hellebore, tansies and monarda line the water's edge and fill the rocks. It is in this area, as nature and garden blend in the distance, that Jekyll's beautiful but invasive weeds are planted; Japanese knotweed (*Polygonum cuspidatum*) and the arresting giant hogweed (*Heracleum mantegazzianum*). Both William Robinson and Gertrude Jekyll emphasised that the garden and nature should blend into one another in the distance. Some strange arrivals are accepted in this natural area. Cyclamen grow of their own accord. Hemerocallis and geranium are as on plans but vincas, hyacinths, scillas and some bergenias have jostled their way in and I have allowed a few dog roses to grow near the planned medlar and quince. Later inhabitants of the house had planted Japanese cherry trees but we have replaced those heavily blossoming trees with the correct, delicately blossomed *Amelanchier canadensis* that Jekyll planned, and with *Viburnum opulus* whose autumn berries are a clear, brilliant red.

Tree lupin (*Lupinus arboreus*) and kniphofia in the Wild Garden.

The berries of *Virbunum opulus*.

The rather phallic erections of kniphofia which lead to the pond.

197

Ros and dogs leaving
the Wild Garden.

I return towards the house along the winding drive that edges the Wild Garden. The drive
is the only part of the garden that is not restored to Jekyll's plan. The holly hedge on one
side is now full and healthy but on the Wild Garden side it has several gaps where plants have
died and my replacements regularly follow ancestors to the grave. Where Jekyll planned beds
of tree peonies to line the drive in front of the holly hedge, Charles Holme had stands of
horse chestnut trees. I have left those large, graceful trees. Someone else can perfect this bit
in years to come when the trees have outlived their beauty.

Walking through the house to the Formal Garden, the contrast in summer is quite
breathtaking, but the beauty of this part of the garden is less enduring than the peaceful,
mature Wild Garden. The Formal Garden puts on a display that is too flamboyant to last, and
that is its particular charm. Assuming the Formal Garden is at its best in all parts as we walk
through – which of course it never is because one area gives way to another from April to
November – I shall start at the house and look over the whole from a first-floor window. It
is important to judge a complete garden because photographs taken of small areas, ignoring
blemishes, can be very misleading and far too flattering. The overall view takes in the context,
the structure and shows the importance of proportion and perspective. There are five
different places in the garden where Jekyll has planned seats (see overleaf) for just this reason,
because, from that particular angle, a view of the garden presents a picture. It took us some
years to replace all those seats but, every time we did, we understood the clever positioning.
Garden owners should be aware of the importance of siting seats though not many have time
to indulge in feet-up moments for admiration of handiwork. I wonder if modern designers
take this into consideration when planning gardens, or do seating areas evolve as the
plants grow.

The Formal Garden has only straight lines. It is geometric, architectural and enclosed with
yew hedges, whilst being cottage-garden in effect in some places and strongly structural in
others. A sturdy pergola runs from the house across the top terrace, carrying sweet-smelling
jasmine, a profusion of roses and the heavy-leafed aristolochia. Its proportions are balanced.
Walk through the pergola, down gentle stone steps between drystone walls whose spring and

Looking over the main pergola from the house. Notice how the pergola has purpose. It leads from the house and its focal point is the rose arbour behind the Tennis Lawn.
Photograph by kind permission of *Bo Bedre* magazine.

Looking towards the main border and Kitchen Garden. This photograph is repeated but it illustrates the text.

The importance of seats and their position in a garden

A grass path running between uncut grasses and wild flowers. It leads to a seat that looks across the Wild Garden towards the church.

The rose arbour behind the Tennis Lawn. The vista from here towards the house is beautiful.

The stone seat that overlooks the Bowling Green.

This seat overlooks the Rose Lawn. All these seats are as on Jekyll's plans.

The Rose Lawn at the height of summer. The iris and wall plants in the background complete the picture.

early summer flowers start the Formal Garden's colourful show, to arrive at the Rose Lawn below. This area is geometrically laid out in a very rigid display, but the double peonies and full-flowered roses have a softening effect. The Rose Lawn represents a typical Jekyll garden to many people. The sheer beauty in early summer of old roses amongst peonies that give way to powerfully scented lilies is truly dramatic. The sight lifts the spirits like a crescendo in orchestral music. Threads of flowers form the background to this display and have equal

Detail of the small
drystone wall planting
with various pinks
(dianthus).

importance in the orchestral piece. Bearded iris, modest omphalodes, hundreds and hundreds of dianthus to edge and control the tempo, make up the structure of the composition. Before the Rose Lawn drops to the Bowling Green, a border, consisting largely of shrubs, contains the area and arrests the eye. The shrubs include *Olearia hastii* and *gunnii* (renamed *phlogopappa*), China roses, *Ruscus racemosus*, lavender and rosemary. Peonies, acanthus, hosta, irises and dianthus grow amongst them. Jekyll emphasised the benefit of using shrubs in her herbaceous borders to give shelter, support and substance to seasonal flowers.

And so on down to the Bowling Green and beyond that to the Tennis Lawn, at the far side of which is our rose arbour. Sitting in there, looking back towards the house we see the garden from below, so to speak, and notice how the steps are edged with aromatic rosemary and how yucca and fuchsia that are planted along the top terrace of drystone walls perform so well against the skyline. The large area of grass that the Tennis Lawn and Bowling Green make up give the garden a dimension of space and a tranquillity. From a distance the planted drystone walls look like colourful vertical flower-beds. They add a further dimension to the garden because walls facing the sun are relatively dry and warm so the plants that grow in them bloom on a different plane and in an earlier season. These walls are another facet of Jekyll's art that I took some time to appreciate fully. They are filled with colour in early spring when only the daffodils and naturalised flowers of the Wild Garden are in flower and virtually nothing but *Iris unguicularis* blooms in the horizontal beds of the Formal Garden. The gentle muted colours of alpine and rock flowers growing in secure tufts from soft green hummocks that cling to earth-filled crevasses include the purple hues of aubretia, *Erinus alpinus, Campanula muralis (portenschlaggiana)* and *carpatica, Pterocephalus perennis*, the yellows and whites of arabis, alyssum, *Cerastium tomentosum, Corydalis ochroleucha* and the small phlox. In *Wall, Water and Woodland Gardens* Jekyll writes of the merits of drystone walls and I quote a large section because her appreciation is so beautifully expressed.

> *I doubt if there is any way in which a good quantity of plants, and of bushes of moderate size, can be so well seen and enjoyed as in one of these roughly terraced gardens, for one sees them*

up and down and in all sorts of ways, and one has a chance of seeing many lovely flowers clear against the sky, and of perhaps catching some sweetly-scented tiny thing like Dianthus fragrans *at exactly nose-height and eye-level, and so of enjoying its tender beauty and powerful fragrance in a way that had never before been possible.*

Then the beautiful details of structure and marking in such plants as the silvery saxifrages can never be so well seen as in a wall at the level of the eye or just above or below it; and plain to see are all the pretty ways these small plants have of seating themselves on projections or nestling into hollows, or creeping over stony surface as does Balearic sandwort, or standing like erinus with its back pressed to the wall in an attitude of soldier-like bolt-uprightness.

Now isn't that a testimony of close observation and love of nature.

The Upton Grey walls need ongoing care because colonies of voles and mice have established themselves behind the stones to feast on fleshy roots during winter months and to burrow frantically all year round, seriously damaging the structure of the walls. We continually tap back loose stones and ram fresh earth into the catacomb-like holes, but I am amused by the tiny creatures and enjoy their fleeting sorties into the flower-beds so we let them be.

Monarda didyma (bergamot).

African marigolds with *Rudbeckia specisoa* and *Gypsophila paniculata*.

When I am asked if I feel too restricted by Jekyll's plans I answer that I can grow what I like in remoter parts of the garden which are not on plans, one of which, the Orchard, is edged with borders and an earth bank. Here we plant surplus stock, of which we have progressively more as the garden matures, but I still have no desire to introduce modern plants. The earth bank in the Orchard stands beneath apple and pear trees; it is fairly barren and partly shaded – not ideal for growing any plant. So this area was allocated to take surplus *Iris germanica* stock which would otherwise have been composted. (Times like these make even the poorest gardener feel rich in resources). The iris bank is quite breathtakingly beautiful in late May when pale sunlight filters through the blossomed boughs onto a mass of flowers, sky blue, deep blue, purple, yellow and violet. I ask all visiting groups to take a detour towards that end of the garden to see the glorious sight. Even when flowers are over, the green strap leaves make an effective display on the earthy bank. William Robinson tried to persuade fellow gardeners of the value of iris used thus but I suppose that devoting an entire border to one flower, particularly one like this iris which only flowers once and relatively briefly, is a luxury only those who own a large garden can afford.

Wandering back through the Nuttery, which in spring is carpeted with bluebells and primulas, reminds me that practical Miss Jekyll never left a utilitarian area unadorned. In the Orchard the gnarled old apple trees are under-planted with daffodils. In the beds that surround the stable-cottage I have planted 'extras', the surplus stock from the main garden, and a few Jekyll favourites like godetia and Iceland poppy (*Papaver nudicaule*), flowers that I also love but which she did not include on her plans for this garden. Whilst pretty in their way and in their season, my whimsical beds do not have the rhythmic art of Jekyll's borders. The difference between mine and Jekyll's can be seen when we return to the last part of our garden, the main herbaceous borders. Whereas my cottage flower-beds are unplanned and represent, as Jekyll described the unplanned border, a mere 'collection' of plants and not a garden, hers are truly works of art. Here colour and texture are important elements of that art. She believed that planting the ground was like painting the landscape with living things. She explained to her readers how colours influence each other and taught them the value of hot stimulating colours, cool soothing colours and of the drama of a bold blob of white in a border, used, like the impressionists used white paint, to draw the eye and to startle. Centranthus (valerian) does this in our Hot Border. By planting in drifts her borders work to conceal and to allow death. There are of course what she described as 'contrivances', plants that are pulled down over

fading neighbours, or ones that are thinned and cut back to extend flowering seasons. Annuals are used as fillings as are large terracotta pots. These pots, when filled with plants like hydrangea, gypsophila or ophiopogon, hide a dying plant well. Container planting itself is quite an art; the very pots are often works of art, as are their contents.

Because I had not gardened before I came to Upon Grey, I look at Jekyll less critically than an experienced gardener might. When I started gardening I decided I did not like certain plants, African marigolds for example and a great many of the composite flowers, few of which are indigenous to England; but I had not seen them planted sensitively. 'It is not the plants' fault, ' wrote Jekyll, 'that they are used in ignorant and foolish ways'. Having had time to observe that family of childishly unsubtle, daisy-shaped flowers, I do now understand their value in extending the border's flowering season to a display of spectacular autumn colours.

I have learnt, through trial and error — the best, if not the quickest or most painless way — that Jekyll was not infallible. However, more often than not her mistake proved to be my misinterpretation of her writing or my mistreatment of a plant. Simply failing to maintain a

Border 5 mid-summer showing centranthus, a stark white, near the strong red centre. My favourite view of the main borders is from above.

The Kitchen Garden rose pergola with *Campanulas persicifolia* and *carpatica* and lavender at the base.

Various views of the Kitchen Garden

Detail of *Iris germanica* (the bearded iris).

The Kitchen Garden and the gardener's cottage with dianthus, lychnis, kniphofia and rue (*Ruta graveolens*) in the foreground. My part of the garden lacks the art of Jekyll's planned parts.

Far left: Some composite flowers, *Helenium autumnale pumilium, Rudbeckia speciosa, Bupthalmum salicifolium.*

Left: Detail of *Helenium autumnale pumilium.*

Rose 'Goldfinch' (1907) growing along the rose walk in the Kitchen Garden.

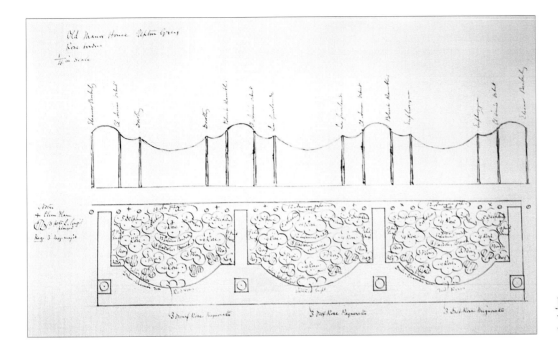

Jekyll's plan for what I called the 'Mystery' border.

good shape or to support a lanky plant can qualify as 'mistreatment'. I am still a little surprised to find meadowsweet (*Filipendula ulmaria*) and bergamot (*Monarda didyma*) planted in a dry chalky border well away from a source of water. However, visitors often remark on how relatively mildew-free the monarda is, so presumably it is happy there. In another border a plant that likes poor soil, the lupin, grows closely beside a greedy plant, a peony, but I suppose that Jekyll's clients had gardeners who were aware of their plants' needs and so gave extra feed where required. Husband John's comment to this was 'How practical to put an easy feeder next to a hungry one to maximise the available nutrients'.

There is one part of the garden which was a necessary compromise and so, although not Jekyll's fault, it is imperfect. The main flower borders are too short. By terracing the natural slope of the garden with drystone walls Jekyll gave maximum length to her herbaceous borders but, ideally, sixty feet is not long enough to allow drifts of flowers to run from cool to hot and back to cool again fluently. In other words the canvas given her was not long enough to fulfil her client's requests. Looking at the borders from ground level you get little perspective on them. They are better seen from the house above. That is my only real dissatisfaction with the garden.

Although the garden is now virtually completely restored there remains one perplexing mystery. Back in 1984 when we unrolled the exciting package of newly arrived Jekyll documents we found one unnumbered plan for what was called 'Old Manor House Upton Grey Rose Border'. There was no indication of where it should stand. I asked advice from our several well-informed garden advisers and, finding no obvious position for it in the garden, we wrapped it up and rather forgot about it. The border depicted is very structured, as the illustration shows, and the planting is beautiful but there is apparently nowhere in the garden where space allows for its inclusion unless it is a substitute for one main herbaceous border and if it were a substitute surely the garden would look oddly asymmetrical. It is possible, but in our opinion unlikely, that it runs along the north end of the Kitchen Garden.

When looking through old photographs in 1995 I noticed the outline of the post and rope structure as background to a picture taken an about 1920 but it was still not apparent where exactly the border lay and it remains a mystery. I suppose someone will eventually solve this vexing problem. However we have used the idea of posts and hanging rope for the rose walk alongside the Kitchen Garden. The inspiration is Jekyll and the result very pleasing. [In June 1999 I was sent a photograph, taken in about 1916, which showed the border standing, as

Two photographs taken about 1914 showing the mystery border as a substitute for Border 5

The mystery border is beyond the Rose Lawn in front of the hedge.

we had suspected in place of one main herbaceous borders. I would like to know if Jekyll was coaxed into providing this odd alteration or if she chose it].

Another view of the mystery border from the top terrace.

I hope that people will appreciate the range of Jekyll's talents and not dismiss her as a gardener who was limited to laborious, colourful herbaceous borders. One of her greatest loves was her woodland garden at Munstead Wood where she drew the surrounding countryside into her garden, gradually and subtly. I believe Jekyll brought together nearly all facets of gardening art, not instinctively but by careful study of the science of her art. In her books and articles she taught gardeners how to make an art of their craft.

Gardens will continue to be barometers of society. Today's gardens are everyman's art, his hobby and his pleasure. Probably the art loses something in becoming a plaything of the masses but arguably the more it is practised the more it develops. In general gardens are becoming smaller, gardeners more practical and, thanks to the media we have a great many styles from which to choose. Gardens of today are more ephemeral than ever (perhaps because people move house more often) and that, for many reasons, is a good thing. It allows each generation to express itself in nature. It gives employment to students of horticulture and it encourages the introduction of new, often improved strains of plants. There are also disadvantages. We should try to retain some elements of gardens of the past as we move on. We should take care not to lose plants which are valuable sources of genetic diversity, and remember that future generations will need some record of the evolution of gardens in order to learn from the past and to progress.

Finally there is the therapy of gardening. I end with this point because it is so obvious and so satisfying. By living with nature one comes to terms with life, disease and death. It is comforting to know that other life goes on. I intend to become a peony in after-life. Quite simple. I shall ask that my ashes or bones be scattered or rot beneath one of the many peonies. They are greedy feeders and will be grateful for my generosity.

Bibliography

Angel, Heather, *A View from a Window.* Unwin (1988).

Anscombe, Isabelle, *Arts and Crafts Style.* Phaidon (1991).

Beale, Reginald, *Lawns for Sports.* Simpkin (1924).

Beales, Peter, *Classic Roses.* Collins Harvill (1985).

Bean, W.J., *Trees and Shrubs Hardy in the British Isles.* Murray 3rd ed. (1921).

Bisgrove, Richard, *The National Trust Book of the English Garden.* Viking (1990).
   The Gardens of Gertrude Jekyll. F. Lincoln (1992).

Blamey, M. and Grey-Wilson, C., *The Illustrated Flora of Britain.* Hodder 1989).

Blomfield, Reginald, *The Formal Garden in England.* Macmillan (1936).

British Rose Growers Association *Find That Rose.* (Annually).

Brown, Jane, *Farrand, Beatrix.* Viking (1995).
   Gardens of a Golden Afternoon. Allen Lane (1982).

Clifford, Derek, *A History of Garden Design.* Faber (1962).

Festing, Sally, *Gertrude Jekyll.* Viking (1991).

Fish, Margery, *We Made a Garden.* Collingridge (1956).

Gradidge, Roderick, *Dream Houses. The Edwardian Ideal.* Constable (1980).

Griswold, Mac and Weller, Eleanor, *The Golden Age of American Gardens.* Abrams (1992).

Gunn, Fenja, *The Lost Gardens of Gertrude Jekyll.* Letts (1991).

Henslow, Geoffrey, *The Rose Encyclopaedia.* Pearson (n.d.).

Hobhouse, Penelope, *Gertrude Jekyll on Gardening.* The National Trust and Collins (1983).

Holme, Charles (Ed.), *Old English Country Cottages* (1906).
   The Gardens of England in the Southern and Western Counties (1907).
   The Gardens of England in the Midland and Eastern Counties (1908).
   The Gardens of England in the Northern Counties (1911). (Published The Studio).

Jekyll, Gertrude, *Wood and Garden.* Longmans (1899).
   ★*Home and Garden.* Longmans (1900).
   ★*Lilies for English Gardens.* Country Life (1901).
   ★*Wall and Water Gardens.* Country Life (1913 – later editions *Wall, Water and Woodland Gardens*).
   ★*Roses for English Gardens.* Country Life (1902).
   Old West Surrey. Longmans (1904).
   Flower Decoration in the House. Country Life (1907).

★*Colour in the Garden.* Country Life (1908 – later editions *Colour Schemes for the Flower Garden*).
   ★*Children and Gardens.* Country Life (1908).

Jekyll, Francis, *Gertrude Jekyll a Memoir.* Jonathan Cape (n.d.).

Jekyll, G. and Elgood, *Some English Gardens.* Longmans (1904).

Jekyll, G. and Hussey, C., ★*Garden Ornament.* Country Life (1918).

Jekyll, G. and Jenkins, E., *Annuals and Biennials.* Country Life (1916).

Jekyll, G. and Weaver, L., ★*Gardens for Small Country Houses.* Country Life (1912 – later editions *Arts and Crafts Gardens*).

Jekyll, F. and Taylor, G. (Eds.), ★*A Gardener's Testament.* (1937)

Johns, C.A. (Rev), *Flowers of the Field.* SPCK (1911).

Lawson, A., *The Gardener's Book of Colour.* F. Lincoln (1996).

Newton, William, *The Work of Ernest Newton R.A.* The Architectural Press (1925).

Robinson, William, *The English Flower Garden.* John Murray (1883).

Royal Horticultural Society, *The RHS Dictionary of Gardening.* Several editions.

RHS Plant Finder. (Annually).

Service, Alastair, *Edwardian Architecture.* Thames and Hudson (1977).

Smith, W. (Ed. W. Stearn), *A Gardener's Dictionary of Plant Names.* Cassell (1971).

Stearn, W., *Botanical Latin.* David and Charles (1966).

Studio Ltd., The, *The Studio Year Book of Decorative Art* (1915).

Tankard, J. and Valkenburgh, M. van, *Gertrude Jekyll.* Murray (1985).

Tankard, J. and Wood, Martin, *Gertrude Jekyll at Munstead Wood.* Sutton (1996).

Taylor, Patrick, *100 English Gardens.* National Trust (1996).

Tooley, Michael & Arnander, Primrose (Eds.), *Gertrude Jekyll. Essays.* Michaelmas (1995).

Victoria and Albert Museum, The, *The Studio High Art Low Life.* Centenary edn. (1993).

Weathers, J., *A Practical Guide to Garden Plants.* Longmans (1901).

White, Gilbert, *Natural History and Antiquities of Selborne.* (Reprint) (1789).

White, J.P., *Garden Furniture and Ornament.* The Pyghtle Works (reprint 1987) .

★ **Reprinted by Antique Collectors' Club Ltd.**

Photographic Acknowledgements

All the photographs in this book (unless otherwise indicated) were taken by me, like the diary notes, as a reminder to myself of what had been. I used cheap camera, film and processing, no tripod and no skill. A few generous friends have lent me good photographs as they visited the garden and from late 1997 Peter Greenhauf provided photographs of a gloriously higher standard than my own. To all those generous photographers I give my thanks and to readers my apologies… but it makes for an interesting record.

Andrews, Geraldine: 52 (top left), 137, 186 (bottom).

Angel, Heather: 45.

Bo Bedre Magazine: 41, 52 (bottom left), 53 (top right), 199 (top).

Coghlan, Ann: 150

Ferguson, Tim: 67 (top).

Greenhauf, Peter: 2, 3, 6, 7 (bottom left), 31 (right), 33 (top and bottom left), 49, 52 (middle left), 53 (middle right), 55, 59, 62, 67 (bottom), 73 (top), 78 (top left), 80 (top right), 94, 95, 97 (top), 99, 101, 104, 108, 113, 128, 129 (bottom left), 132, 144, 158, 161, 163, 170 (top right), 175, 179 (top), 182 (top left), 190 (top), 191 (top, bottom left), 193, 195, 198, 199 (bottom), 206, 207, 208, 211.

Lawson, Andrew: 109.

Nohl, Sebastian: 19.

Sykes, Christopher: Front cover, 124, 141.

Woodyard, Cynthia: 22, 93.

General Index

Page numbers in bold refer to illustrations.

Complete Plant Index

Page numbers in **bold** refer to illustrations. Entries without a page reference are plants grown at Upton Grey but not illustrated or mentioned in the text.